THE WORLD OF THE

OREGON
FISHBOAT

A Study in Maritime Folklife

JANET C. GILMORE

WSU
PRESS

Washington State University Press
Pullman, Washington

Washington State University Press
P.O. Box 645910
Pullman, Washington 99164-5910
Phone: 800-354-7360   FAX: 509-335-8568
©1999 by the Board of Regents of Washington State University
All rights reserved
First printing 1999

Originally published by UMI Research Press, Ann Arbor, Michigan, 1986

Cover illustration from a drawing by Janet C. Gilmore

Library of Congress Cataloging-in-Publication Data

Gilmore, Janet Crofton, 1949-
    The world of the Oregon fishboat : a study in maritime folklife /
Janet C. Gilmore.
        p.   cm.
    Originally published: Ann Arbor, Mich. : UMI Press, 1986.
    Includes bibliographical references (p.   ) and index.
    ISBN 0-87422-171-4 (alk. paper)
    1. Fishing boats—Oregon—Coos Bay. 2. Fishing boats—Oregon—
Charleston. 3. Fishers—Oregon—Coos Bay. 4. Fishers—Oregon—
Charleston. 5. Maritime anthropology. I. Title.
SH344.8.B6G55 1999
979.5'23—dc21   98-54419
                                                                    CIP

Contents

*To the independent, individualistic,
professional, full-time commercial fishermen,
their families, and the small water-oriented
businesses of the Charleston-Coos Bay area*

Twenty Years Later
Preface to the Reprint Edition

The opportunity to re-present this book has offered me another welcome excuse to revisit the Coos Bay area and renew old fieldwork relationships. But like the fisherman grappling with an existing boat, I am limited as to what I can do here. I can only hint at changes in Coos Bay area fishing businesses, only provide the barest outline of what has occurred in the lives of the fishermen and boats documented in 1977-78.

Oregon's economy went bust in the late 1970s, reeling from painful adjustments in the timber industry. The Coos Bay area was hit hard with 20 percent unemployment. Through much of the 1980s, the port remained suspended in time, retaining its rugged and depressed look. But by the late 1980s, state and federal funds flowed in. Besides improvements to port facilities, Coos Bay's downtown received a face-lift, a waterfront boardwalk and interpretive center, and a replaced public dock. Charleston's marine facilities benefited too.

Charleston now looks a bit neater and brighter. Where the highway meets South Slough, a new restaurant perks up the parking lot of the former Peterson's Seafood, softening the eerie quiet of the fish plant that changed hands several times before folding. Across the highway, Kelley Boat Works now houses the Charleston Post Office, but the marine ways for small and medium boats—and modest budgets—have closed. Beyond Kelley's and Englund's Marine Supply, formerly Hanson's, a substantial shipyard, do-it-yourself boat yard, and metal fabrication plant have inhabited Hanson's drydock site. Qualman's Oyster Farm has built a tidy plant with adjacent oyster market, and the Port of Coos Bay has replaced the "transient boat" docks with a more substantially engineered "Distant Water Fleet Facility."

The quaint green steel swing drawbridge that crossed the slough and plunged the traveler into the sights, sounds, and smells of fish plants, boats, and decaying matter, is gone. A sterile concrete lift bridge affords a more distant, less visceral view. Downtown Charleston has lost Red's Tavern but remains anchored by the Old General Store, the Breakfast Barn, Davey Jones Locker, a beauty salon, and an expanded Chuck's Seafood. A new visitor's center has joined them.

Across the highway, the looming Oceanic Tavern and a gas station have yielded to a brightly painted Mexican American restaurant, gift, video, and espresso shops, and the entrance to an RV park beyond. The creative ferment of Bill's Machine and Welding has vanished with the occupation of Chuck's Seafoods' sedate oyster operation. The expanse between the bridge and the boat basins has burgeoned with additions of fish plants, a new fish market, fishermen's associations, and more services devoted to both recreational and commercial groups. Still hugging the hillside, the Oregon Institute of Marine Biology has grown denser with expanded and new structures.

Charleston may now be attracting retirees and vacationers less focused on recreational fishing. But the place still keeps its "junkyard" character, remaining an honest nuts-and-bolts working community not overly prettified and emasculated for the benefit of the tourist trade.

The boats in the boat basins still reflect the remains of the past and the ongoing struggle to adjust to present and future conditions. Many of the "old girls" are still in service, but there are fewer wooden ones, many are in need of a bottom cleaning and paint job, and too many are for sale. Looming over the old boat stock are relics from the joint venture binge of the past decade: large, black, ominous, steel trawlers, some built locally, paid off but expensive to maintain, now enlisted for fishing performed most effectively by vessels half their size.

Surprisingly, many more people, some with overly effective fishing machines, entered the fishing business during the past two decades, even as varieties and quantities of fish stocks seemed to dwindle while adjusting to warmer ocean temperatures. Fishermen have expanded into fishing for black cod with pots, for lingcod with longlining gear, for scallops with dredges, and for squid and "assorted rockfishes" with "hook and line" gear of Vietnamese origins. Wild coho salmon are now on the endangered species list but the formerly scant wild chinook are more plentiful. With El Niño weather patterns, pilchards and their pelican predators have reappeared offshore, and fishermen have enjoyed a nearshore bounty of albacore tuna. Stricter regulation, including limited entry, extremely curtailed fishing "seasons," individual fishing quotas, and fisheries review board processes, has created more turbulence in the commercial fishing industry and, as retired fisherman Floyd Green says, may be 50 years too late.

There are as many fish processors and buyers in the port as in the 1970s, but many have retrenched. Hallmark's, the longest-lived, has a "buy everything" policy that accommodates many of the oldest fishing families and may contribute to its endurance. Eureka, another veteran, looks vastly curtailed. Another processor, now named Pacific Seafood, located beside the small boat basin in the late '70s, assuming Lazio's and the Alaska Packers facility. A fish by-products operation and a fish broker built alongside. Three fish-buying stations between the boat basins and Hallmark's serve the broker and a fish marketer based at the Portland airport. The former Barbey plant burned down.

Committed to logging and ocean-going industries, area businesses dedicated to the supply, production, maintenance, and repair of marine equipment have persisted, with closings balancing new enterprises, and perhaps a dozen firms weathering the past two decades. Hillstrom Shipbuilding fell under the weight of too many new, big jobs taken on too quickly. Nelson Log Bronc changed to Mid-Coast Marine and assumed the Hillstrom yard. After considerable expansion and Port support, it also closed, but it is now reincarnated as a shipbuilding facility on North Spit. Meanwhile a tug- and barge-building arm of Sause Towboat thrives near Eastside. At the Charleston Shipyard, Giddings Boat Works, dedicated to building and maintaining mid-size steel boats, has assumed some of the jobs that Hillstrom's and Nelson's once accommodated. While the shipyard workforce has survived, however, the big yards and Charleston's do-it-yourself facility have not replaced Kelley's or Hillstrom's, and most fishermen now take their boats to ports like Winchester Bay for upkeep and repair. While the ranks of craftsmen with decades of wooden boat experience are fast dwindling, there still is a handful of young practitioners who perpetuate the traditional knowledge.

Despite material changes in the fisheries and marine worlds, fishing families continue to pass on their marine expertise and enthusiasm to new generations. Many of their well-tended elderly vessels live on. The following updates on fishermen and boats illustrate the ups and downs that fishing people have weathered over the past two decades.

Leonard Hall, 69 when interviewed, had retired already and sold his boat, the *M.S. Electron*. "Through luck and some perception," he wrote in February 1985, "I got out of the fishing business just in time." His three sons all fished commercially, but only one persists in the business, and another switched to towboating. Hall passed away in 1995 at 87, but the *M.S. Electron* still fishes out of Newport.

Willis R. Short (alias Cyrus Little), 78 when interviewed, retired in 1966 but helped maintain his son's two boats well into his 80s. Sadly the *Christina J* (alias *Maria E*) sank in 1981, taking his son's stepson, the fourth family member lost at sea. Short passed away at 88, in 1988. After ill health, his son followed in 1995, at age 69. Willis, Sr.'s daughter's son, who helped his grandfather build and fish the *APO* in his youth, has crewed on a trawler since the Weyerhaeuser mill closed in 1990, putting him out of work. The *Wind Song* (alias *Silver Wave*) still fishes.

Charlie Ells had also already retired when interviewed at age 68. Hale and hearty at 89, Ells is still involved with his son Alex in the cranberry and fishing businesses. In 1990, Alex quit fishing and turned his attention to cranberries. He and his father lease the *Amak* to a fellow Port Orford fisherman ("doing very well" fishing for sole), who worked on the boat with Alex for many years. In 1995, the Ellses "renailed the whole boat."

Joe Easley (alias Jake Harlan), fortyish in 1978, soon after left the business and remains active in fisheries regulation. "In 1982 my vessel the *Estep* [alias *Puget*], which was under charter, was sunk with no loss of life. All the safety equipment worked like it was supposed to. With the *Estep* gone I have stayed on here longer than I intended."

Fred Anderson, 50 when interviewed, took his boats and "boys" to Alaska to enter the joint venture mid-water trawling business for several winters. He paid off the *Sleep Robber*, but when the joint ventures slackened he returned to Charleston for good. He then built another steel trawler, the *Jeanette Marie*, at Giddings. Afflicted with diabetes and a bad leg, he retired from fishing two years before he died in 1990. Never one to give up, he talked about building another boat, and he worked on nets in his gear shed every day until his death. The International Port of Coos Bay later dedicated the "Distant Water Fleet Facility" to him. Fred's wife Betty sold the three boats (including the *Betty A*), which still operate in the area. Both sons quit fishing.

Norman Walker, 52 when interviewed, built a 57-foot by 17-foot steel drag boat in his backyard in 1980 rather than buy a bigger boat in the East and bring it through the Panama Canal. He took the *Briny W* to Alaska to crab one summer, and sold the boat in 1988-89. It now works out of Brookings alongside the *Elaine Dell* and *Frank F*. Norman semi-retired from fishing in 1987 as he and Virginia built a new home on a few acres well inland from the coast. As Walker retired, nephew Tom Hockema began leasing the *Rambler*, which he is presently purchasing. He has removed the flying bridge that Norman installed, which needed repair. He fishes the boat for salmon and crab, its customary use, but also for the newer "hook-and-line assorted rockfish" fishery. Walker was diagnosed with an incurable lung disease in 1994 from which he died in 1996. His four daughters all "had their turn of summers on the *Rambler*," two of their husbands fished for Norman for over a decade, and all three of Norman's last boat pullers now fish their own boats.

Floyd Green, 51 when interviewed, retired from fishing in 1987-88. He liked fishing, but he lost interest as it got harder to make money at it. He sold the *Oregon* in 1987. It sank in 1996 while crossing the bar at Winchester Bay. It was later stripped and burned. Green now enjoys hunting and camping, and he and his wife have moved away from the water. No family members have followed him into fishing.

Carl Harrington was 40 when interviewed. Now 61 and semi-retired, he has experienced a dizzying array of ups and downs. In 1982, after the sudden death of his first wife, he sold the *Kodiak*. He had just rebuilt the hull and installed new hydraulic winches. The boat has since spent a season fishing halibut in Alaska, and currently works out of Newport. After remarrying in 1983, he and his present wife

Eileen purchased the 40-foot *Pioneer Lady,* fishing it for salmon and crab, then adapting it for bottomfishing. He was pleased with the boat's performance, but it leaked while trawling, so he sold it. For the next several years he ran a string of trawlers for various owners. He arranged to purchase one of the boats, but the deal fell through when he suffered a massive heart attack in 1987. He next purchased the *Oregon,* fishing it for crab and salmon for a couple of years. After selling it, he ran several more boats, including a small troller/crabber which sank during a risky trip over the bar. He kept fishing, operating a 68-foot shrimp boat for a couple of years, but then quit, took contracting classes, got a license, and did contracting work for a year or so. When his brother-in-law wanted to buy a fishing boat, he returned to fishing, running his 40-foot crab boat for a year until more health problems put him ashore again. He presently fishes on a limited basis. His stepson, who at 16 started fishing with Carl, spent 10 years fishing commercially, including several winters in Alaska, before entering college.

Basil Warnock (alias Cecil Crockett) was also 40 when interviewed. By 1981 he had sold the *Flo-N* (alias *Lou-R*), which sank with loss of life a couple of years later. Meanwhile he had purchased an 80-foot wooden Gloucester schooner type built in Massachusetts in 1944, which he brought through the Panama Canal with stops to outfit the boat. He trawled for bottomfish and shrimp for five to six years until a log pierced the hull and sank the boat off Cape Blanco. Over the next two years he built 30 trawl nets for other fishermen. Then he purchased the *Impala,* a 40-foot wooden troller built in the Columbia River area, which he fished for crab. He later moved up to a 48-foot steel dragger built in Fort Bragg, California. He has since sold his bottomfishing and shrimp permits, but still crabs. He hopes to retire at 62, if he can sell his boat. A son and son-in-law fished with him for over a decade, and a grandson is learning.

Dick Lilienthal, 48 when interviewed, retired in 1989 after his arthritis became bad. He turned the *NelRonDic* over to his son Rick, who had worked with him since he was 15. Rick has since installed all new electronic gear and replaced the sturdy, slow mechanical winch with a hydraulic version. He focuses on crab and trawls for bottomfish, but has quit shrimping, which Dick says became too crowded for smaller boats. Rick might quit trawling altogether, due to increased restrictions on fishing in the shallow nearshore waters which the Lilienthals have long favored. Besides maintaining an extensive rhododendron garden, Dick welds and repairs up to 40 crab pots a year for his son, who wraps and knits them. One grandson had worked on the *NelRonDic* since he was 15 until, tired of low wages, he went to college. Another grandson is learning to make gear and is working on the boat.

Arnold Hockema was 58 when interviewed. Back problems complicated by anemia compelled him to retire in 1983 and sell the *Elaine Dell,* which now works out of Brookings. His son Tom built a 41-foot steel dragger, *Brandy,* in his parents' backyard in 1978 to fish for salmon, tuna, crab, and bottomfish, but he lost the boat to the Production Credit Association in 1984. Arnold succeeded in purchasing the boat back in 1985 but Tom had meanwhile assumed his uncle's boat. Arnold's grandson Devin began running the *Brandy*, which he fishes for crab, bottomfish, shrimp, and squid. Arnold helps him finance it and keep it in crab pots, which he welds, wraps, and knits. Arnold's son John still fishes the same boat he operated in 1977-78 for crab, and after adapting the boat for trawling, he also fishes for shrimp and bottomfish.

I marvel at the persistence and dedication of these determined fishing people who so love their work, the fish, and their environment. Their traditional small family business strategies have kept them in good occupational health and have fostered the stamina to endure. As politics, marketing, climate, exotic species, and contaminants seriously threaten their livelihood, the important role that traditional, sustainable fishing businesses play in nurturing the fisheries, in providing food for the public, and in supporting local economies, must be recognized and respected.

For updates and reviews of the summaries I am most grateful to Betty Anderson, Joe Easley, Charles and Alex Ells, Floyd and Nancy Green, Carl and Eileen Harrington, Paul Heikkila, Arnold and Doris Hockema, Dick and Verna Lilienthal, Lila Short, Holly Hall Stamper, Viola and David Steege, Virginia Walker, and Basil Warnock. Any inaccuracies in rendering their stories and advice are of my own making.

Janet C. Gilmore
Mount Horeb, Wisconsin
November 1998

Acknowledgments

I owe my introduction to Charleston and the fishing world to the spring-term programs of the Oregon Institute of Marine Biology (1973–76) and to students and staff who participated in them; Joe Parker, Jim Wright, and Bob Terwilliger were especially inspiring. For taking me in and educating me in things that they do not think are important because they know them so well, I am particularly indebted to Fred Anderson, Cecil Crockett, Charlie and Jessie Ells, Floyd Green, Leonard Hall, Jake Harlan, Carl and Lynne Harrington, Arnold and Doris Hockema, Art Horton, Dick and Verna Lilienthal, Cyrus, Sr., and Violet Little, and Norman and Virginia Walker. Thanks as well to most of these people plus Betty Anderson and Eileen Harrington for graciously responding through the mail to recent requests for updates and additional information. I am also especially grateful to Marine Extension Agent Paul Heikkila for sharing with me his incredible knowledge of all aspects of the local commercial fisheries obtained not only from his extension work and a solid grasp of fisheries-related research, but mostly from his upbringing and current active involvement in the fishing business. Also for their knowledge and willingness to share it, I would like to thank Norm Anderson, Roger Boyington, Helen Cardwell, Bill Chard, Ruth Hallmark Day, Darrell Demory, Nathan Douthit, Lorance Eickworth, Bob and Jim Green, Lucille and David Hanson, "Bud" Hartley, William Hillstrom, Jr., Mike Hosie, Fred Humbert, Terry Irick, Jack Kelley, Harold and John Knutson, Mike Lane, Jerry Lukas, Virginia Maine, Keith Ott, Butch Schroeder, Kurt Swanson, Burley Young, Jack Wilskey, young fisherman Mark B., and Mr. Smith of Koontz Machine Shop.

I would especially like to acknowledge Joe Parker, Ward Robertson, Charles Kocher, Betty Anderson, Charlie Ells, Mr. and Mrs. Floyd Green, Holly Hall, Doris Hockema, and Virginia and Norman Walker for furnishing many of the photographs presented in this work. I thank Jean Hanna and Paul Rudy for use of the Oregon Institute of Marine Biology darkroom, and Jim Carman of Madison, Wisconsin, for making prints from my negatives at cost and according to my exacting specifications. For general encouragement, moral support, and hospitality during the fieldwork phase of the project, I am indebted to Dorothy and Art Loftus, Anne and Bill Karl, Bonnie and Bruce Wiegman, Mary Lee Flanagan, and most of all, to my parents, Dorothy and Phil Gilmore of Eugene.

The original version of this work could not have been completed without Warren E. Roberts's patient support over many years. The project also benefitted from W. Edson Richmond's interest in the subject and his eye for catching dangling modifiers, Mary Ellen Brown's thorough readings and editorial advice, and Rita C. Naremore's commitment over a very long period of time. The writing and revising phases of this work would have been impossible but for generous "grants" from the James P. Leary Foundation. During the revision process, an Honorary Fellowship bequeathed by the Department of Scandinavian Studies at the University of Wisconsin–Madison gave me indispensable access to the university's library collections and photographic equipment, facilities, and services. Of course, a published, revised version of the original never would have seen the light of day but for the enthusiasm and encouragement of Simon Bronner and Marie Low.

To protect their immediate identity, I have used pseudonyms as requested for three of the major fisherman-informants, their spouses, their boats, and the boats and people they mention in this study.

Introduction

Charleston, Oregon

After skirting the Coos Bay estuary for six miles, the Cape Arago Highway sweeps down into Charleston where it crosses South Slough, continuing for another seven miles out to state parks that face the Pacific Ocean. The low drawbridge spanning the slough thrusts motorists suddenly into the heart of the area's fishing industry and the midst of a concentration of smallish, fairly modern, low-lying buildings—residences and businesses—stretched along the waterway on sands deposited against forested hills that border the confluence of the slough, the Coos Bay estuary, and the sea. The sprawl of Peterson's fish processing plant, its extensive graveled parking area, stacks of crab pots, and strings of fishing boats docked alongside grace the northern side of the highway as it approaches the bridge. South of the approach, joined together with a pitted, sandy and graveled road and wide parking areas of similar caliber, cluster a blocky marine supply store with a small charter boat office out front, a remodeled house trailer turned workingman's cafe, and the looming, weather-worn buildings that house Kelley's bustling boatbuilding and maintenance facilities. Beyond these businesses, to the south, a number of small cottages nestle in crab grass, backed by a motley assemblage of boats in dry dock, in turn surrounded by docks edging the slough and harboring an eccentric range of fishing boats.

The crossing exposes a bank of additional fish processing plants rambling off to the north, and a stretch of small homes lining Roosevelt Boulevard to the south, hugging the far side of the slough. Buffeted by briny wafts of sea air, the bridge affords a wonderful view of fishboats engaged in a variety of activities on the waterway—docked at fish plants delivering fish or taking on ice in preparation for a fishing trip, or pulled out of water, up on the ways at Kelley's undergoing repairs—and traffic is often halted on the bridge while it swings open to let the fishboats through.

The other side of the span ends in downtown Charleston, a busy intersection saddled with locally important small businesses that serve as both tourist

1. Cape Arago Highway
2. Downtown Charleston
3. Roosevelt Boulevard
4. Bill's Machine & Welding
5. Hanson's Boat Dock
6. South Slough
7. Joe Ney Slough
8. Pacific Ocean
9. Coos Bay Bar
10. Inner Boat Basin
11. Outer Boat Basin

12. Coos Bay Estuary
13. Alaska Packers
14. Lazio's
15. Barbey Fisheries
16. Hallmark Fisheries
17. Cape Arago Highway
18. Peterson's Seafood
19. Hanson's Landing
20. Kelley Boat Works
21. Boat Graveyard
22. Joe Ney Moorage

Photo Courtesy of Ward Robertson

traps and informal meeting places for the community. To the south, heaps of rusting metal parts and equipment and a herd of customer cars and trucks attend a squat marine machine and welding shop. A laundromat, curio shop, restaurant-bar, and a gas station complete the line up, with access to Roosevelt Boulevard residences shortly beyond. The northern strip lodges a tiny post office, a combination general store and gas station, a barber shop, one of two seafood shops in the area where one can purchase fresh local ocean produce, another general store featuring antiques on display and a false front façade to entice tourists, a small drive-in, and finally, the well-worn, well-loved Red's Tavern, a local hangout central to the community and renowned for its crusty customers and wild times.

An immediate right off the highway after leaving the bridge leads behind several fish processing plants, past a church, into a sandy, crab-grassy area interspersed with small cottages, house trailers, and more small businesses—the other seafood shop, another curio shop, another restaurant-bar, a motel, a marine electronics firm, a fiberglass boat repair shop, and Leonard Hall's miniature Snug Harbor Railroad, which he runs around his house on weekends at 25 cents a passenger. Broadway continues north beyond this area past a series of modest buildings of varying ages backed against the hillside, which variously house the Oregon Institute of Marine Biology, a branch of the Oregon Department of Fish and Wildlife, and the U. S. Coast Guard. Fanning out between this string of institutions and the block of homes and small businesses in 1978 lay a wasteland of sand and gravel fill staked out for storage and parking spaces for summertime RVs and small pleasure boats, hemmed in by general parking areas which finally look over the Charleston Boat Basin; new storage buildings have since filled much of the void.

The masts and trolling poles of some 500 to 700 local fishing boats wave and whistle above the rock retaining walls that rectalinearly define the two boat basins and set them off some from the slough, the rest of the estuary, and the ocean. The basins harbor the overwhelming majority of local fishing boats and support along their banks two cafes and the Fisherman's Library where fishermen congregate; a tavern; marine electronics, engine, and bait and tackle shops; further fish processing and landing stations; and more Coast Guard facilities.

Rough and cluttered with the ugly signs of recent, quick, unsophisticated development, Charleston contrasts sharply with the raw beauty of its natural surroundings–tall evergreens rising from sandy banks lining a seemingly unabused waterway that trails off to the south, and a brooding expanse of clouds and ocean that engulfs the northwest. Equally contrasting characters ply this cool, interrupted setting, running the gamut from people intent upon making a good living and enjoying it while they do, to calculating businessmen, shady speculators, sloppy tourists, derelicts, losers, and people hiding from the world, society, or the law. Rudely defying the natural environment, packed with outlaws, eccentrics, and independent types of all kinds, Charleston is indeed an energetic, modern frontier town, hardly the quaint and curious quiet fishing village that some people would like to think it is. Less staid than the older, more established northern Oregon ports which are more heavily influenced by ethnic groups and the "old Portland," New England Yankee-based traditions of the state, Charleston remains dominated by a kind of speculative optimism that characterized the Californians who first seized the Coos Bay estuary for business in the mid-1800s.[1]

Origins of the Project

Born east of the Cascades, brought up in the Willamette Valley, I was accustomed to visiting more uninhabited regions of the Oregon Coast 70 miles north of Charleston during winter and spring weekends and vacations. Occasionally during the summer, I also visited the more exploited coasts of northern Oregon and northern Washington. I had passed through Charleston on the way to state parks in the early 1960s when I was a teenager; except for a blurry yet colorful memory of crossing the bridge, however, the experience did not make much of an impression. At that time many of the current buildings did not exist, the boat basins were not yet complete, and the area did not churn with as much activity as it does now. Charleston did not make a real impact upon me until I went to the Oregon Institute of Marine Biology in March 1975 to teach folklore during its spring-term program.

Homesick for my native Oregon and at a critical juncture in my folklore studies at Indiana University, I had returned to the Pacific Northwest in 1974 to do fieldwork for my dissertation. That folklorists and cultural geographers deemed the territory an area of "utter darkness" early in 1975 gave me additional impetus.[2] Soon after my return home, I obtained the teaching job and spent two and a half months living at the marine biology station along with 7 other University of Oregon faculty members and 45 students. The program then was interdisciplinary in scope, aimed at developing a comprehensive understanding of the Coos Bay area through study of its geological, biological, and cultural makeup; its history and geography; and various economic, political, and social issues facing the local population. Each student pursued a major term project based on local issues, sources, and fieldwork that could integrate scholarly concerns and approaches of several of the disciplines represented in the program.

While I conducted my own fieldwork and made observations and contacts trying to comprehend the area on my own terms and get a jump ahead of the students, I did not pay much attention to aspects of the fishing industry that are so heavily present in Charleston until students brought me an unexpected wealth of observations regarding local fishermen, fishwives, their politics, superstitions and attitudes, meeting places, daily routines, clothing styles, and boats.[3] I still did not take a vested interest in these matters until the following spring when I again moved to Charleston from the Willamette Valley to teach a second term in the program. Further student reportings of fishing ways, especially regarding fishing boats, fatally piqued my interest.

In particular, several students had observed how the local fishboats could be classified according to fisheries use, hull shape, and hull material.[4] The persistent Joe Parker turned up the late extraordinary Wilbur Humbert, "the last great wood-boat builder on the West Coast," and evidence that fishermen were substantially involved in maintaining, repairing, altering, and even building their own boats and fishing gear to suit their individual tastes and local fishing.[5] In short, student inquiries pointed to active local traditions of building, maintaining, and altering a variety of fishing boats for a number of purposes. Since I was then mostly interested in user-based practices of altering existing structures for personal use, Charleston's fishboats seemed to form a much more compelling, concentrated, easily identifiable, common-sensible, natural corpus of artifacts to study than did any selection of houses I might isolate in the southern Willamette Valley or on the southern Oregon coast. Inspired, I decided to follow up on my students' leads, not realizing that in turning from land-based to water-oriented structures I would enter into an entirely other world of folk traditions that appear to be typical of fishing communities wherever they might be, well beyond the port, the state, or even the region.

Studying the Fisherfolk

I settled in the Charleston-Coos Bay area for two years, after completing my teaching responsibilities in June 1976. While holding down a part-time job to finance my research, I spent the first year (1976–77) contacting local authorities and marine officials; perusing archival sources and governmental records for information regarding the Charleston fisheries, fishing boats, and potential contacts; conducting inventories of fishing boats moored around the bay, recording their names and the kinds of fishing gear they had on board; and locating, observing, mapping, and photographing local marine service shops. During this time I also began lurking around the docks observing and photographing boats, watching fishermen at work on them, and engaging in conversation with fishermen when the opportunity arose.

Since I felt I needed some analytical method for selecting a small but representative number of fishermen and boats to study in depth, I distilled from the mire of fisheries statistics a fairly tricky system for determining informants. Following Marine Extension Agent Paul Heikkila's advice, I decided to concentrate on fishermen engaged in the "combination-type" fisheries, or, in terms of the groups outlined in Stevens and Liao's 1972 study of Oregon commercial fishermen, crab fishermen (who might also fish for salmon, tuna, shrimp, and/or bottomfish) and drag fishermen (who fish for bottomfish and/or shrimp and maybe also crab and/or tuna).[6] With such a focus I could eliminate the overwhelming majority (over 90 percent) of people who obtain commercial fishing and vessel licenses to fish only part of the year only for salmon (and maybe tuna). In contrast, the small remainder (about 200 fishermen along the Oregon Coast and about 60 in Charleston) represented full-time, year-round fishermen whose home towns coincided with their home ports. These men also had many more years of fishing experience and years spent as skippers of their own boats; they had much less nonfishing employment experience; their fathers and/or fathers-in-law were more likely to have been fishermen, too; they spent more days fishing and more days devoted to the maintenance and repair of their boats and gear during the year; they operated larger, more expensive boats and more expensive equipment; they seemed to be more successful businessmen earning good incomes despite the high costs of their operations; and they are better documented in federal, state, and port records. In short, this focus led me to the hard core of the occupation, the self-proclaimed "professional, full-time, commercial fishermen" for whom fishing is often a family tradition and most certainly a way of life.

Next, using Oregon Department of Fish and Wildlife records, I compiled a list of 21 boats that had been fishing out of Charleston and/or nearby ports for comparatively conspicuous lengths of time, representing about one-fourth of the Charleston crab fleet and a little less than one-half of the drag fleet (more than half of the bottomfish-only fleet, and about two-fifths of the bottomfish-shrimp set) in 1976–77.[7] From this list, and using Charleston Boat Basin records, I in turn generated a list of fishermen which pleasingly dovetailed with a growing list of contacts recommended to me by locals.[8]

I began interviewing in July 1977 and continued intermittently through May 1978, when my funds were dwindling and I felt I had enough data to begin writing. During this period I also conducted another inventory of the local fishing boats, this time estimating their lengths and noting the hull/stern shapes and materials, color schemes, the placement and features of pilothouses, and the kinds of fishing gear they had aboard. With these data I could estimate numbers of boats and participants in both year-round and summertime fisheries — statistics sadly lacking for individual Oregon ports. I could also use the information to make rough correlations between boat forms and fisheries uses, hull materials, and color schemes. Appropriately enough, I ended the fieldwork phase of my project by attending the launching of a fisherman-informant's newly built steel fishing boat.

Ultimately I formally interviewed twenty-five people involved with the local commercial fishing industry: eleven fishermen, four boat shop managers/ boat designer-builders, three marine machine and welding shop managers, one machinist-welder-hydraulics expert, one propellor and general marine fabrication expert, one marine electronics expert's son, two marine supply store managers, and two old-timers (one former gillnet fisherman and former manager of one of the marine supply stores; one former manager of one of the older local fish processing plants). I must have spoken casually with at least eight more fishermen. Additionally I badgered three friends occasionally for information and help, each of whom worked with or for some of the above shop managers and paved the way for me to interview them.

I interviewed roughly half of the fishermen designated on my list of twenty-one boats—ten owner-operators and the fisherman-father of an eleventh—and I spoke casually with a twelfth and his brother. Five were predominantly drag fishermen (three bottomfish-only, two shrimp and bottomfish); three were bottomfish, shrimp, and crab fishermen; another three were crab fishermen who fished also for salmon during the summer; and one was a crab fisherman who fished either salmon or shrimp during the summer, depending on how he felt.[9] They represented perhaps one-sixth to one-eighth of the 1977 crab fleet, and one-fourth of the 1977 drag fleet (more than one-half of the bottomfish-only fleet).

The 12 marine shop informants accounted for perhaps one-tenth of those engaged in such businesses in 1977, but they represented all of the local boat shops, all but one of the marine machine and welding shops, the two major marine supply shops, and one of several marine electronics firms. Most of them also commanded years of experience in the business and/or area and could speak with great authority—compared to at least half of the waterworkers who are young men, new to the business or the area, and who do not really want to wax eloquent about their work anyway, at least to a woman.

Contacting fishermen initially to arrange for interviews, let alone catching them at just the right moment to interview them, took a great deal of patience and persistence. Because of the nature of their work, they are likely to be at any one of several places on land or at sea at any moment. Generally, fishermen get up very early in the morning, an hour or two before daylight, in order to check the weather and get ready to go out fishing—if the weather and tide permit, about half an hour before dawn, when light is just breaking and they can see their way across the bar better than in complete darkness. A good portion of the year, fishermen get up and get to work much earlier in the day than does the average landlubber. If they go out fishing, they might be gone for only part of the day or up to more than a week. And if they go out fishing, they generally work many more hours of the day than the average of other kinds of jobs— sometimes 16 to 18 hours a day for day-fishermen, and 'round the clock for two to three days for drag fishermen—so they get into port "after hours," late in the evening or any time during the day or night. While crab fishermen generally return to port at the end of a day of work, draggers stay out of port from two to five days, and salmon or tuna trollers stay out up to two weeks. When the season is busy and the weather is good day after day, fishermen are impossible to locate. They are out fishing intensely, home tending to family emergencies and snoozing in between runs, or frenetically racing around town gathering parts and supplies, mending their boats and equipment to get ready for the next possible day of fishing.

I found that the best times to locate fishermen were slack times — during mid-season slumps (after the first-of-season rush, before the end-of-season push), when fishing had not been too good, when the weather had kept them in port for so many days that they had long since completed immediate preparations for the next day of fishing, when they were on strike for better prices and had not been fishing for a while, when they were in between fishing seasons and were outfitting their boats from one fishery to another (as the weather permitted), when they were waiting to take their boats out of water for an annual checkup, or soon after they had retired from fishing "for good." November through May were the best months to catch fishermen ashore with aught to do but chat; the worst times were late spring, summer, and especially early fall, not only because of the "last chance" fishing mentality but also because, after the end of the fall season, many fishermen escape to the woods to hunt for three to six weeks.[10] Sometimes Fridays were good days to find fishermen ashore, since superstition keeps some of them from beginning a trip then. Even so, it took weeks to catch certain fishermen, even when they were quite willing to be interviewed.

In general, my most successful method of netting interviews was to learn to identify specific fishermen by association with their boats, and then to approach them face-to-face on the docks. A less successful but necessary procedure was to contact fishermen sight unseen by phone — I got a few more acceptances than refusals this way. But after the initial contact, whether by phone or on the docks, I had to call up the fisherman repeatedly until, usually aided by his wife or a crewman, I caught him at just the right moment when he felt he had the time and inclination to be interviewed and when he could not find an excuse to get out of it.

No matter how I presented myself to fishermen initially — on the docks or over the phone — I sensed some discomfort and suspicion from almost all of them. During the course of interviews I could actually see the relief spread over their faces once they had realized that my interest was sincere and my questions relatively harmless, or once they had grilled me and lectured me about my affiliations with the Oregon Institute of Marine Biology and educational institutions in general, my means of employment ("Are you working on a grant?"), and my origins. In some cases, I still do not think I passed the "test."

Much of the initial testing I encountered—even among some shop workers—appears to be the result of past bad experiences with interviewers, of whom there have been too many in the area in recent years, I gathered. Also, fishermen value their reclusiveness and many feel that much of their hard-earned money unjustly goes to taxes that support governmental and educational institutions, which in turn sponsor data collectors whose bad jobs studying fishermen inevitably and derogatorily influence fishermen's politics and economics. In fact, two fishermen would not allow me to interview them because of the bad experiences they claimed they had had with data collectors and subsequent publicity. For similar reservations, three of the eleven fishermen who did grant me interviews preferred that I retain pseudonyms for them and their boats in this book.

As an aside, in response to many colleagues who have asked me about the subject, I cannot deny that my gender may partly explain the difficulties I experienced in obtaining interviews. However, in my position as a nonparticipant observer—more specifically, a data collector with an education—I felt I had an advantage. Young male college students without the appropriate family ties to the fishing community often encountered more trouble seeking information than I did. One fellow, unwittingly looking like a classic case of someone seeking work on a fishing boat, could not get any fishermen to talk to him but one who took pity on him and explained why he was being so carefully avoided. Another student, while getting fishermen to speak to him, spent more time defending his choice of going to school instead of gaining a "real" education by fishing than he did discussing topics centering on the fisherman. Yet another, in showing his inquisitiveness, was absorbed into the industry, getting a job on a fishing boat and forsaking academic studies altogether. In short, as a woman, I did not run as great a risk of appearing a prime candidate for a job, provoking avoidance or enticement behaviors; I was less likely to become a fisherman in the future, thus less worrisome as a potential gossip in the wrong contexts, and more trustworthy as a confidant; and I was not expected to know much about fishing or mechanics, so fishermen were more likely to take pains to explain things to me.

On the whole, marine-related craftsmen and shop managers were much easier to contact, regardless of how busy they were. They could usually be located at their offices or shops or at their work phone numbers, Monday through Friday, eight to five. In almost every case, calling or showing up without previous introduction worked well, in order to make arrangements for an interview and a tour of the shop right then, later in the day, or later in the week, month, or season when the informant knew he would have some slack time (something a fisherman can never quite determine). I suppose that because of the nature of their businesses—services rendered to the public at large—craftsmen and shop workers are accustomed to receiving calls or shop visits from strangers.

In almost all cases, I contacted initially and interviewed craftsmen and shop managers at their shops or in their offices, and I received tours of their shops from them at the time of the interviews. In contrast, I interviewed most of the fishermen in their homes and in the presence, or within earshot, of their wives—the result of calling them at home, often having spoken to the spouses about the interviews over the phone in trying to reach their husbands. Interviewing fishermen in their homes with their wives present was unexpectedly rewarding, however. Not only did I get to see the fisherman's landbase, but the wife's presence eased the awkwardness of the confrontation and she often increased the productivity of the interview. Interviews were fuller and longer, and often the two would take over the discussion, trying to get facts straight, discussing this angle and that in depth, and reminding each other of things they had left out or that they thought would be particularly interesting to me. Actually, fishermen's wives usually know quite a bit about commercial fishing. Many are active partners with their husbands, often managing the family fishing business, promoting cooperative relief organizations for fisher families who suffer losses, and sometimes lobbying for legislation favoring their businesses. Further, many wives come from fishing families themselves, and often were instrumental in getting their husbands into the business in the first place. Granted, the wife's presence may have precluded the discussion of some matters (raunchy stories and jokes, experiences that might "tell on him" such as dangerous fishing experiences not told to wives to keep them from worrying, detailed particulars of boat maintenance), but I felt the advantages of her presence far outweighed the disadvantages, and besides, my presence alone was probably enough to curtail some kinds of talk.

I interviewed only two fishermen on their boats (one of whom was accompanied by his wife); I spoke with two others aboard their boats; and I spoke with another in the storeroom of a restaurant (where I could tape-record him without excessive noise). For the most part I interviewed each fisherman only once, and I did not get tours of all of the boats, although I did get tours of several boats not on my "select" list.

In interviewing fishermen, I sought, (1) a brief life history that would launch into an account of personal fishing experience; (2) an account of the fisherman's experience with boats, a history of his boat ownership, and a history of his present boat and his experiences with it (fulfillment of fishing requirements, adaptations made, upkeep needed); and (3) a description of his daily, seasonal, or yearly work and boat maintenance routines, the amount and kind of work put into boat and gear maintenance, and specialists consulted for maintenance service.

In interviewing craftsmen or shop managers, I asked for a brief life history, a family history if pertinent, and a history and description of the business or trade. I was particularly interested in determining the kinds of work certain craftsmen or businesses do for fishermen, which fishermen constitute their clientele, and what kinds of contracts or arrangements they make with fishermen for the work they do.

While my approach to each interview was broadly standard, I let the informant dictate the course of the interview, and I guided it as minimally as I could. To my delight, many of the fishermen embellished their descriptions with sayings, jokes, anecdotes, and general discussions pertinent to their businesses. One man loved to tell stories about the bizarre kinds of paraphernalia he brought up in his fishing nets over the years. Another fisherman liked to tell stories about near fishing disasters, in particular, about people falling off their boats while at sea. Another man got to telling old Norwegian halibut fisherman dialect jokes. Yet another expounded on fishermen's superstitions. Several fishermen informed me about local fishermen's politics, while one fellow chose to educate me about international fisheries politics, the American democratic system, and his ideas about life, death, and education. And another fisherman suggested how I should have conducted my research! Indeed, talking to fishermen about the concrete and familiar aspects of their environment—artifacts and behaviors that they know well—indirectly elicited oral forms of folklore that, while interesting in themselves, illuminate fishermen's attitudes about their work and its technology. In contrast, I found many of the shop managers and craftsmen much more direct, almost curt, in their responses to my questions, and unlike fishermen, they made generalizations about fishermen very easily, and some liked to gossip about them at great length.

I was able to tape-record a third of my informants. Three informants would only allow me to take notes and in other cases I did not ask to tape-record because the informant was testy, the environment was too busy, or I did not have the equipment with me. Whether I tape-recorded, took notes, or depended on my memory, after completing an interview I wrote down what I could recall of it. Then referring to any interview notes or tape-recordings, I amplified the recall and wrote an assessment of the interview. Altogether I completed 293 handwritten pages of interview write-ups, recorded 9 hours and 42 minutes of tape, selectively transcribed 151 pages (typed, double-spaced) from the tapes, and shot over 500 black and white photographs and nearly 100 color slides of Charleston boats and scenes of boat work.

For this volume I succeeded in corresponding with nine of the original eleven fishermen (three fishers, five fisher couples, and one's wife), two student mentors, and the propellor man. I gratefully received back updates on fishing businesses, standard information I failed to obtain during interviews, corrections of information printed in the dissertation version, photos of some fishermen and boats which sadly I had not taken while working in the field, and, in several cases, hearty approval and encouragement of my work!

The World of the Fishboat

While I had intended to study the local commercial fishing vessels, alterations that fishermen had made in them, and the impact that fishermen as users and designers had made on local boat forms, constructions, and building practices, I did not collect the kinds of hard evidence — such as precise measurements and scale drawings of altered boats before and after the changes vis-à-vis those of locally built new boats, over at least a decade of time — that would render the appropriately precise judgments. Instead, while keeping boats and fishermen-induced alterations as my focus but relying on oral testimony and the fishermen themselves to elucidate the artifacts and work done to them, I netted quite different results. I discovered less about the specifics of boat design and building than I did about the ideas that inform them and the general context of the artifact. Through talking to fishermen about their boats, I learned partly to see the boat as the fisherman does, to understand how he uses it to express attitudes about his work, the tools of the trade, fellow fishermen and water workers, and in turn, to comprehend the fisherman's way of life, the nature of his work, and his worldview.

When I began this project, searching for some cosmic affirmation of my intent, I consulted the *I Ching*. To my amazed gratification, the oracle directed me to the hexagram meaning dispersion, whose "image of wood over water," says the discourse, "gives rise to the idea of a boat."[11] It continues: "They scooped out tree trunks for boats and they hardened wood in the fire to make oars. The advantage of boats and oars lay in providing means of communication." In the context of my study, this appropriately mysterious message is both apt and profound. It implies a broader purpose, a greater functional field, and a larger web of human relationships than are ascribed to the boat when it is perceived more narrowly, as it usually is, primarily as a means of plying and exploiting a certain environment.[12] Looking at the boat as both means and point of communication helps illuminate an ancient maritime world of human endeavor, interaction, and psychology, of occupational and family networks, customs, and beliefs, which is today not very accessible nor well understood.[13] The boat provides a way of delineating a characteristic geography of ideas and of isolating and understanding a distinctive kind of community; it offers the scholar a means not only of gaining access to this world and of communicating with its inhabitants, but of discussing pet concepts with colleagues in the scholarly world (if he does not become so absorbed in the esoteric terrain, as so often happens, that he loses the ability to translate).

Seen as a means of communication in the most conservative sense, the boat clearly transfers information from point to point. Before the advent of mass media, boats were often used in coastal and riverside communities as primary vehicles for relaying news. Today the exchange of information is usually both a secondary and inadvertent function. For example, with their boats, fishermen from many ports meet at sea and in other ports as they journey to and from fishing grounds, pursue fish along the coast, escape bad weather, tend equipment failures, deliver their catches, restock supplies, or even seek camaraderie. Face-to-face or over the radio they pass gossip and much purposeful misinformation. Indirectly through their boats, equipment, and the manner in which they keep and use them, they communicate additional information. Indeed, keen observation of other fishermen's movements, equipage, and use of equipment often aggravated by tricky radio game-playing appears to be a common and possibly essential custom among offshore fishermen.[14] A joke (paraphrased) that retired commercial fisherman Charlie Ells tells accentuates this point:

> This Norwegian fisherman kept getting tremendous catches. Another man kept following him and watching him with binoculars. One day the Norwegian brought his boat over to the other's and said, "We just lost Martin overboard." The other said, "Never mind [that]. What are you using for bait?"[15]

Consequently, through first-hand experience and gossip, fishermen are very knowledgeable of the personnel and technology involved in the fishing industry in ports throughout the immediate region. Partly out of common interests, and partly due to this esoteric mode of communication enhanced these days by mail-order catalogs, other widely available specialized publications, extension agents, and personal correspondence, both coastal and inland fishermen (at least in media-gorged North America) are often quite well-informed about fishes, fish-taking equipment, methods, and boats, not only in adjacent regions but in far distant parts of the world.[16] Thus the boat contributes to the formation of a special maritime geography of ideas extending from port to port, coastline to coastline, and throughout entire river systems, far beyond state, national, and broad regional lines, which accounts in part for widely shared varieties of fishing technologies.[17]

As a point of communication, the boat also is, in one sense, a place of communication. Typically an all-male environment physically and visually isolated from the immediate land-based community and the society at large, the fishing boat is the arena for distinctive kinds of human behavior and communication. Outside the bounds of land-based society, yet besieged by stresses of a hostile environment, hard work, close company, and the necessity of cooperation, the members aboard create a society in microcosm, with well-defined roles, rules of appropriate behavior, and an esoteric system of communication based on the boat and its operation.[18]

A tool for achieving different environmental, and thus different behavioral, social, and mental states, the boat is also a way of coping with these experiences. A companion at sea whose performance is critical to all aboard, the boat provides a common experience and topic of conversation, and it is discussed and sometimes addressed as a person. Offering means for working with the environment in prescribed ways, her parts and behaviors receive names, dominate exchanges during periods of intense work and sometimes during leisure moments, and may comprise the bulk of esoteric vocabulary used on board.[19]

While the experience at sea is often unsettling and not always the most positive for a fisherman, it gives him an underlying camaraderie with people who have shared the same experience, even if they have not fished together, and it puts him at odds symbolically, if not actually, with the social order back home or with society in general.[20] Even for a fisherman who fishes alone, his ability to isolate himself so overtly with his boat from land, society, and the known, and to traverse two worlds with distinctly different ways of operating, promotes a kind of perspicacity, aloofness, and uneasiness in his attitude toward things ashore. Indeed, fishermen and old salts are often stereotypically thought to be soothsayers; one of the more recent, vivid, and well-publicized examples is the late Robert Shaw's portrayal in Steven Spielberg's movie *Jaws*. The fisherman's treatment of the fishing trip as an otherworldly, mystical experience that he cannot fully articulate—or simply as an esoteric experience that he does not wish to take the trouble to explain to outsiders—his preference ashore for the company of the initiated, and his conspicuous avoidance of outsiders attracted to the docks to view the fishing boats give physical form to his psychological distance. His discomfort, his knowing muteness, and his cliquishness ashore, serve to foster the aura of mystery and romance and a plethora of ancient stereotypical notions that most landlubbers associate with the fisherman's life, work, and character. Indeed, for the public at large, the boat is the most visible manifestation of the fisherman and his work; its appeal, colorfulness, and strangeness of form are used to substantiate an imaginary world of colorful eccentrics, idyllic work, and quaint and curious fishing villages. Thus the "experience of the boat"—for both insiders and outsiders—contributes to the existence of a separable, truly marginal, fishing community defined by the associations fishermen do make with those who support their existence and occupation ashore.

Ashore, the circle of discussants and the range of talk involving the boat expands. As fishermen clean, mend, maintain, and alter their boats, they also seek advice and help from fellow fishermen and a variety of water workers, and they gossip about the attributes of each other's boats and habits of boat use and upkeep. This kind of boat talk coupled with observation of a variety of boats gives fishermen a real education in boat description, history, design, construction, and performance. It also demonstrates the heavy expressive load that fishermen place on their boats and the way they use them to rank their colleagues, endorse particular water workers, show solidarity with certain fishermen, yet project a distinctive identity and a particular fishing philosophy.

People who talk boats together pass among themselves certain ideas about boats and a detailed vocabulary specifying boat behaviors, shapes, parts, construction techniques, and features and locations in the boat's environment.[21] How people talk about boats, what words they use to describe boats, and where and to whom they choose to talk boats in depth express as well important folk networks of individuals. Forming "conduits" through which certain kinds of information are promulgated, circulated, and kept alive, these networks explain the existence of several schools of thought regarding fishing, fishing technology, and boatbuilding practices, indicate the seats of personal power and influence within the fishing and waterfront community, and provide clues to the forms that boats do take.[22]

This book concentrates within the sphere of relationships and communicative behavior that integrate the world at sea with the world ashore through the medium of the fishboat.

Charleston Fishermen

Charleston, Oregon, today harbors a wide range of commercial fishing vessels that differ from one another in size, shape, structural makeup, construction materials, original use, present fishing use, builder, ethnic and regional origin, age, and color scheme. Indeed, the Charleston Boat Basin is a veritable museum of boats chronicling stages in the development of West Coast fisheries and fishing technology. Most of the boats were not built locally but have been imported from other coastal areas. While many have impeccable folk origins, some have been designed at the tables of marine architects and engineers, some have been built in modern industrialized shipyards that hire school-trained personnel, and still others have been mass-produced in factories according to standardized plans. Even boats that were built locally are not necessarily ideally suited to the locale or their present uses.

Charleston seems a haven for boats rejected elsewhere — boats that have outlived their original purposes, have grown outmoded, or, like some of the Gulf shrimpers now found in the port, have fully depreciated in value in their native territory. Characteristically, most of these fishboats are old, anywhere from 20 to 70 years, and they have been adapted from a variety of past uses to fish one or more of the present five major fisheries of the region: salmon, albacore tuna, Dungeness crab, shrimp, and bottomfish. Old wooden or iron lifeboats have been substantially revised for salmon trolling; salmon trollers built during the 1920s and 1930s have been geared up for modern-day trolling and crabfishing; old cannery and fish trap tenders, halibut schooners, and purse seiners are now used to capture shrimp, bottomfish, tuna, crab, and even salmon; older pleasure boats and a variety of former workboats such as tugs and icebreakers have similarly been fitted out.

Fishermen have been responsible for adapting the boats for present uses: they have usually done the work themselves, but often they have enlisted the services of experts to make the alterations to desired specifications. Engineering these changes in common ways for similar reasons, they have replaced, refashioned, removed, and added a variety of components themselves widely divergent in ages, places of origin, original uses, materials, and manufacture, to come up with new composite forms. The new compositions resemble each other, however, so that each boat expresses an individual interpretation of ideas prevalent in the area about how to accommodate a boat to fish the local grounds successfully — ideas individually perceived and individually expressed, but similarly interpreted. Thus, typical adaptations not only unify the wide assortment, but lend the boats a certain "fishboat look" that distinguishes them from other use-types of boats on the bay and, so it is said, from the fishing boats of other West Coast ports: the presence of certain kinds of fishing gear particularly identifies each boat as a regional commercial fishing vessel; a smaller, older boat that has been converted to present fishing use frequently designates Charleston as its home port; and a prevalence of converted boats distinguishes Charleston's fishing fleet from the fleets of other major West Coast ports.[1]

These boat conversion practices represent a user-based boat design tradition which has a logic distinct from local new-boat design practices and provides an interesting counterpoint to them. Perhaps at its most flamboyant in the Charleston area, this tradition is common among Pacific Northwest coastal commercial fishermen, and it appears to be an extension of their regular, active involvement in the daily, seasonal, and yearly maintenance and repair of their own boats.

In these days of handy disposables and built-in obsolescence, the longevity of Charleston's boats is truly outstanding, especially in view of the abusive manner and environment in which fishermen work them. The length of time the boats remain useful proves the economic uncertainty and the rapid rate of technological change that have so characterized the Pacific Northwest fishing industry over the past century. Their endurance is additionally a tribute to the high standards of craftsmanship and materials that generally have gone into Pacific Northwest boat construction, particularly in the case of older, wooden boats which were built when the region was thick with suitable Douglas fir and Port Orford cedar, when wooden boat- and shipbuilding were common, vibrant activities vital to local transportation and commerce, and when a surfeit of talented ship carpenters existed. Indeed the endurance of some of the boats also commends the multifunctional utility that some builders and fishers, faced with the creation of so complex and expensive an artifact for such changeable conditions of use, have succeeded in building into boat forms and constructions. The longevity of Charleston's boats attests primarily, however, to the high regard in which fishermen view their boats and the care they take to prolong the lifespan of a boat once it is built, even if it does not match their notions of the most appropriate boat for their purposes.

Perhaps at the core of the fisherman's care and respect for his boat is the artifact's critical importance to his work and his survival at work. Because of the nature of the work place, offshore fishermen everywhere depend absolutely on their boats: they use them as vehicles for entering and traversing a strange and risky realm, as platforms from which to work, as shelters from the elements while at work, as homes in which to live on the ocean for days at a time, and as companions with whom to gauge and discuss the experience.[2] Simultaneously the fisherman's sole protection and an essential tool for engaging and deriving income from a tricky environment, the boat demands and gets a lot of regular care and constant adjustment so that it may stay in good enough condition to fish as dependably and as often as possible.

The special nature of the typical fishboat of the region contributes as well to the economically hard-pressed Pacific Northwest coastal fisherman's interest in making it last. Complex, expensive, and today an esoteric artifact, the fishboat, especially a wooden one, is not easy to build, procure, or replace. Many fishermen have at one time attempted—and a few have in fact succeeded—building their own boats to cut costs and give form to desired fishboat traits. But the majority of boats used for commercial fishing have been built by specialized builders, and in general, committed, full-time fishermen have had to entrust the complicated construction, for which they seldom have both the skills and the time, to experts. Even second-hand, fishboats thus represent a formidable commitment of capital—which is often elusive in a barely surviving industry. Built anew, they require great fishing success and business solvency—a rarity among fishermen—and to many fishermen, they are somewhat suspect in craftsmanship or materials until thoroughly tested through use. Since woods of appropriate quality and builders with appropriate skills are currently thought to be too dear, too scarce, or nonexistent, a well-built wooden boat tested through time is thus virtually irreplaceable and, accordingly, fishermen revere it and the "vanished" crafts tradition that it articulates. But any boat, especially a new one, is something from which a fisherman wishes to eke as much service as he can.

Indeed, fishboat maintenance and repair chores are endemic to the off-shore fisherman's lot, and as integral parts of the operation of fishing equipment, they command a significant share of his work effort (even though scholars traditionally ignore these aspects of the fisherman's occupational life).[3] What makes the Charleston fisherman's involvement in these tasks distinctive is that, like small-time, often part-time (nonspecialized), generally inshore, often self-employed fishermen in many parts of the world, he owns his boat, he is immediately responsible for its upkeep, and he is usually the primary participant in such work.[4] Unlike them, however, but like the specialized skippers of large fishing operations such as deep-sea trawlers and tuna seiners, his boat is a much more complex artifact and he has usually not built it himself.[5] Unlike the skippers of fishing ships, however, he rarely delegates the immediate supervision and the actual work to a range of specialists on board.

Like a self-sufficient farmer, the typical Charleston fisherman is a jack of many trades, master at keeping an entire complex in balanced, working order. He assembles, installs, adjusts, repairs, replaces, and often creates from scratch a variety of complicated fishing equipment; he keeps engines and related mechanical and hydraulic parts operating smoothly; and he takes steps to ensure that the basic boat structure, especially its "skin," remains safe and sound. Additionally he can describe down to fine detail the components and features of the boat and all equipment on board; he can diagnose a problem and make minor repairs; and he can knowledgeably dismantle, reassemble, and often overhaul most mechanical and hydraulic equipment, as well as parts of the boat's superstructure.

To be sure, not all Charleston fishermen claim outstanding skills as mechanics, machinists, welders, or shipwrights. In fact some fishermen, the better off and the larger their operations, will employ crew members specifically for their welding or mechanical talents. And all local fishermen, regardless of how handy they are, depend on the expertise of specialized marine craftsmen for several essential aspects of boat upkeep such as the annual hull checkup; necessary hull repairs; propellor, shaft, and electronics repair; serious engine and mechanical failure; and most engine overhauls. Indeed, many Charleston fishermen claim that, had they the money, they would gladly give over all maintenance and repair work to the experts. Certainly the specialists would like nothing better!

However, in affording current levels of mechanization and sophistication of equipment, local fishermen can barely make good livings; so they often give work to the ever-expensive shipyard and specialists only when they must. Even if they felt able to afford more specialized care of their boats and equipment, it is doubtful if all Charleston fishermen would, or indeed could, hand over all maintenance and repair work to experts. Again, partly to cut expenses and partly to afford mechanization and larger boats, Charleston fishermen hire as few crew members as they can; local fishing operations rarely involve even four fishers including the skipper, and some—summertime salmon trolling operations—get by with only one person. With so small a crew (or none), typically composed of one or two young hands who are only moderately technically skilled in the mechanics of fishing and operating a fishboat, the skipper must be able to handle effectively a wide variety of breakdowns at sea, where no specialists are easily available. Moreover, he must keep himself fully cognizant of the condition of all parts of the boat complex in order to prevent breakdowns, which can always be life-threatening.

Perhaps more important than economic necessity in guaranteeing his involvement in boat upkeep, however, is the typical Charleston fisherman's image of himself as independent and self-sufficient. The primary reason he gives for enjoying his work, for adopting it as a profession in the first place, and for distinguishing it from other kinds of work, is that fishing allows him to be his own boss.[6] He likes to work alone or with only a few other people, and to be absolutely responsible for his work, even though his independence is certainly an illusion once he returns to port and to some extent even while he is at sea.

This solitary, self-sufficient, highly competitive, and miserly fishing style is rooted in Pacific Northwest salmon troller tradition, "first effectively settled" by Norwegian and Finnish immigrants during the early decades of the twentieth century.[7] According to this pattern, the Charleston fisherman begins fishing for his father or another older male relative or friend of the family, with or without additional crew members, on a small- to medium-size fishboat; later he may hire on to a larger boat with a larger crew, again usually operated by a male relative or friend of the family. But when the young fisherman comes of age and has saved up enough to purchase his own boat, he will usually buy a small- to medium-size boat which he will use at first mainly for salmon trolling, and which he may operate alone or with only one other person. He may later graduate to a larger boat and other fisheries, and hire a larger crew, but his first experience of owning and operating a boat single-handedly has a powerful effect on the formation of his "fishermanliness," conditioning his status among fishermen and encouraging the cultivation of adversarial relationships with peers, shoreside specialists, and society in general. With his own boat the young fisherman really begins to prove his competence as a Charleston fisherman, which involves to a great extent the demonstration of his control over the technology of the occupation, and eventually his mastery of a diversity of technical skills.[8] Indeed his acceptance of second-hand boats, which must be converted for local and personal fishing use, signifies his confidence in his technical abilities and his willingness to practice them.

The adaptation of boats for local and personal fishing use is thus a natural consequence of the Charleston fisherman's basic disposition toward the fishing business, and hence the active and responsible role he plays in operating and maintaining the entire "fishing machine," his intimate knowledge of fishboat components and repair procedures, and his practice of purchasing second-hand boats. Most boat conversion practices are based upon the replacement of parts, common maintenance and repair routines with which the fisherman is amply familiar. Many replacements—of planks and fittings, or of an entire subsystem such as an engine, for example—are made precisely to result in as little change as possible, in order to preserve the integrity of an existing system such as the hull, or the entire fishboat complex.[9] Such exchanges, involving the replacement of a part (usually worn or damaged) with one nearly identical, can result in subtle changes in the long run, for better or worse, but they do not represent significant departures from well-established rules of thumb. Even so, the fisherman may use the occasion to color the boat with his choice of materials, brand-names, or repair persons to make the changes, or with the care he takes to replicate the original or produce a piece of better fit.

Other kinds of replacements, usually those involving major components of the boat or its equipment, are made specifically to change the performance of the entire boat or any one of its subsystems, and here the fisherman makes overt conversions and exercises greater freedom of thought as a matter of course. The most frequent and obvious of such replacements generally involve fishing equipment. Since the full-time, professional Charleston fisherman must fish all year long, usually for more than one fishery, in order to make a living from fishing, he switches one complex of fishing equipment for one of another order at least twice a year; consequently, he subjects his boat to different kinds of use according to equipment, fishery, and season. He makes much the same sort of exchange of equipment and change of use when he buys a "new" second-hand boat from a region where different fisheries or gear prevail, or from a local fisherman whose choice of fisheries or equipment do not match his own.

At less frequent intervals the fisherman also faces the replacement of other major subsystems such as the engine or steering apparatus, as they inevitably malfunction and wear out. Especially if the original was not his selection, as is frequently the case with second-hand boats, the fisherman often uses the opportunity to make a change in the quality and capacity of the component, usually with the intent of improving the overall effectiveness of his fishing machine and thus any number of facets of his work. Responsive to trends in the fisheries, the region, the port, or among colleagues, he is ever on the lookout for new ideas—from a wide variety of sources—that might help mitigate recurrent technological problems.

While the fisherman makes replacements of certain components with those of different capabilities and compositions with the expectation of specific results, he frequently finds additional, often substantial, adjustments necessary because of the unforeseen effects of using new equipment or of using the boat in new contexts. To some extent such secondary adjustments are unique to the specific fishboat and the fisherman's manner of handling it. But many fishermen will make boat and equipment alterations in anticipation of these secondary effects.

Not unlike the traditional boat builder when he plots a new boat, the experienced Charleston fisherman appears to perceive the fishboat complex as a finite set of relationships that require specific solutions to achieve desirable results.[10] Through operating one boat in a variety of contexts and several boats in the same contexts, sharing with colleagues experiences with quite a range of different boats in similar contexts, and comparing notes with boat builders and other specialists while inspecting and repairing a number of boats, the Charleston fisherman learns to discriminate the fishboat's essential components and to understand the critical relationships among key subsystems. An excellent observer and a student of his own material culture, he acquires the ability to correlate a boat's performance characteristics with its formal attributes.

More like the totality of West Coast builders over the past century than any one builder or designer, however, the Charleston fisherman tolerates a simpler, more basic concept (a "deeper" structure) of what qualifies as an appropriate fishboat, and he accepts a broader range of surface structures, solutions to the problems of fitting boat form to boat function. While the fisherman, like the builder, appreciates certain features that can be consciously executed in building a particular boat, and disparages clumsy articulations, he is more willing than the builder usually is to put up with less than ideal structural details (shape, materials, joinery, overall good looks, for example), if a boat can fulfill rather general expectations of usefulness and comfort (size, sturdiness, and feel, for example), and cost. To the Charleston fisherman, being stuck with one boat that he must use in a variety of contexts over many years and in the face of many innovations, every boat represents a compromise in some way, no matter how well and conscientiously built it may be. Certain boat characteristics may work well for one use but not so well for another; adjustments may improve characteristics for one but not another purpose; a new boat may not be able to resolve the problem any better, and even if it does, it might not prove effective for long. So the fisherman opts for boat characteristics that fulfill a preferred or primary use, or he settles for a common denominator of boat traits that will work for all of his uses; a suitable boat need not have been built specifically as a fishboat.

From his experience of boats of many origins and original uses, and his involvement in the maintenance, repair, and alteration of such a variety of boats, the fisherman is also cognizant of a wide range of new and old boatbuilding technologies — differing solutions to similar problems. Accordingly, he is aware of the shortcomings of the boat builder's art: that one builder's practices and coveted embellishments may not be the only answers for achieving certain ends; that builders, try as they might, generally lack close control over some boat performance characteristics; and that standard kinds of compensatory adjustments such as the addition of ballast and stabilizers often must be made after completion of a boat. This acquaintance fuels his confidence that he, just as well as any builder, can improve imperfections in a particular boat's performance; simultaneously it encourages his tolerance for, adoption of, and inclination to experiment with new and old ideas from a multitude of (outport) sources. Indeed, he welcomes a range of boat and fishboat possibilities that would be found excessive and irreverent in a community such as Winterton, Trinity Bay, Newfoundland, where builders and fishers, often one and the same, steadfastly hold to one or two boatbuilding traditions.[11]

Importantly, the Charleston fisherman recognizes — perhaps "senses" is the more appropriate word — that the builder places different expressive demands on the boat than he does. As specialists, builders and fishers seldom share the same fishboat experience, design problems, or audiences for their boat work. The builder's most fascinating problem is "new work" in George Sturt's terms, the refinement of "proven theories and well-tried fashions" in conceiving and building a new boat, the best articulation he can make of his interpretation of the fisherman's desires within the context of a strongly maintained building philosophy.[12] His performance in fashioning the boat—selecting and preparing the materials, fabricating the components, putting the pieces together in a particular arrangement and sequence, and adding the finishing touches—is perhaps of equal (or more) importance to him as the performance of the boat as a fishing tool. The builder is perhaps as interested in pleasing and impressing other builders—mentors, peers, and apprentices—as he is his clients—fishermen individually and collectively. He may regard repair work as a necessary evil—a way of earning his bread and butter, but a gray area of unique circumstances and annoying arbitrations with strong personalities—even though it provides him with the grounds for perfecting his ideal and subsequent statements of it.

In contrast, the fisherman takes the builder's composition, an already completed work, and as he uses it, rethinks it through recomposition to make it fit another expressive context. The performance of the boat as a fishing tool is of primary importance to him, but so is his performance in making the boat as effective a mechanism and as positive a reflection of his fishing abilities (competence) as he can. He addresses other fishermen—mentors, peers, and hands—primarily; a specific highly respected builder only occasionally and usually secondarily; and in a backhanded way, builders collectively. In the Charleston context, what Sturt says in contrasting wagon-making repairs with new-work seems appropriate more to the fisherman's than the typical builder's involvement with and orientation to fishboat design:

> From repairs, in fact, came the teaching which kept the wheelwright's [boat builder's] art strongly alive. A lad might learn all about the tradition—all that antiquity had to teach—but at repairs he found out what was needful for the current day; what this road [sea] required, and that hill [estuary]; . . . repairs called for ingenuity, adaptiveness, readiness to make shift. It wasn't quite enough to know how to do this or that; you needed also to know something about why, and to be ready to think of alternative dodges for improvising a temporary effect, if for any reason the time-honoured methods known to an apprentice [a boat builder] could not be adopted.[13]

While the construction of a new boat represents an important, although rare, communicative and educational event for both the builder and the fisher, more significant are the more frequent meetings of minds over major maintenance and repair problems and, in particular, the annual hull inspection at the yard. Here the fisherman, hoping for approval, uneasily submits for review his boat, abused by another year of hard use, and his own work in the form of upkeep and personal adjustments. Builders and mechanics receive an update on the efficacy of certain designs and constructions, they observe (often not without ridicule) "new" ideas that the fisherman may have implemented during the year, and in turn they get ideas for making improvements in future new and repair work. Together builders and fishers share ideas as they reach an appraisal of the boat's condition, decide upon the work that needs to be done, figure out how to engineer certain repairs and adjustments, and then do the work. While the fisherman needs the builder's expertise, he is not particularly fond of relying upon it, or of negotiating and articulating work that he wants done, when he knows he may not be pleased with the result because of gaps in communication, lack of negotiating power, and basic differences in the ways the boat and boat work are perceived. He may use the builder's advice merely as food for thought instead of a dictum, and he may choose someone else, including himself, to accomplish the suggested work at some future time. Through this reluctant association and clash of design expectations, however, the fisherman gets a valuable part of his education in boatbuilding technology, and the builder most of his education in the fisherman's way of looking at boats. Together they establish a forum for the discussion of certain ideas, stimulating the boat design process, maintaining its vibrancy in both camps, and, through a kind of dialogue of experimentation, searching for ideal statements of new and already built local boats.

In spite of his isolationism and his own sort of specialization, the fisherman participates in, contributes to, and benefits from a greater maritime occupational community of specialists, representing a wide variety of callings, who address and discuss among themselves common problems of working at sea and of equipping people for work at sea. As a distinctive, implacable, predictably eccentric constituency, however, fishermen influence by opposition. Acting as gadflies they induce an intellectual ferment by flaunting their own tradition of working things out for themselves, testing and often flying in the face of established shoreside building practices. As an individual, each fisherman influences through cooperation and exertion of his personal (persuasive) powers. Often following the predilections of his coterie of fishing colleagues, he allies himself with a small selection of shoreside specialists. Through this consortium of specialists and fishers, often cemented by longstanding family and pedagogical connections, the fisherman fosters (or hopes to foster) preferred, often traditional notions of doing business and of articulating boat work.

Several distinctive communicative networks of this kind make up the greater occupational web.[14] Interconnected, they form the core of a broader maritime community of families set apart from the workaday world ashore by common patterns and perspectives of daily life dictated by common features of work.[15] Representing different fields of ideas and personal relationships, they give the community its texture and account in part for local fishboat variation on several themes, and the perpetuation side-by-side of several philosophies of fishboat technology.

The Coos Bay Fisheries

A Regional Perspective

The Coos Bay estuary merges with the northeastern Pacific on the southern Oregon Coast, midway between two major West Coast centers of the commercial fishing business (see fig. 2). Puget Sound lies roughly 500 miles by sea to the north and east of Coos Bay, and San Francisco and one-time influential Monterey Bay lie some 500 miles to the south. These two centers handily mark the northern and southern boundaries of one primary West Coast commercial fishing region that comprises the coastal fisheries of Washington, Oregon, and northern California (see fig. 3). More specifically, the stretch of coast between Fort Bragg, just north of San Francisco, and Cape Flattery (Neah Bay), the northwest tip of the Olympic Peninsula, delineates the region.[1] Though influenced by developments in Puget Sound and San Francisco fishing enterprises, the coastal fisheries region distinguishes itself from them, and also from those of Alaska and southern California, in the amount and kinds of fish caught there, in geographical features, and in the extent and kinds of fishing effort possible, given predominant weather, market, and political conditions.[2]

Chief among the classes of fish sought throughout this region are troll-caught salmon, Dungeness crab taken by pots, troll-caught albacore tuna, shrimp taken by otter trawl, and bottomfish taken by otter trawl, in order of decreasing value, according to Oregon catch statistics in the early 1970s (see figs. 12–24 for examples of gear types).[3] Purse seines are by and large absent from the roll call of gear used to fish the area. The coastal region as a whole then produced the bulk of the Pacific Coast catches of albacore tuna, Dungeness crab, bottomfish, and lower West Coast shrimp (*Pandalus jordani*), but less than one-fifth of the salmon catch, much of which was caught by gillnet on the Columbia River, a fishing district distinct from the coastal zone.[4] Oddly enough, the majority of fishermen of the region employed themselves only in pursuit of salmon.

Certain ports within the region have been associated with certain species, at least through the 1970s. Westport, Washington, and ports at the mouth of the Columbia River have generally ranked first for their Dungeness crab catch. Astoria, Oregon, and Ilwaco, Washington, in particular, and Oregon in general have received most of the West Coast albacore catch, when El Niño has not adversely affected tuna runs and the related canning business as it has the past several years (the only albacore tuna canner in the region, Bumble Bee in Astoria, recently closed). A substantial portion of lower West Coast shrimp used to be caught off Newport and Coos Bay, Oregon, but decreased shrimp stocks irregularly distributed along the coast in recent years have discouraged a regular pattern of landings and the shrimp fleet has not only dwindled by two-thirds, but it has become a "migratory" fleet much like the salmon trolling fleet. Northern California used to dominate all other West Coast districts in bottomfish landings, but with a significant intensification of effort in this fishery during the late 1970s and early 1980s, landings have increased in all ports and no major port currently outshines the others.[5]

Fishing in the coastal region occurs offshore in the open ocean, as it does in western and central Alaska and southern California, in contrast to inshore fishing in the protected waters of the Columbia River, Puget Sound and the Strait of Juan de Fuca, and southeastern Alaska. The majority of fishermen work waters less than 30 miles away from land. Crab fishermen place their pots in 2 to 25 fathoms of water, not far offshore.[6] Bottomfishermen must venture 10 to 30 miles out to find their prey at depths between 5 and 250 fathoms, while shrimpers head for similar waters at depths of 50 to 100 fathoms, and as much as 250 fathoms.[7] Salmon trollers range offshore, sometimes at distances of 30 miles or more, while tuna trollers rarely find their catch as close in as 30 miles, and can locate it 300 miles out — their average ranges from 50 to 150 miles offshore.[8]

Drag and crab fishermen not only wander less distance offshore than do trollermen, but they also do not stray as far north and south, generally keeping within the specific territory unofficially assigned to their home ports (between 30 to 60 miles north or south). Too, after a turn of fishing, they return to home port, unless bad weather or bad markets make harbor in another port more feasible. Moreover, crab and drag fishermen do not stay out at sea as long as trollers do to seek their catch. Crabbers day fish by and large, heading out to their fishing grounds in the early morning hours and returning with their catch later in the day, weather permitting, of course. Draggers fishing for either shrimp or bottomfish, trip fish, averaging two to five days out since it takes some time to get to requisite grounds and return home from them, and more time yet to locate and fish adequate stocks.

The nature of the tuna and salmon fisheries dictates otherwise. Albacore begin their annual sweep up the Pacific Coast starting around Baja California about the middle of June; by July they are running off the Oregon and Washington coasts; and by September, they swing west or south towards the Hawai-

Figure 2.   The Northeastern Pacific Ocean.
*(Map based on Robert J. Browning, Fisheries of the North Pacific: History, Species,
Gear, and Processes [Anchorage: Alaska Northwest Publishing Co., 1974] p. 4 and
John Earnest Damron, "The Emergence of Salmon Trolling on the American
Northwest Coast: A Maritime Historical Geography" [Ph.D. diss., Univ. of Oregon,
1971] figs. 2 and 51)*

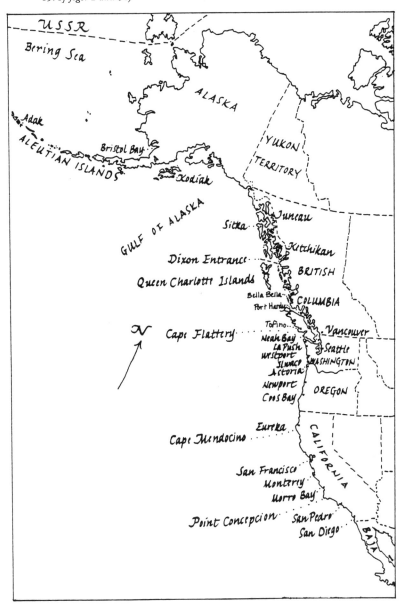

Figure 3.   Pacific Northwest Coastal Fishing Ports.
(Map based on John Earnest Damron, "The Emergence of Salmon Trolling on the American Northwest Coast: A Maritime Historical Geography" [Ph.D. diss., Univ. of Oregon, 1971] fig. 3 and Oregon State Univ. Dept. of Agricultural and Resource Economics, Socio-Economics of the Idaho, Washington, Oregon and California Coho and Chinook Salmon Industry, vol. B [Corvallis, 1978] fig. X-3)

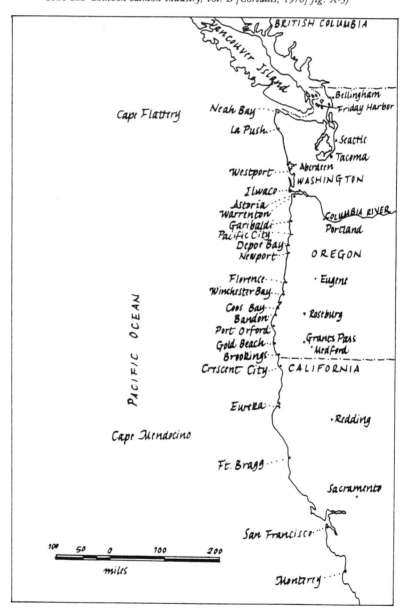

ian Islands.[9] Salmon likewise, in April and May, depending on the species, begin their return to spawning grounds, proceeding north up the coast from northern California and south to coastal rivers from northern reaches.[10] In both fisheries, the fishermen must find and follow the paths of these fish up (or down) the coast, requiring trip fishing. The average trip lasts three to five days. In the past a fishing trip could run up to fifteen days at sea, but today the most many trollers have stayed out is seven to ten days. With the earlier opening of salmon season in California, or reports of the first tuna bites off California, trollermen from California, Oregon, and Washington head south to begin their treks north along with the salmon or tuna. Hence, during salmon and tuna seasons (salmon generally April through September in California, May or June through October in Oregon; tuna whenever they run), fishermen spend little time in their home ports except when the "bite's on" in waters adjacent to them. Trollermen deliver fish and utilize the services in a number of ports over the season as they move north with the fish. As the fish progress north, ports overflow with transient boats (pronounced "transit")—boats from many different ports and states—and the fish plants, docks, and local bars burst with activity around the clock.

Indeed, late spring, summer, and early fall are the busiest times of the year at the coast with the entire fishing fleet in action pursuing salmon, shrimp, tuna, or bottomfish. But summertime does not necessarily grace the busy season with good weather. Storms from the southwest are fairly infrequent from the end of April through the end of September each year. But sturdy northwest winds can pick up and end a day of fishing prematurely or keep fishermen hemmed in port for days, unable to venture out to the fishing grounds at all, despite deceivingly clear skies. During the winter, northwest winds have their days, but storms from the southwest prevail, often lasting three to four days at a time and locking the crabbers and bottomfishermen, who work through the winter season, in port.

Offshore fishing under any circumstances is a pesky business, and the coastal region provides its own distinctive hazards to navigators—tricky offshore ocean currents, complicated access to the predominant estuarine type harbor of the area, and fairly large tidal changes, which, along with weather typical of the area, make harbor access all the more difficult. Ten of the twenty-one primary Oregon estuarine systems, and one lesser system, serve as fishing ports in some capacity (see fig. 4).[11] The remaining two of Oregon's thirteen fishing harbors lie directly on the coast in waters protected by headlands from the prevailing northwest winds of the summer months, and unprotected from southerly winds the rest of the year.[12] Three of Washington's four coastal fishing ports and two of northern California's three are likewise posited in estuaries.

Most of the boats of the region must thus cross a sandbar at the mouth of a

Figure 4. Oregon Fishing Ports.
(Map based on inside front cover of Oregon Coastal Conservation and Development Commission, Summary, Final Report, 1975 [Florence, OR, 1975])

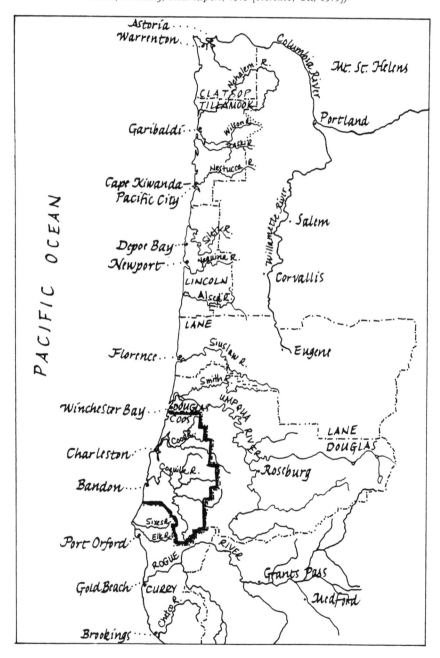

small river system modified by jetties in order to gain safe harbor in an estuarine bay. Jetties and the channel between them are subjected to relentless abuse over the year and need constant repair and upkeep. Frequent lack of upkeep (and poor channel design to start with) and the constantly shifting bar and sands in shallower in-bay waters approaching moorage facilities hinder passability and make bar crossings treacherous. It can be disastrous to cross the bar at the wrong turn of the tide or in the wrong kind of weather, or to take the wrong path through the channel. In fact, most "boat deaths" occur while trying to cross the bar.[13]

Additional geographical features set this stretch of coast apart from the contiguous land mass to the east. The rugged and impassable Olympics block direct east-west overland routes from the western Washington coast to the Puget Sound-Hoods Canal areas and the population centers of that state (see fig. 5). Oregon's coastal mountain ranges hamper travel and commerce up and down the coast as well as between the coast and Oregon's population centers inland—the Willamette Valley and the adjacent Roseburg-Medford-Grants Pass area directly to its south. Likewise, the Siskyou Mountains of southern Oregon and northern California have not encouraged population growth nor easy east-west access to the adjacent inland areas where growth has occurred.

Early settlers did pass through the mountains from inland to the coast, but many of them gained the coast by water, sailing north up the coast from San Francisco and southern California ports, traveling down the Columbia from Portland to Astoria and embarking from Astoria to coastal points north or south, or sailing to points along the perimeter of the Olympic Peninsula from areas surrounding Puget Sound.[14] (Vancouver Island, British Columbia, still has no north-south road along its west coast.) Because of the difficult terrain besetting north-south travelers on land, Oregon early proclaimed its beaches highways during low tide, hence public property under the jurisdiction of the state's department of transportation. (Thus, Oregon today has some 300 contiguous miles of public beaches, more than any other coastal stretch in the United States.)

Modern transportation and highway conditions have greatly enhanced east-west and north-south overland contact, yet Oregon's coastal politicians and businessmen bitterly complain even yet of their isolation from the inland markets, which they attribute to bad roads and inlander attitudes that the coast is not a place where people live but where they play. Eugene, Salem, and Portland average about 80 miles to the coast as the crow flies, but residents of Oregon ports are often in closer contact with people in sister ports sometimes 200 to 500 miles north or south. Coos Bay, for instance, seems in better touch with San Francisco, Eureka, and Newport, than it is with Eugene, the closest large outlet to Willamette Valley commerce.

The modern-day commercial fishing industry, with its necessary emphasis

Figure 5.   Physiography of the Pacific Northwest Coast.
          (Map based on John Earnest Damron, "The Emergence of Salmon Trolling on the
          American Northwest Coast: A Maritime Historical Geography" [Ph.D. diss., Univ.
          of Oregon, 1971] fig. 3 and Charles B. Hunt, Natural Regions of the United States
          and Canada [San Francisco: W. H. Freeman and Co., 1974] figs. 1.1(D), 18.1,
          18.2, and 18.26)

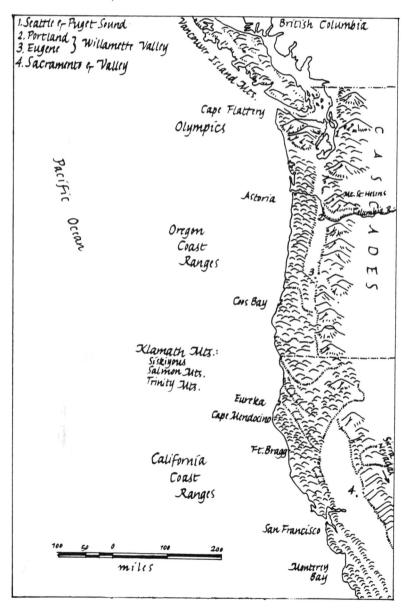

on transportation and access by water, has perhaps best preserved the mentality of coastal living without automobiles. Movement of fishermen from other ports acts as a means of maintaining communication along the coast for thousands of miles. West Coast commercial fishermen are much more cosmopolitan than landlubbers may realize in that they keep current with information regarding fisheries from Alaska to the Gulf of Mexico, the common coastline providing continuity and great breadth of vision and contact across state and national lines. Indeed, I think West Coast fishermen are better informed about international politics through observations and interaction with Russian, Polish, and Japanese fishermen at sea than are average U. S. citizens who have access only to the news media.

Fish marketing affiliations have followed much the same north-south direction that communication among fishermen has. While gossip always has a market in the fishing world, and it often only gets better with age, the case is the reverse for fish products, and marketing them from geographical outreaches like the coastal area is a tough problem. Coastal populations are not (yet) large enough (and willing enough) to absorb the quantities of locally produced fish, and until recently, insufficient and inadequate means of preservation and transportation hindered deliveries to major population centers.[15] Even so, lack of popular demand for fish in general and competition with cheaper prices of foreign fish products protected by international agreement have often made the transport of local produce self-defeating.[16]

Thus market conditions of the coastal stretch are somewhat depressed, which just makes commercial fishing throughout the region, especially in southern Oregon, all the more difficult than it already is due to geography and weather. Fishermen of these grounds have to work long and hard hours to earn moderate incomes from their jobs. Fishing operations on the average are quite small, with boat lengths ranging roughly from 20 to 75 feet and averaging around 40 feet, and crew sizes running from one to four men. Comparatively, Puget Sound, Alaska, and southern California fisheries feature larger boats with larger crews, and more efficient, modern gear. Coastal fishermen also fish with older boats, theoretically less ideally suited for the fisheries uses to which they are put.[17] One of the Coos Bay shipyard managers called Coos Bay fishermen 15 years behind Puget Sound in boat and gear sophistication, which if they could manage would make their fishing operations more efficient and safer.[18] But as fisherman Fred Anderson claimed, the Coos Bay markets are so bad that they do not make it worth gearing up to the level of modern-day technology.[19] If a Coos Bay fisherman wants desperately to keep up with modern technology and build himself a boat of the times, he has to take it to more lucrative grounds and markets to pay it off. Anderson was then considering taking his new boat to Alaska to pay it off in a few seasons; indeed he has now been fishing in the Bering Sea for the past 3 or 4 years.[20]

Despite the odds, these coastal fisheries continue to thrive and bring good livings to those who pursue the business assiduously. Almost in defiance, in fact, the Coos Bay fisheries grew persistently from the 1930s through the boom period of the 1970s—when Coos Bay was known as one of the two fastest growing fishing ports in the region—and they retrenched and persevered after the bust of the early 1980s.[21]

Coos Bay as an Oregon Fishing Port

Among Oregon's commercial fishing ports, Coos Bay contended for second place with Newport, after first-ranking Astoria, during the 1970s (see fig. 4); today Coos Bay and Newport vie for first place.[22] In 1973, Coos County fish landings accounted for 22 percent (18,821,000 pounds) of the Oregon catch by volume, and 24 percent ($6,462,000) of the catch by value.[23] From 1966 through 1973, Coos Bay and Newport's catches resembled each other in amounts and proportions: salmon accounted for half of each port's total, followed in decreasing but similar quantities by shrimp, tuna, groundfish, and crab.[24] Comparatively, Astoria (Clatsop County ports), Oregon's number one fishing port for the past century, hauled in the primary quantities of tuna and groundfish, and in 1973 represented 39 percent of the total Oregon catch in volume and 34 percent of the total value.[25] During the late 1970s and early 1980s as salmon, shrimp, tuna, and even crab landings have fallen off mostly from the effects of El Niño and low ebbs in fishery cycles, bottomfish landings have overshadowed all others, and Newport's and Coos Bay's have bettered Astoria's (see n. 3).

Only in the past 20 years has Coos Bay begun to offer serious competition to the older more established ports of the northern Oregon coast, and over this period, the growth of the area's commercial fishing industry has dramatically outstripped that of fellow fishing ports. Since 1958 the number of fish processing plants has more than doubled, and employment in them has increased nearly tenfold from 39 in 1958 to 337 in 1973.[26] Since 1973, at least two more fish landing/fish plant operations have located in Charleston.

The fishboat count has grown, too, over the years. One resident fisherman estimated that 2 to 3 drag boats, 10 to 12 crab boats, and 25 to 30 salmon boats worked out of Charleston-Coos Bay before World War II.[27] Nineteen forty-five saw 40 to 60 year-round fishboats in Charleston, with 75 to 100 during the peak salmon season in summer, and through 1960–64, the year-round fleet averaged 113.[28] In 1977–78 Coos Bay moorages accommodated approximately 360 commercial fishing vessels year-round, only 70 to 80 of which actually fished all year, and approximately 100 additional commercial boats showed up during the summer months.[29] Furthermore, 100 or so sports fishing and other "pleasure boats" tied up around the bay during the winter, increasing to more than 300 during the summer months.[30] Since the late 1970s, the number of working commercial fishboats has dwindled probably to about 200 boats, a little less than half of which fish all year: the number of crab boats has remained stable, bottomfishing trawlers have doubled, the shrimp fleet has decreased by two-thirds, and the salmon fleet by half.[31]

Numbers of fishermen have increased accordingly from at least 59 in 1945, double that number through 1960–64, to between 850 and 1,000 in 1977–78.[32] However, the more recent numbers comprise only 200 or so year-round, resident, full-time, "professional fishermen"; another 200 to 300 fishers reside locally but fish for less than half of their annual income, and another 500 or so live more than 30 miles away from the ocean most of the year, coming to Charleston only during the summer to fish for salmon.[33]

Not only have the numbers of boats and fishers increased radically over the years, but so have the amount and quality — and sometimes, too, the size — of each boat's fishing gear.[34] Unfortunately, fish stocks have not increased proportionately, so roughly five to six times as many boats are bringing in only twice as much fish today as they did during the Second World War.[35] Perhaps the greatest discrepancy has existed in the commercial salmon business where the number of boats and fishers (who fish for no other species but salmon) has continued to rise despite the fact that salmon stocks are presently taken at 90 percent maximum sustained yield.[36] Despite an unsurprising wealth of business failures in this fishery year after year, a tremendous turnover in personnel, and some exceptionally bad fishing years, the fishery still attracts newcomers, hoping, no doubt, to strike it rich quick.[37] (Such hope seems to be directly proportionate to the greater geographical distance of one's residence from Charleston, one's lack of experience with the occupation and its longstanding professionals, and one's dependence for information about the returns of salmon fishing upon well-ripened gossip.)

On the contrary, the numbers of year-round fishers and boats have not risen nor fluctuated so wildly over the years, and have perhaps only doubled in the past two decades. These few, representing roughly one-fifth of Charleston fishermen, bring in more than half of the port's annual catch, and they all fish for a variety of species over the year — some trawl for bottomfish all year, others alternate bottomfishing with shrimping and sometimes crabbing and trolling, and still others crabfish most of the year, switching to salmon, shrimp, and/or tuna fishing during the summer when they cannot crab. And it is within this group that one finds the more experienced fishermen, who operate (or work on) the larger fishing boats and run the most successful fishing businesses, who are more likely to be native Oregonians (often third, fourth, or fifth generation) tied by family, and thus historically, to the occupation, and in many cases, to the Coos Bay area.[38]

Historical Aspects

Until the mid-1930s, development of Coos Bay's commercial fisheries mirrored but lagged behind the examples set by its sister Coquille River fisheries to the immediate south and the front-running Columbia River fisheries to the north (see fig. 4). Commercial exploitation of the salmon resource had commenced upon white settlement along the Columbia River, but through the 1820s, 1830s, and 1840s, it was native-caught Columbia River salmon that was packed in barrels and shipped to the Hawaiian Islands in trade.[39] Not until the mid-1800s does it appear that whites became engaged in the actual process of taking fish for commercial purposes on that river.[40] Whites began settling Coos County in the early 1850s and several years later, in 1860, John Flanagan is said to have done the first commercial fishing on the Coquille River.[41] By 1877, when the county's population edged 4,000 in number, the Coquille fisheries were sending 3,000 barrels of salmon at a time to San Francisco.[42]

Until the fish canning process reached the West Coast during the 1860s, however, the commercial fisheries were slow to develop, and probably the bulk of fishing done and fish taken up to this point had been for home and local use — as had been the case for thousands of years among the native populations prior to and coincident with the early years of white settlement.[43] The first West Coast salmon cannery went into operation on the Sacramento River (California) in 1864; by 1866–67 the first had started up on the Washington side of the Columbia River; and another appeared on the Oregon side in 1869.[44] By 1880, Oregon claimed fifty-five such operations, thirty of which graced the banks of the Columbia, and only one of which hailed from the southern Oregon coast at the mouth of the Rogue River.[45] Salmon canning finally came to Coos County during the 1880s — three canneries went in on the Coquille, and two on Coos Bay, followed by a third in the late 1890s, while the county's population had increased to more than 10,000 (see fig. 7, nos. 11 and 12).[46]

In 1900 a little more than a third of the county population had settled within the area of the Coos Bay and the river systems that fed into it (see fig. 6), while the Coquille River system, a watershed distinct from Coos Bay, perhaps boasted the remaining majority (see fig. 4).[47] Despite apparent differentials between the two systems, development of the fisheries in both areas through the 1920s roughly paralleled each other. Common to both were difficult access by land and sea and poor, unreliable modes of transportation.[48] For the first 65 years of settlement, transportation within these river valleys and between them was almost entirely by water. Mail was delivered by boat, milk delivered to the creamery by boat, children took the milkboats to school, farmers took their own boats to town, picnickers rode the boats to picnic grounds on weekend outings. Ferries abounded to link trails and roads; materials and supplies from the outside world came in with steamers as did newcomers arriving to settle in the

Figure 6.   The Coos Bay Estuarine System.
(Map based on State of Oregon, Division of State Lands, Tideland Map: Coos Bay [Feb. 1973])

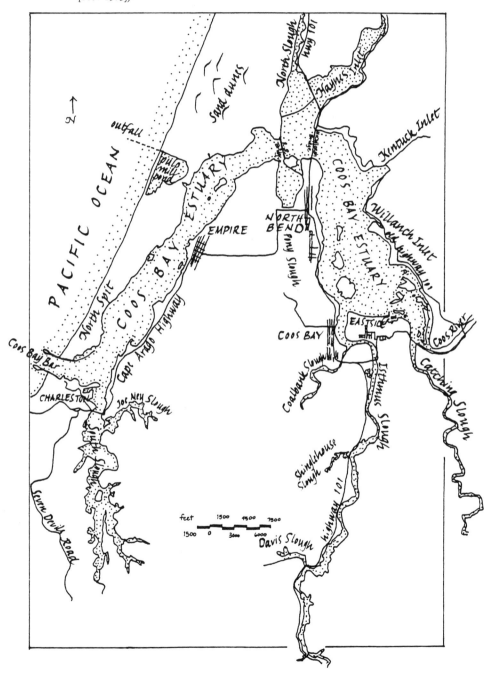

area, and locally produced goods shipped out on them along with residents traveling to points up and down the coast.[49] As John Koontz testifies:

> . . . there was no transportation by cars at all, see, there was no cars. And they were all on boats. Well, everybody had a boat. . . . they all went in the boats, and stuff like that, row boats, and every kind of a boat you could think of . . . every farmer had a boat, you know, and they got gas engines in it and they all come to town with their boats. They didn't have no roads to go on. No roads at all.[50]

The first automobile arrived in Coos Bay in 1914, and the railroad connecting Coos Bay with the inland Valley and Eugene was completed in 1915. Travel by car on plank roads over marshlands, mudflats, stream beds, and sand remained precarious for many years more. The McCullough Bridge, completed in 1934, spanned the bay, conjoining the north and south sides of the bay in one short, direct route, sending the coast highway, U. S. 101, through the heart of the population and business centers of the area (see fig. 6). This move symbolically brought to a close an era of coastal living in all ways oriented to the water, and it signified the demise of a special coastal landscape of settlements isolated by land, connected by water.

Throughout this early period all of the fish canneries located upriver, from 6 to 15 miles from the ocean (see fig. 7), indicative of the kinds of fish sought commercially at the time, the predominant location of fishing grounds and the nature of commercial fishing of the day. Salmon, steelhead, striped bass, and shad (these latter two were artificially introduced in 1871–85 and 1914, respectively), are anadromous species that then could be caught in the bay, or "inside," during certain times of the year when the fish were running inland and upstream to spawn.[51] Until the 1930s, the majority of fishing in Coos Bay was carried on upriver and in the bay, inside as opposed to "outside" in the open ocean, and it was seasonal work, frequently accomplished at night. Thus fishermen usually complemented fishing with other kinds of work over the year or during the day. At the time, fishing was more supplement to other modes of employment than the major means of income. The Lilienthal family augmented farming with fishing, leaving the farm in care of the hired hand during salmon season, while a family friend, Ed Brown, fished during the summer and worked in a sawmill in the winter.[52] Carl Sandstrom alternated fishing with gardening, woodcutting, and occasionally shipping out on a steam schooner.[53] Lorance Eickworth fished with his partner at night and worked at a lumber products mill during the day.[54] A roster of some 80 fishermen who delivered to the Charlie Feller plant in Coos Bay in 1916–17 attaches each man to one or another of the rivers, inlets, and sloughs that drain into the bay upstream and inland (see fig. 6), further demonstrating the primary locale of fishing grounds and the concomitant ready access to other mainstream kinds of work such as farming, logging, milling, or working in town.[55]

Furthermore, fishing in Coos County bays in the early years was readily accessible to anyone who had the urge: it took a minimum of gear and investment, especially since most residents already had the use of a small boat for transportation that could double as a fishing boat at night. In order to fish, one needed a small open boat (that might range from a "scow" of 8 to 10 feet, to a "Joe McGee" of 16 to 18 feet, to a "dory stern" of 18 to 24 feet, to a "Columbia River fishboat" of 26 feet, or a "seine boat" 26 feet long and 8 feet wide) with or without a gas engine, and a net (set net, drift net, gillnet; haul, beach, or horse seine).[56] For gillnetting, the fisherman could work alone or with a partner. For seining, however, he usually worked as a member of a team of three or more individuals plus or minus a horse. Often with seine operations, a cannery would provide the boats and net as well as a barge on which to pile the catch for shipment to the cannery; in return the cannery would claim a percentage of the value of the take, or, more likely, pay the fisherman scant wages.[57] Only closure of Coos Bay in 1949 and the Coquille in 1955 put an end to inner-bay netfishing operations. By then, however, the majority of commercial fishing was being conducted outside with larger, engine-powered boats specialized for commercial fishing and more elaborately equipped for taking a wider variety of fishes.[58]

The adoption of gas engines to power fishing boats in the early 1900s again introduced change to the young West Coast fishing industry. Motor power encouraged fishing in the open ocean in small boats, the design of larger and stronger small fishing craft, and the widespread shift to trolling for salmon (luring them with lines while they run up the coast feeding frenzily before entering the bays to spawn) instead of netting them.[59] By 1915 the entire West Coast trolling fleet was motorized; indications are that some boats were motor-powered in Coos Bay as early as 1900.[60] Trolling, introduced through southeastern Alaska and Monterey in 1905, premiered off the Columbia River in 1912 and had reached Coos Bay by 1916.[61] It boomed and peaked off the Columbia in 1919 with 1,000 to 2,000 boats in the water.[62] Despite the tremendous impact of this powerful new fishing combination along the entire coast, in-bay fishing appears to have remained predominant in Coos Bay throughout the 1920s.[63]

The 1930s were a significant period for Coos Bay and Oregon's commercial fisheries. By then logging and mining practices had significantly altered stream beds along the coast, and had taken a heavy toll on fishing returns inside the bays. Competition between sports and commercial fishermen, detrimental fish catching methods, overfishing in general throughout the Pacific Northwest, and the voracious interloper, striped bass, had further helped deplete salmon stocks; fishery efforts to supplement the native stocks with hatchery breed had not as yet been very successful. Hence, people were on the lookout for new stocks and new species to exploit. Further, the national economy was depressed and many people turned to commercial fishing as a means of earning good money to make a living when jobs were scarce and well-paying ones even scarcer.[64]

The state of Oregon, doubtless in response to this multitude of variables, passed legislation in 1933 freeing up restrictions on the commercial taking of Dungeness crab and, in 1935, pilchards (Pacific sardines); this led to sharp increases in landings of the two species, considerable growth in the fishing industry, and increased activity outside.[65] With the 1935 revision of pilchard legislation, four plants for receiving and reducing pilchards to oil sprang up in the Coos Bay area almost overnight, and a fleet of some 75 purse seiners arrived from Monterey each carrying a crew of six to eight Italians or Portuguese to catch the fish.[66] A year later, however, the great numbers of pilchards had apparently vanished, the Californians departed as quickly as they had arrived and the plants closed down.

The pilchard fiasco, however, set the stage for the inception of two of today's major commercial fisheries.[67] The example of the pilchard fishermen with their large crews, large boats, and large nets, apparently gave new impetus to the development of the trawl fishery for bottomfish which had been flailing since the 1880s. Furthermore, discoveries of albacore tuna by fishermen searching for pilchards off Coos Bay in 1936 spurred development of a commercial fishery for that fish. By 1937, commercial fishing in each department had begun off the Oregon Coast; for once, the Coos Bay fisheries were right in step with the northern Oregon fishing ports.[68]

Meanwhile, the Hallmark family moved to Charleston, at the mouth of the Coos Bay estuary, in 1936 to commence processing Dungeness crab.[69] The Hallmarks had previously developed a small, successful crab canning business on Alsea Bay 80 miles north of Coos Bay. Since the Alsea had no improvements at its mouth and the fishing had to be confined to small boats that could operate only within the bay, however, Charleston looked like a better prospect for the expansion of their operation.

When they arrived in Charleston, evidently few people remained fishing commercially in the bay or in their corner of it, and the only other fish plant on the bay was Feller's, 15 miles upstream. In Charleston then there was only a small fish buyer and during peak salmon season, a buying station further south at Sunset Bay, on the coast. Further, commercial fishing in the area at the time seemed a fairly marginal activity to the family, attracting to it only marginal types:

> . . . so many of the fishermen were just [the] kind of people who weren't very successful at anything else, who didn't want to work steadily, or who couldn't hold down a steady job, or just wanted to fish enough that they could go on a good drunk, or that sort of thing. And they could make a living with just a little boat and just a minimum of gear, and make enough living to suit them . . .[70]

In contrast, "the fishermen who came with us were family men, and steady, pretty steady men who really made a business of it."[71]

Hallmark's processed crab in the winter and salmon in the summer in the early years, and thus could offer fishermen full-time, year-round employment fishing commercially. This first for the area, together with Hallmark's timely location in Charleston with ready access to the ocean, prompted long-time area fishing families to move permanently to the vicinity from upstream, attracted fishermen to Charleston from other coastal parts, and, notably, drew a number of people (some Hallmark family friends and acquaintances from the Alsea) to Charleston to try their hands at fishing for the first time (many of whom have become today's old guard in the fishing business).

Hallmark's arrival signaled a major transformation in the nature of local commercial fishing, from one of many local occupations that a person might alternately pursue throughout the year, to a profession, a person's sole occupational pursuit. This change ultimately contributed to the formation of a geographically concentrated fishing community, socially and occupationally distinct from the surrounding majority of the population. Despite these new developments, the mouth of South Slough where Charleston sits was not improved for many years to come. Only the small (26- to 50-foot) motor-powered boats used to fish for crab or salmon could navigate the shallow waters, which were subject to radical changes in depth overnight and were unprotected from storms and damaging wave action. In times of rough weather, the Charleston-moored boats had to move 11 miles up the bay to safer moorage in North Bend, or further yet, in Coos Bay. Many of the transient salmon boats would bypass the port because Charleston's moorage facilities were so minimal and those of the upper bay too far upstream.[72] Larger boats landing halibut, bottomfish, or tuna still had to go 15 miles up the bay to Feller's plant, or 11 miles up to plants that operated off and on through the 1940s and 1950s on the North Bend waterfront (see fig. 7, nos. 4 and 6).[73]

By 1937–38, however, Hallmark's presence in Charleston was apparently giving Feller something to think about, for his plant began processing crab too. By 1942 he had opened a receiving dock in Charleston, and thence joined local efforts in lobbying to get state and federal monies to improve the harbor in Charleston.[74] In efforts to attract the annual traffic of transient salmon boats, as well as to provide good facilities for the increasing numbers of Charleston fishermen, some 59 local fishermen put together a petition for a boat basin in 1945 which, with the backing of the local fish processors, received approval in 1947.[75] Construction of the Charleston Boat Basin began in 1948, but it was interrupted by the Korean War and not completed until 1957.[76] In the meantime, 1951 brought another competitor, Eureka Fisheries, to settle six miles up the bay from Charleston (see fig. 7, no. 13).[77] A Seattle-based fisherman's cooperative formed, building a processing plant on the site of the new boat

Figure 7. Fisheries-Related Businesses and Services in the Coos Bay Area.
(Map based on State of Oregon, Division of State Lands, Tideland Map: Coos Bay
[Feb. 1973])

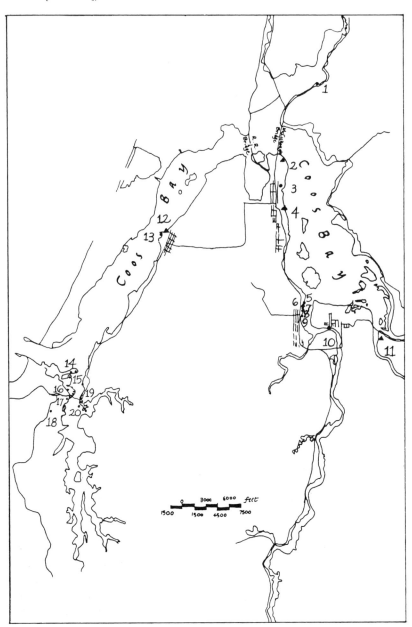

Key to Figure 7

1. Humbert's Boat Shop

   North Bend Waterfront
2. Former Site Simpson/Kruse & Banks Shipyard
3. Present Site Oregon-Pacific
4. Former Site Oregon-Pacific, Several Fish Plants

   Coos Bay Waterfront
5. Hillstrom Shipbuilding
6. Former Site Feller's Fish Plant
7. Koontz Machine Shop
8. Knutson Diesel and Machine
9. Coos Bay City Dock
10. Nelson Log Bronc (Eastside)
11. Former Site Several Fish Plants

12. **Empire Waterfront**
    Former Site Snyder Fish Plant
13. Eureka Fisheries

    Charleston Businesses
14. Alaska Packers
    Lazio Seafood
15. Boat Basin & Basin Cafe
16. George's Marine Electronics
    Barbey Fisheries
    Hallmark Fisheries
17. Bill's Machine & Welding
    Roosevelt Boulevard Net Loft
18. Ott's Machine Shop
19. Peterson Seafood
20. Hanson's Landing
    Galley Cafe
    Kelley Boat Works
    Hanson's Dock
    Boat Graveyard
    Joe Ney Dock

basin in 1958, adding another competitor to the industry.[78] By 1965, Feller had sold to a firm that closed down the plant far upstream and expanded the Charleston facility; and another operation, Peterson's Seafood, locally formed in North Bend in 1961, also moved down-bay to Charleston.[79]

With the completion of the boat basin, subsequent concentration of all of the fish processors in or near Charleston (see fig. 1), and the 1957 discovery of yet another species (shrimp) in substantial quantities directly off Coos Bay the Coos Bay fisheries at last came of age.[80] Since then, all of the fish processors but one have changed hands. Hallmarks sold to a corporation based in England in 1969, and the Co-op, which went bankrupt in 1971, was bought out by a Newport firm, and later, in 1976, by Alaska Packers; both firms are currently owned by Cal-Shell.[81] Feller's plant has changed hands three to four times since 1958; in 1978 it was known as Barbey Fisheries, but it has since gone out of business.[82] During the late 1970s Peterson's gave in to a large West Coast fish processor; the plant has changed hands several times since.[83] The California-based Eureka Fisheries plant located up the bay has remained steadfast since 1951.[84] In 1977–78, a recently formed receiving dock for Chuck's Seafood, a local fish marketer, changed color to Tom Lazio Food, based, I think, in California; it is still in operation. Since the extension of U. S. jurisdiction to 200 miles offshore in 1978, successful local efforts to capture and market Pacific whiting have resulted in the creation of a new processing plant specifically for the fish off the small boat basin.[85]

Just as contemporary commercial fishing goes hand in hand with moorage facilities and fish receiving, processing, and marketing establishments, so does it depend on a host of dockside businesses which sell, service, or repair all manner of fishing equipment, from component materials and parts to complete outfits, boats, gear, and mechanical, electrical, hydraulic, and electronic systems. In 1977–78, there were at least 26 marine support firms operating in the Coos Bay area, employing 150 to 170 people (in 1979 employment doubled, only to fall with the collapse of the major shipbuilding company) and catering directly to commercial fishermen (see fig. 7).[86] Fifteen were located in or near Charleston, and eleven on the upper bay. Another dozen or so carried marine materials, parts, and equipment, or offered various marine repair services (welding, marine electrical, refrigeration) in addition to their main lines of supplies and services for automotive, logging, farming, or industrial concerns—only one of these businesses was located near Charleston.

The Charleston businesses included one of the four major boatbuilding and repair shops in the area, three of five marine electronics shops, two of four marine machine and welding (and hydraulic) shops independent of the shipyards, one of three marine engine dealers, one of the two major marine supply stores in the area, several small-time bait and tackle shops, and three cafes where fishermen hang out (see fig. 1). The establishment of these support services in Charleston over the years has reflected the growing pains of the local commercial fishing industry upon which they partly depend. Hallmark's settlement in Charleston in the late 1930s evidently inspired the location of a boatbuilding shop and a couple of bait and tackle shops before World War II, but only one of the bait and tackle shops remains.[87] The wartime and postwar fishing boom apparently attracted both John Kelley, a veteran worker in Northwest Coast shipyards, and Emery Hanson, who had sailed the high seas, to come to Charleston to open, respectively, the present boatbuilding and repair facility, and a bait shop that expanded over the years into one of the major marine supply stores in the area.[88] Most of the remaining bait and tackle shops and fishermen's cafes followed the completion of the boat basin in 1958 — and at that time Hansons expanded their shop by moving to larger quarters. Commercial fishing slumped for about 20 years (1948–68),[89] but its resurgence in 1968 was attended by the gradual arrival of the marine electronics firms, a marine engine dealer, and the marine machine, welding, and hydraulics shops (and another cafe in 1976) through the late sixties and early seventies. And in 1968, Hansons moved into the large new building with which they were identified through the 1970s — they recently sold out to Englund Marine, an Astoria-based company, I believe.

On the other hand, shops on the upper bay have followed trends in the fishing industry to a lesser extent. Their continued presence on the upper bay proves their continuing commitment to the bay's entire fleet of workboats (besides fishboats, Coast Guard boats, harbor tugs, log broncs, and towboats used for maneuvering log rafts about the bay or barges of lumber between ports), and their primary orientation to the needs of the logging industry, the nexus of which has been the upper bay for more than a century. These shops thus form an overlap among distinctive industries, specifically, logging and fishing, and thus owe a debt to Coos Bay's occupational heritage and its past dependence on transportation by water.

The location of lumber interests on the bay in the early 1850s originally opened up the area to settlement and economic development.[90] The lumber companies offered a myriad of jobs: land-based milling and logging, maneuvering logs downstream and around the bay to mills, loading lumber aboard ships for export, nudging lumber ships through the difficult estuary, navigating lumber ships from port to port, and, most spectacularly, building the lumber ships themselves. Simultaneous with their commencement on Coos Bay in the 1850s and 1860s, and on the Coquille in the 1870s, the lumber companies introduced shipyards, where at first they built wooden sailing vessels to carry their lumber to West Coast ports and, later, wooden steamers and gas- and diesel-powered varieties for local as well as export use. In a span of almost a hundred years, these early yards and their successors and offshoots turned out several hundred large wooden boats; for decades they employed a good portion of the local labor force and attracted dozens of waterworkers from afar seeking employment.[91]

The increased facilitation of land transport in the area, a concurrent decline in the demand for boats for local interchange, and innovations in lumber ship technology encouraged the demise of the old shipyards between the two world wars, and put a number of skilled waterfront workers out of work.[92] Moreover, in the 1940s and 1950s, huge wood products corporations such as Weyerhaeuser, Georgia-Pacific, and U. S. Plywood subsumed most of the local lumber industry—putting numerous small independent sawmills out of business—and bought tremendous portions of the waterfront.[93] There they created extensive plants where they store their products and load them onto huge steel freighters for export, effectively blocking public access, both visual and physical, to much of the estuary. Recent environmental restrictions have moved storage and movement of logs even more off the water. The waterway has thus become the jurisdiction of only those few whose occupations still depend on it, and it has ceased to be the integrating influence for the entire occupational community that it once was.

The persistence of the commercial fishing industry and small, independent logging and harbor operations still justifies the existence of waterfront firms to build, outfit, maintain, repair, and operate a variety of small workboats for local as well as export use, albeit technologically different from those of former days. Further, despite the development of marine services in Charleston, many fishermen still prefer or need to use the larger, more extensive facilities (and often the more expert care) that the upper bay marine support businesses can offer. These businesses have thus continued to locate on or near small surviving portions of the original upper bay waterfronts. They are the legacy of Coos Bay's past; the healthy offspring of the old water trades and the old water-oriented way of life, still performing an integrative function for all of the area's water-related occupations, both lower and upper bay industries, both fishing and logging enterprises.

The Commercial Fishing Boats
of Coos Bay

Charleston fishboats are less the focus of this book than are the traditional behaviors surrounding and influencing their upkeep and modification: the habits and aspirations of individual skippers, skipper identification with other fishermen, and the interaction of fishermen and marine craftsmen. As major referents throughout this work, however, they will be described below in some detail: in the first part, according to characteristics that distinguish fishboats from other local workboats; in the second part, according to the features that assign fishboats to a limited number of form, construction, and use types; and in the final part, in terms of the circumstances that make each boat unique.

The Fishboat: A Distinctive Kind of Workboat

Fishing boats, when at rest, cluster at several points around the Coos Bay estuary (see figs. 1 and 7). The majority of them berth in the Charleston area, near the mouth of the estuary, along with pleasure boats — sports fishing boats, sailboats, recreational motor boats of all kinds — and a few vessels used for marine research and exploration. Most of these boats can be found at the Charleston Boat Basin, which is owned and operated by the Port of Coos Bay. Three of the Charleston fish plants also provide dock space where smaller numbers of boats regularly congregate; two additional sets of privately owned docks provide space for more boats.

Only a few fishing (and pleasure) boats are moored regularly on the upper bay along with the majority of other kinds of local workboats, tied up at Eureka Fisheries in Empire, at the ramshackle Coos Bay City Dock, or alongside waterfront businesses adjacent to downtown Coos Bay. More fishboats can be located for inspection on dry ground. In addition to vessels under construction and others brought out of water for repair and routine upkeep at boatbuilding establishments in Charleston, North Bend, Coos Bay, and Eastside, collections of boats stand in hopes of repair at the Charleston boat graveyard, while some unfortunate hulks, rejected, lie dying along the shoreline. And backyards and garages throughout the area harbor retired boats and new ones in the making.

More than distributional factors isolate most commercial fishing boats from other local types of workboats. Larger than most pleasure boats, smaller than most tugs and tows, the local commercial fishing vessels range from 20 to 75 feet in overall length. Mostly of wood, secondly of steel, or thirdly of fiberglass, commercial fishboats are much sturdier in build than the lighter, mostly fiberglass pleasure boats that are mass-produced according to standardized plan. Yet fishboats are not as burly as the tows and tugs, nor as sleek and trim as Coast Guard vessels, which, these days, are all professionally designed and stoutly constructed of steel. Powered by single diesel or gas engines with 40 to 300 + horsepower, fishboats, further, hum to a different tune than the deep-throbbing twin diesels of towboats, or the loud, whiny late model engines of dredge launches and smaller Coast Guard vessels, or the faint, tinny purrs of outboard motors attached to open recreational boats.

Fishing boats are especially distinctive, however, in general shape. Conventional commercial fishing vessels feature rather slender hulls—fairly narrow and deep for their lengths—with graceful sheers—high and fairly sharp at the bow, lower at the stern (see figs. 8 and 9 for terminology). These hulls are fully decked over with covered openings to the hold, and on salmon boats, with a small cockpit set into the deck toward the stern. A squarish, upright pilothouse, usually one story (deck) high and one or two compartments long, rises from the deck of such a hull; it is usually positioned forward of amidships (but old-style, sometimes on the stern [see figs. 36 and 69]), taking up less than half the amount of deck space.

Comparatively, tugs and tows feature more massive above-deck quarters, several stories high, claiming a generous portion of deck space (see figs. 10 and 11). Their hulls seem much beamier for their lengths, and their bows higher proportionately to their lower, flatter, and broader sterns. Though graceful—marked—in sheer, their bows have a pug-nosed look to them rather than the clean profile of most fishboats. Pleasure boats, on the other hand, are not only small, but fairly fat (short and wide), shallow, and low with little sheer (see fig. 11). They are frequently undecked except over the bow, and some contain low steering shelters built into the sides of the boat, placed forward of amidships and just back of a decked bow (beneath which lie the living quarters, if any).

Since boats which originally were designed as sports or tug boats are sometimes now used for commercial fishing, the amount and kind of rigging present on a boat are particularly significant in distinguishing the commercial fishing vessels from boats of other classes. Log broncs, dredge launches, and most Coast Guard and pleasure boats (excepting sailboats) boast little or no rigging; tugs, tows, and larger Coast Guard vessels feature only a low mast to which little is attached but lights and radar equipment. Commercial fishing

Figure 8. Glossary Illustration of Fishboat Parts.

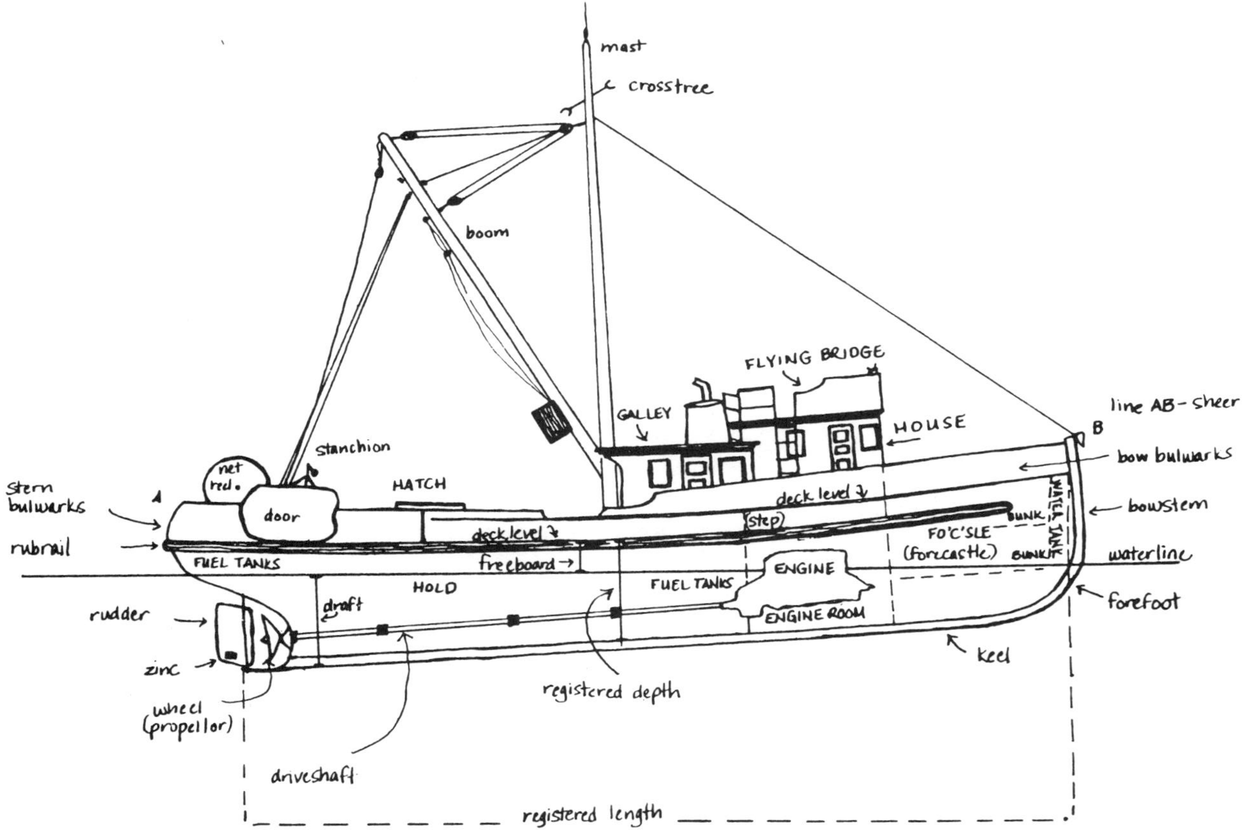

Figure 9. Deck Plans and Terminology.

The *Kodiak* detailing living accommodations above and below deck (not to scale).

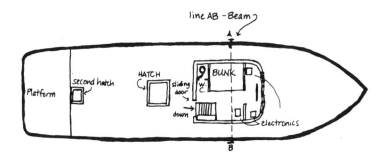

The *Puget* above deck, detailing house interior (not to scale).

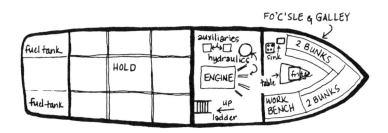

The *Puget* below deck, showing fo'c'sle containing galley (not to scale).

boats, however, display a plenitude of lines, posts, blocks, gurdies, and such equipment that is associated with local trolling (salmon or tuna), trawling (shrimp or bottomfish), or potfishing (Dungeness crab). Most distinctively, the majority of fishboats bear one sturdy fixed mast (a pole of wood or a pipe of steel) to which are strung lines and braces that steady it and guy 1) at least one pair of long, slender, tapering trolling poles which, straddling and roughly paralleling the mast, are attached to the sides of the boat (see fig. 12); and/or 2) a boom, another sturdy pole or pipe which angles acutely from below mid-mast toward the stern of the boat (see fig. 8). There are some newer contraptions on the market that take the place of the pole mast or single boom, but nevertheless the sheer amount of paraphernalia rising rigged and tall from the deck of a proportionately small- or medium-size boat is a good sign that the boat is for fishing.

Predominant colorings further set the fishing boats off from their cousins. Fishboats as a group show greater diversification in color scheme than do the other fleets of workboats, which, above the waterline, generally feature black or dark brown nether parts and white uppers, perhaps touched off with some yellow, red, or mast buff, and trimmed in black or dark brown. Many fishboats, too, wear a dark color below and white above, trimmed with a dark color, but they display a greater range of dark colors, including dark green, grey, even blue, and black. Many boats are painted entirely white above the waterline, as are most Coast Guard vessels, but they are set off with trim of a wider variety of light or dark colors compared to the Coast Guard boats. Some feature dark hulls with lighter solid color uppers (not white); some are painted wild solid colors such as red below, black above, and trimmed in black and white, respectively; and some are entirely painted in one color such as light blue, pale green, or turquoise, set off with trim of another color, light or dark. On the other hand, light blues, turquoises, pale yellows, white, extraordinarily bright colors such as orange, or fake wood grain or real varnished wood, frequently not touched off with colored trim, prevail in the pleasure boat arena— a variegated yet different order of colors than those used on fishboats.

Finally, the fishboat fleet displays not only a broader spectrum of colorings and color combinations and a wider range of materials used in construction, but more variety in hull, house, and gear configurations from one boat to another than do pleasure boats or the other groups of workboats. Further, the prevalence of wood construction among the fishing boats testifies to the greater longevity of many of them. Hence, as a group, fishboats span a greater range of ages than do the other classes of local boats, thus reflecting more tangibly their own historical record—the evolution of their design in partial response to the vicissitudes of the local fishing industry.

Such variegation is indicative, perhaps, of the flamboyance of (the area's) fishermen, but more certainly of the tremendous instability that is typical of

Figure 10. Oceangoing Towboat with Fishboats in the Background. Coos Bay City Dock.

Figure 11. Pilot Boats with Pleasure Boat and Harbor Tug in Foreground.

the fishing industry, of the economic restraints endured by fishermen, who are independently employed, and of the individual ownership of boats. Comparatively, other workboats are owned by the government or companies linked to the lumber products industry, which has enjoyed relatively great stability and prosperity for decades. The companies and the Coast Guard have been able to keep their fleets updated with modern designs and equipment and to contract to have their boats kept in tip-top shape, effectively yielding them preferential treatment at some of the local shipyards. Since these businesses have not been besieged by frequent radical fluctuations, their boats have achieved a certain uniformity in design. (Their boats also have a very well-tended look about them.) Fishing boats, however, which have been so linked to the flights of fortune and the requirements of individualists, clearly have posed exasperating and demanding problems for the local boat builders, marine repair specialists, and fishermen alike; the creation and upkeep of these boats have surely required some of the most ingenious of design energies.

Kinds of Fishboats

In early 1978, there were somewhere between 670 and 750 spaces on Coos Bay where individually owned boats could be moored.[1] That winter, I counted 362 commercial fishing boats parked together with 103 pleasure/sports/ miscellaneous boats at various facilities on Coos Bay.[2] These numbers represented approximately 79 percent of the summertime commercial fleet, and 40 percent of the summer hoard of sports/pleasure/miscellaneous boats.[3] Of these winter commercial craft, 286, or 79 percent, were of conventional fishboat design, or otherwise showed themselves to be serious commercial fishing vessels.

The remaining 76 commercial boats (21 percent) were what I call "rigged pleasure boats," that is, pleasure boats in form that have been rigged for commercial fishing. I excluded these 76 boats from deeper descriptive analysis for several reasons. In design and rigging they do not show themselves to be the boats of serious "professional fishermen" nor boats to be used for serious and conventional commercial salmon trolling. Rigged only for salmon fishing, they carry newer, lighter-weight, mostly store-bought varieties of gear compared to regular commercial salmon boats. With minimal hold space and living quarters and questionable overall stability, they are basically used for day fishing only, in contrast to the roomier, stabler, and sturdier conventional salmon boats which stay out on the ocean for days at a time when in use. As day-only, summer-only boats, prospects are good that their skippers reside far from the immediate locale most of the year, holding down full-time jobs of other kinds during the remainder of the year. There is some feeling among the local hard-core commercial fishermen that skippers of these boats are in fact using them more in the fashion of sports fishing vessels, while deriving certain benefits (like tax write-offs) by being able to designate them commercial boats:

> And too many people have bought commercial licenses for the wrong reasons. Let's take a little thirty-thousand-dollar Chriscraft down there, put commercial gear on it, first thing you know you got a tax write-off, instead of a luxury item. And people with weekends and summer vacations and schoolteachers, and everyone's into the business, you know, 'cause it's a wide open field.[4]

Conventional fishboats fall into groups according to the kinds of fishing gear they have aboard; the size, shape, and material of their hulls; and their color schemes.

Use

Fishermen differentiated boats most often on the basis of what kind of fishing they do, in other words, according to their fishing use. For example, they will refer to a fishboat as a "troller," "salmon boat," or "tuna boat"; as a drag boat or "dragger"; as a "crab boat"; or as a "combination boat" or "general purpose boat." Indeed, one of the easier, more conspicuous means of differentiating Charleston's fishing boats is according to the types of fishing gear they have on board (despite tremendous variety in actual makeup of specific kinds of gear), which in turn aligns them with one or several of the local fisheries. In winter 1978, when only bottomfish and Dungeness crab were in season, 248 of Charleston's 286 commercial fishboats bore trolling gear for catching salmon or tuna, 48 carried gear for collecting Dungeness crab, and 37 displayed trawling gear for taking shrimp or the many varieties of bottomfish (see figs. 12–24). The fishing boats best divide up into four categories, however: trollers only, trollers with crab gear, trawlers only, and trawlers with crab gear. Two hundred and fourteen boats (75 percent) carried trolling gear only (around 189 fished only for salmon, 25 for tuna and/or salmon); 34 boats (12 percent) carried both trolling and crab gear (28 salmon and crab, 6 tuna/salmon and crab); 14 (5 percent) carried both crab and trawl gear; and 24 (8 percent) carried trawl gear only (of the trawlers, 18 apparently fished only for shrimp, 11 for shrimp and bottomfish, 5 for bottomfish only, and 4 were of undetermined affiliation).[5]

Trolling.   Trolling is the sole means used at present for catching either albacore tuna or the several varieties of salmon off Coos Bay. The most distinctive of trolling components is one pair of tall, skinny, usually wooden poles (usually from 30 to 40 feet in length) that are braced upright astride the mast when not in use (fig. 12). "There is a rough rule that says the main poles should be close to the length of the boat itself."[6] Each pole is hinged to the top rail of its respective side of the boat. In order to manipulate and stay the poles in their

Figure 12.   Salmon Troller with Trolling Poles Braced Astride Mast.

Figure 13. Salmon Troller Showing Gurdies and Cockpit. Cockpit is covered. Fisherman has temporarily removed davits and blocks or works without them.

various positions, lines are rigged in a number of ways from each pole to the sides of the boat and the mast or house. More lines run from the poles to the stern of the boat and, depending on how they are rigged, indicate whether they are trolled for tuna or salmon.[7]

On salmon trollers, usually two to three lines emanate from springs positioned separately toward the tip of each pole. These lines, "tag lines," "outriggers," or "inhauls," often three to a side, stretch to the stern of the boat, adjacent to a cockpit or "trolling pit" set down into the deck toward the stern, whence the trollerman can operate both his boat and the fishing gear while trolling (see fig. 13). When in use, each tag line is snapped on to a fishing line to hold it at a proper distance from the boat. The fishing lines are run from power-operated gurdies or spools (one per line, three per side) set near the cockpit. More elaborate riggings involve threading the fishing lines through blocks hung from davits on the stern, one per side, three blocks per davit (see figs. 16, 28, 32, 39, 41, 61, 65).

In operation, the poles are lowered to an angle of 40 to 50 degrees from the vertical, "about five degrees forward of a right angle to the center line of the craft."[8] Stabilizers may then be put over each side, one suspended from each pole close to the side of the boat and riding from 5 to 10 feet below the surface of the water. A "cannonball" sinker is set to the bottom of each fishing line; "spreads" carrying each a lure or bait are set at specific intervals along each line; floats may be fastened to the outer lines; and ultimately each fishing line is fastened to one tag line, before being thrown overboard and reeled out from the gurdy (see fig. 14). The lines are set out one by one, positioned and weighted differently so hopefully they will fish at different depths but not foul with one another. A fisherman may attach bells to the outriggers at the pole to warn him when a fish (or some other unknown) is tugging a line. To retrieve the catch, he reels in his line.[9]

For tuna trolling, the fishing lines are run directly off the poles and sometimes also from the stern of the boat, theoretically up to eight lines per pole and two to the stern, but more like four per pole and two to the stern (see fig. 15).[10] The fishing lines are evenly distributed along the entire length of the pole rather than stretching from the top fifth of the pole as on salmon boats. While these lines are further attached to haul or tag lines that are controlled from the stern area of the boat, they are not rigged through power gurdies or davit blocks, and they are not set with spreads, sinkers, or floats—just bait or lures that differ, further, from those used to attract salmon. Tuna lines are operated to and from the boat through simpler "power line haulers," usually one set on the stern rail to each side of the boat (two altogether). Apparently some tuna boats do not feature a trolling pit. However, since many tuna boats also are used to fish salmon, the more complicated salmon gear is often left aboard during tuna season and utilized somewhat. Since many of these boats

Figure 14. Simplified Salmon Trolling Gear.
(Source: After John Earnest Damron, "The Emergence of Salmon Trolling on the American Northwest Coast: A Maritime Historical Geography" [Ph.D. diss., Univ. of Oregon, 1971] fig. 47)

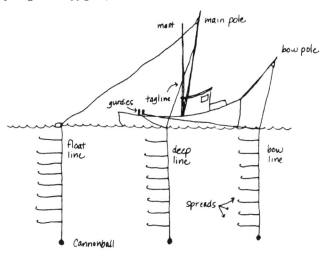

A Spread

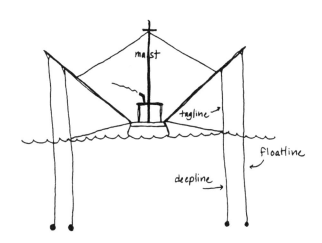

Figure 15.   Albacore Trolling Gear.
(Source: After Robert J. Browning, Fisheries of the North Pacific: History, Species, Gear and Processes [Anchorage: Alaska Northwest Publishing Co., 1974] p. 221)

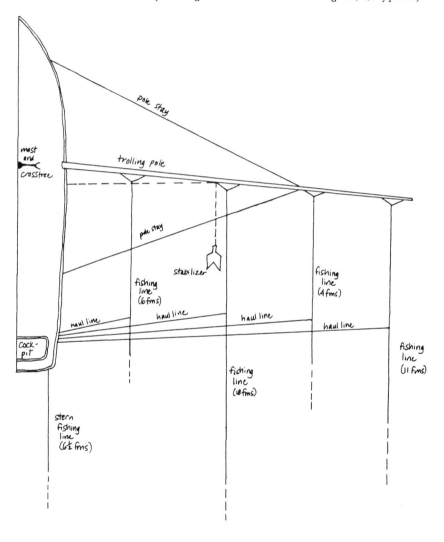

start and end the summer season with salmon trolling, when I did my winter inventory, not surprisingly, most trollers only looked like salmon boats to me; if their rigging were only partly complete, I took it to mean "off season" rather than perhaps "tuna boat." Hence I have not been able to differentiate the tuna from the salmon trollers on the basis of my inventory.[11]

Crabbing.   The major means of identifying a boat participating in the local Dungeness crab fishery is a "crab gurdy" (see figs. 16, 63, 65). This large, hydraulically powered disc, usually of brass, hangs from a sturdy, short boom of metal pipe that angles from a similarly stout vertical post, which in turn is fastened amidships to the top rail of one side of the boat (usually the starboard, or right, side). Hydraulic hoses, reaching from the gurdy to controls on the house, are wrapped around the boom and post. Additionally a large, upright and squarish steel tank — a "live tank" filled with sea water in which to keep the catch — may be positioned amidships, just aft of the cabin (fig. 16). Early or late in the season, or from time to time throughout the winter, crab pots may be stacked on the stern deck of the boat, usually on the entire after-end of the boat, weighing it low in the water (fig. 17).

Local crab pots are squat, wide cylinders, about 36 to 38 inches in diameter, and 9 to 14 inches high. They consist of a frame of round steel rod wrapped with rubber strips cut from inner tubes and covered with a woven stainless steel wire mesh. Weights made of various metal stock and frequently engraved or marked with the maker's or owner's special signature are welded into the bottoms, and escape rings for undersize crabs are welded to upper frame members. There are several (secret) ways of weaving into the pots the entry tunnels and interior traps. Half of the top round of the pot folds back on inner-tube hinges to give access to the catch and removable bait box (see figs. 18, and 19).[12]

Throughout the season, these pots, from around 150 to 300 per boat, are kept at sea in fairly shallow waters close to shore. Pots are set in "strings," each pot marked by a buoy fastened to a line that is in turn fastened to the pot which rests on the ocean bottom. Crab fishermen basically tend their pots when the weather allows, journeying out to their grounds to unload and rebait the pots. The boat must be brought alongside each pot's buoy, the line brought on board with a boat hook and sent over the crab gurdy, and the pot raised and swung on board for emptying and rebaiting.[13] Protective planking or horizontal strips of ironwood may be built onto the hull beneath the power block to protect the boat from pot damage. Additionally, a crab boat may feature a "flying bridge," an open-air enclosure mounted on the roof of the house from which the fisherman may steer the boat and get a better view of the crab grounds than he can from within the wheelhouse (see fig. 17).

Figure 16.   Assorted Crab Fishing Equipment.
Crab gurdy (*right of center*), protective planking beneath, live tank (large black box, *left*), live box (slatted crate for keeping crabs alive and fresh in water next to boat while awaiting processing). Note stanchion for holding otter board (*left foreground*). Davit and blocks for trolling on boat to the right.

Figure 17.   Crab Boat.
This boat features flying bridge above house and pots stacked on stern.

Figure 18.   Crab Pots with Buoys and Line Inside for Storage.

Figure 19. Crab Pots under Construction.
Note the wrapped frame, the tunnels woven into the frame, the weights welded to the bottoms, and the escape rings to the sides. Also note the homemade "pot holder" for working on the pots.

Trawling. Several pieces of gear mark a trawler, also called a dragger or drag boat. Of most heuristic value, at present, is a large boom of steel pipe, comparable in length and diameter to the mast, which angles acutely from the lower portions of the mast, toward the stern of the boat, along its centerline (see fig. 8). Wire cables strung through blocks run between upper portions of the mast and the boom; several more sturdy wire cables run up the boom from winches at its base, pass through a number of blocks hung from the upper end of the boom, and run again toward the boom base or to various points about the after sides of the boat. Accompanying the boom contraption are one or two large reels holding a net and mounted on the stern deck, and a pair of large, rectangular "doors" or "otter boards" that are hitched high on a pair of triangular shaped "gallows" or "stanchions" which rise above each side of the boat — one to each side — just forward of the transom and/or net reel (see figs. 20–23).

To fish this gear, the net ("found in sizes up to 100 feet across the mouth with a depth of 20 feet and a length of 150 feet") is towed by cables behind the boat along or close to the ocean bottom (see fig. 24). The funnel-shaped net is lowered slowly over the stern, cod-end first, into the drink. As the net comes off the reel, the doors are disconnected from their mounts on the stanchions and fastened to cables which stretch from the doors to each side of the mouth of

Figure 20.   An Otter Board or Door for Trawling.

the net. The doors are then lowered into the water. Additional cable leads from each door through each stanchion to a winch stationed aback of the house (either to one common winch at the mast or to separate winches, one to each side of the house and deck). As the boat tows the net through the water, the doors, floats attached to the top of the mouth opening, and weights attached to the bottom of the mouth opening keep the mouth open and help herd fish into the net. The net works to force the fish to the end of its length.

To complete a tow, the net and doors are winched in, doors remounted on the stanchions, and net wound up on the reel to its mid-section. Then the boom and overhead cables come into action, hoisting the net high enough for the boat to swing its stern under it, positing the net end to one side of the boat. The cod-end is brought aboard and emptied in "splits," with the continued aid of the boom, cables, and hydraulic winches. To reset the net, or rewind the remainder of the net, the net is once again hoisted high, while the boat swings itself under it to reposition the net once again directly behind the stern of the boat.[14]

Figure 21.   Empty Net Reel with Stanchion to the Right.
(Photo courtesy of Joe Parker)

Figure 22. Commercial Fisherman Fred Anderson Surveys the Loaded Net Reels on the Double-Rigged *Betty A*.
Note stanchion on right (and on far left) and winch on left side of boat just back of the house.
(Photo courtesy of Joe Parker)

Figure 23. Typical Charleston Trawler (Shrimp).

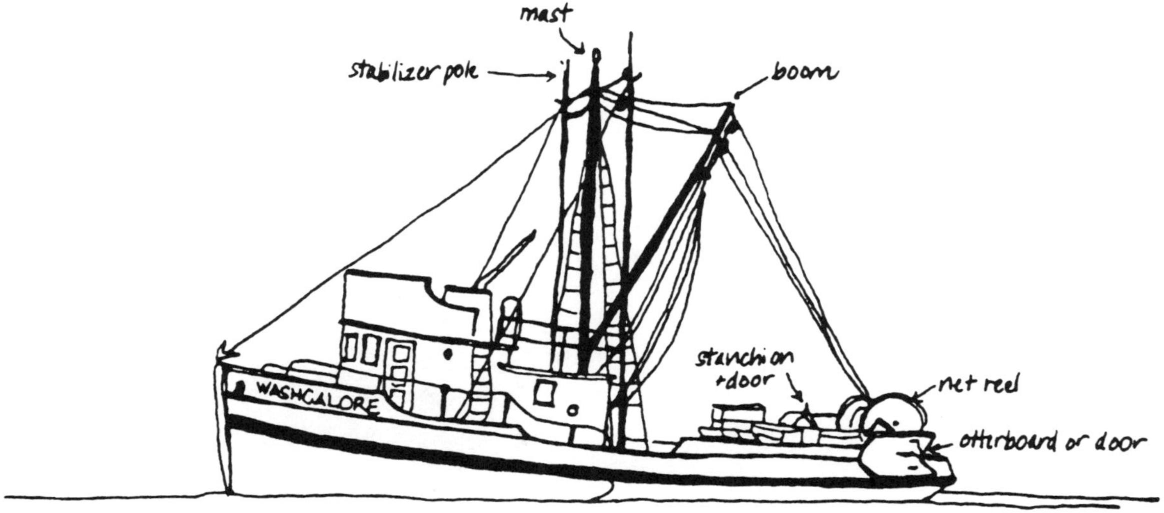

Figure 24.   Trawling Net in Tow.
            Not to scale.
            (Source: After Robert J. Browning, Fisheries of the North Pacific: History, Species, Gear and Processes [Anchorage: Alaska Northwest Publishing Co., 1974] p. 128 and A. K. Larssen and Sig Jaeger, The ABC's of Fo'c'sle Living. [Seattle: Madrona Publishers, 1976] p. 45)

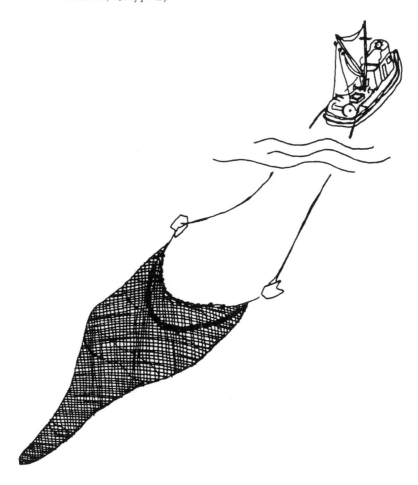

Especially when discussing specific boats or boats within fishing (use) classes, fishermen most often mention the size-range of the boat—"little," "in the 70-foot class," "50- to 60-foot range"—frequently referring to the boat in terms of its overall length in feet—"40-foot boat," "86-footer." According to my estimates, Coos Bay's commercial fishing boats ranged from a low of 20 feet in length to a high of 78 feet. I divided these boats into three size ranges inferentially on the basis of informant talk: small (20 to 35 feet), medium (35 to 50 feet), and large (50 to 75 feet and more). One hundred eight boats (38 percent) fell into the small-size class, the majority hovering around 30 to 32 feet. The medium-size class comprised the most boats, 138 (48 percent), more than half of these falling between 35 and 40 feet. Forty boats (14 percent) made up the large-size class, half of them in the 50- to 60-foot range, and one-fourth each in the 60-foot and the 70-foot-and-greater ranges.

Indeed, different fishing uses require boats of different sizes and power capabilities. Draggers, with their heavy, bulky equipment and huge tows of fish, require a fairly large boat with a lot of horsepower, and a lot of hold space in which to store tremendous quantities of fish for several days during a fishing trip. Thirty-one of Coos Bay's 40 large-size boats were used for dragging; 31 of 38 draggers fit into the large-size class. A 78-foot trawler constructed locally in 1978 touted a 450 horsepower diesel engine, quite a bit of power for Coos Bay, where trawler horsepower ranges from around 100 to over 300 and averages around 200 (boats which fish only for bottomfish generally reflect the greater horsepower figures).[15]

Crab boats do not need near the power of draggers, but they can do with a certain amount of deck space—more than most small boats allow—on which to carry, load, and unload crab pots. Like draggers, crab boats take a lot of abuse from the fishing gear, and as winter fishing boats, they are safer the larger and sturdier they are. Thus, most of Charleston's crab boats (whether troll/crab or drag/crab) fall into the middle-size range of fishing boats: of 48 crab boats, 31 (65 percent) are medium-size, 11 (23 percent) are larger-size, and only 6 are small (12 percent). I estimate their horsepower average to be around 100, with a range between 80 and the low 200s.

Charleston's 248 trollers (including the 34 troll/crab boats), definitely corner the market on the small- and medium-size boats: 131 of 138 middle-size boats, all 108 small boats, and only 9 of 40 large boats. Their horsepowers range from well below 100 (40) up through the upper 100s, and rarely above, averaging around 110. Salmon-only trollers make up the overwhelming majority (90 percent) of smallest boats and a good number of the medium-size vessels (60 percent). Generally only one man, occasionally with one helper, operates a salmon boat and runs the gear entirely by himself. Alone he can operate and

Figure 25. Variety of Sterns out of Water at Kelley Boat Works. *Left to right*: double-ender, square stern (transom), rounded square stern, and round stern. All boats have round bottoms.

Figure 26.   Variety of Sterns in Water.
Left to right: rounded stern (trawler), square stern, double-ender, rounded square stern, bow, square stern, double-ender, round stern, and double-ender.

work with only so large a boat and catch only so much fish. A larger boat, however, offers more stability and hold space, and more comfortable accommodations for the often requisite trip fishing, which can keep the trollerman out on the ocean for several days at a time to follow his quarry up the coast. Tuna trolling requires a larger-size boat than does salmon trolling, since it demands a larger crew of two or three, and more extensive trip fishing (weeks) farther from shore. Evidently tuna boats, and trollers in general, can do with high-speed capabilities for fishing and for quick transport back to shore over long sea distances.[16] Thus the ideal troller is strong but light, and adequately powered, whereas drag and crab boats preferably are strong buy heavy and abundantly powered.

Shape

As a matter of course, a professional fisherman becomes well-acquainted with boat forms, particularly hull shapes, as he tends his own boat in and out of water year after year, observes and compares his colleague's boats, both in and out of water, and discusses boats with fellow fishermen and boat craftsmen. In fact, he can become so well-attuned to the shape of his boat that, like Leonard Hall, he can spot one of identical design should he chance to meet up with one:

> I tied up alongside a boat in Newport one time, noticed the hulls were identical. The cabins were a little different, but the hulls were identical. We got our documents out, got to checking around, found out they were both built in the same yard off the same plans the same year. That was pretty interesting.[17]

Local fishermen often refer to particular models of boats which embrace the look of the entire boat, such as "double-ender" or "halibut schooner." But more frequently they refer only to features of a boat's hull, significantly, the shape of the bottom and the shape of the stern. Bottom descriptions I encountered were "round," "flat," "V-shaped," "rounded V hull," and a hull with a "hard chine," these latter two terms referring to boats of recent creation in the Coos Bay area. The three stern types I heard mentioned were the *square stern*, the *round stern* and the double-ender. Some fishermen will also describe proportions of specific boat hulls and some of their riding characteristics: "it's real deep and narrower than it should be, and rolls like a son of a gun."[18]

I was concerned with getting a broad rather than a detailed understanding of Charleston's boat forms, since they were not my major focus. Hence I was not able to observe the bottoms of most of the boats, and I cannot describe them in the detail to which most boat scholars are accustomed. I did, however, record the stern type of each fishboat that I included in my inventory, which only suggests, perhaps rather poorly, the kind of bottoms the boats may have. I followed John Damron's stern-type designations for salmon trollers: the double-ender or "canoe stern," the "transom" or square stern, and the "seine" or round stern (see figs. 25, and 26).[19] These stern types roughly correlate with those that Richard Lunt specifies in his "Lobsterboat Building on the Eastern Coast of Maine": the canoe stern with his double-enders ("Melon Seed Hull," "Torpedo Stern"), seine or round stern with his "steamboat," "washtub," and "planked around" sterns, and square stern with his "cut-off" sterns.[20]

Of Charleston's 286 boats, I determined 94 of them to be double-enders (33 percent), 107 to be square-sterned (37 percent), and 85 to be round-sterned (30 percent), although many of the round sterns appear to be modified square sterns, and may thus belong to the square stern category. Within categories there is tremendous variation, attributable to boatbuilding trends and mostly to the individuality and ethnicity of boat builders.

The double-ender.   In the Charleston context, a double-ender, or canoe stern, basically comes to a point at the stern, as it does at the bow, the side planking joined to a roughly vertical stern post as it is similarly joined to a roughly vertical stem post at the bow. The only acute, sharply angular points on the surface of the hull come at the juncture of the sides of the boat at the bow, stern, and along the keel which runs the length of the bottom between bow and stern (see figs. 27, 28, 30, and 32). Besides the round hull bottom, the forefoot (lower end of the bow stem that joins the keel) is curved, as is the lower portion of the stern post (the aftfoot?), in contrast to the angular stern profile of Jonesport and Mount Desert lobsterboats (compare square and double-ended sterns in figs. 25 and 27; see fig. 8 for forefoot location).[21]

The Charleston double-ender is almost exclusively a salmon troller and most often a smaller-size boat. Only five of them are salmon/crab boats. Sixty-two of them measure less than 35 feet in length, and most of the remaining 32 are no longer than 40 feet.

Damron specifies three types of West Coast double-enders, which can be found among the Charleston double-enders. These types evolved rapidly around the turn of the century with the addition of motorpower to sail-powered boats of similar shapes such as the Columbia River gillnetter and San Francisco-built Mediterranean types.[22] This shape of hull is rarely if ever built today; it flourished during the late 1920s and early 1930s, and by the 1950s it had been superseded by boats with square or round sterns that could handle greater power and several types of fishing uses more easily.[23]

Perhaps the greatest number of Charleston double-enders fit Damron's "Norwegian-style troller" type, bearing an almost vertical bow stem, a deep forefoot, no flare to the bow, and a straight stern post above the waterline that angles very slightly away from the boat (opposite of "tumblehome").[24] An excellent example is Charleston's *Capistrano*, built in 1925 at Sagstad's in

Figure 27. *Capistrano*, a Norwegian-Type Double-Ended Troller.
Registered measurements: length, 29.0'; breadth, 8.8'; depth, 4.2'.

Figure 28. *Petrel*, a Finnish-Type Double-Ended Troller. Registered measurements: 39.4′ × 11.9′ × 5.8′.

Seattle (see figs. 12, 13, 25, and 27). These boats are deep, fairly beamy, with their fullest beam just about at amidships. The bow stem rises higher than the stern post—which, however, rises higher than the stern profiles of many other kinds of fishboats—giving the boat, with its beamy middle, a graceful curve of a sheer. The house sits tall, often with a door to its back rather than to either side; house, mast, and engine sit just forward of amidships, with the fo'c'sle below extending forward of the house and engine room (but in a style different from other troller types); the after half of the deck is taken up with hatch, trolling pit, and some deck space surrounding them. According to Damron, these boats were built mostly by men of Scandinavian or Finnish background from northern California to Alaska; their hull lines are similar to the larger halibut schooner type that evolved on the north Pacific Coast, but the forward part of the boat, with the house tall and forward resembles the purse seiners that were common to the northwest coast from California to Alaska (cf. figs. 36, 55, 57, 69, 71).[25]

A fewer number of Charleston's double-enders fit Damron's "Finn-style troller" type—I spotted six: the *Oregon* (built in 1926 in Astoria by Matt Tolonen of the Columbia Boat Building Company; see fig. 65), the *Veni, Tinker, Sharon, Wendy R,* and one unnamed boat (see fig. 28).[26] These boats resemble the Norwegian type, but they are shallower, their bow stems are not vertical but continue the curve of the shallow forefoot, and their stern posts, while vertical, appear to have slight tumblehome, angling toward the centerline of the boat. These boats appear to be less beamy; the sides and bulwarks do not rise quite as high as those of the Norwegian troller, and the sheer line from bow stem to stern is likely to be much more of a curve than that of the Norwegian version. The house sits low in the boat, featuring a door on both sides; the house and mast sit forward of amidships, the fo'c'sle filling the entire area of the boat forward of the cabin, entrance to it being through the cabin rather than through an engine room below. The engine sits in its own compartment directly aft of the house, and pretty much at amidships—rather than below the house—and aft of that stretches the deck, hatch, and cockpit. The Finn-type troller was developed and built by people located in the vicinity of the mouth of the Columbia River, an area heavily populated by Finns (many of whom emigrated from temporary settlements in northern Norway, according to Juha Pentikäinen, June 1981). Damron does not know if the type was called "Finn-boat" because it was Finnish-built, or because the fishermen who usually fished the boats tended to be Finns.[27]

I counted ten boats that fit or take after Damron's third double-ender type, the "Monterey clipper."[28] Charleston's *San Pietro, Prosit,* and *Elaine* are particularly good examples, as is the *Eager Star,* a fiberglass boat moulded to the Monterey clipper shape (figs. 29–32). These boats have high bows, with a graceful sheer line that curves down to a low and slightly pointed stern. Of

Figure 29.   Variety of Bows.

The *Eager Star* is based on a Monterey Clipper, and *Elaine* next to her appears to have been modeled after one.

Figure 30.   Monterey Clippers *San Pietro* and *Prosit*.
Measurements for the *San Pietro* are 28.1′ × 10.2′ × 3.7′; for the *Prosit* they are
29.1′ × 9.9′ × 4.1′.

Figure 31. *Prosit*: Side View.

Figure 32. Monterey Clipper Bow (Bowsprit) and Stern Detail.

generous beam, they are shallow for their lengths, and decked with wide waterways fore and aft (29-foot length, 9-foot beam, 3-foot draft). The sides flare out from the deck in the forward section of the boat and exhibit slight tumblehome on the after sections. Perhaps the most notable feature of the boat type is its clipper-style bow: the bow stem curves outward away from the boat, ending in a short, stout, bowsprit (see fig. 32). The stern profile resembles that of the Norwegian troller, although the stern ends in less of a point (see fig. 32). The house is small, set amidships, and the engine may sit directly behind it, not below. They were not designed to be trip boats, and thus the fo'c'sle space is limited and does not extend far forward into the bow area as on the other two types. Trolling pit and hatch are similarly set into the deck aft of amidships. The design of these boats developed in the San Francisco Bay area, the result of adding motor power to sailing craft introduced by Italian and Portuguese immigrants.

Many of Charleston's double-enders fit into none of the three classic types. These remaining miscellaneous boats are usually the smallest of double-enders, less than 30 feet long, and their hulls were not originally intended to be those of commercial fishing vessels. Some of them (I counted nine) appear to be converted U. S. Coast Guard life boats, for example, Charleston's *Precious*, *Anne Marie*, and *Sea-Ne-Ma*. Others, such as Charleston's *Jody*, resemble the riverboat and sailboat forms from which today's larger double-enders and trollers allegedly emerged. These latter boats sit low in the water, they are beamy and not very deep, the sides are not often heightened with bulwarks, bow stem and stern post are almost identical in curve and height, and the sheer is graceful. They offer little if any living quarters in the fo'c'sle; the house (at or forward of amidships), after deck, hold, and cockpit are diminutive in size. In appearance, those with wooden sail- or rowboat hulls resemble the Finnish-type double-enders.

The square stern. The square-stern category comprises boats that end with a transom, a relatively flat crosspiece (of frame and planking) that is placed between the extreme stern-ends of the sides of the boat and is attached to the extreme stern-edge of the bottom. The transom abuts the sides and bottom abruptly, creating clean and distinct edges at the seams, in contrast to rounded sterns where the stern sides do not end in an edge or a center post, but wrap smoothly around the stern-end. Whereas the double-ender comes to a point, or a V, the round stern comes to a non-angular U, and the square stern to an angular U. Most of these transoms are straight up and down in profile, and sit vertically with respect to the waterline — some rake outward slightly, a few have tumblehome. Occasionally bulwarks with tumblehome have been positioned atop the transom, and they will extend forward along the sides of the boat (see figs. 25 and 26).

Figure 33. Gulf Shrimper with Square Stern.

Charleston's square-sterned fishboats range in size from about 28 to 50 feet (with the exception of some of the 70-foot class Gulf shrimpers of that stern shape that have recently arrived in the area; see fig. 33). They dominate the medium-size class of boats, comprising 63 (46 percent) of the 138 medium-size boats. However, the majority of square sterners (78; 73 percent), range between 30 and 40 feet in length, most falling in the mid-30-foot range, as Damron observed (only 4 are smaller than 30 feet, and 25 are 40 feet or longer).[29] Most of them (87; 81 percent) are used only in the troll fisheries, competing closely with the number of double-enders (89) that are so employed. On the other hand, for joint trolling and crabbing ventures, square-sterned boats (16 of them) outnumber the double-enders (5) by far, and boats with round sterns only slightly (13); very few of them (4) are found on drag or drag and crab boats.

The transoms of Charleston area square-sterners do not all take the roughly rectangular shape of Jonesport and Mount Desert lobsterboats.[30] Instead, some take the fancy "wineglass" form or bear a close resemblance to it. Many appear to be angular variations on that theme, especially some of the square-sterned, V-bottomed fishing boats that have been built recently on the southern Oregon coast in the 35-foot range, apparently along the lines of local dories (figs. 34 and 35).[31] Boats with the shapelier transoms (those that curve along the sides, bilge and bottom), and those with fairly narrow, rectangular transoms, seem to be smaller, older boats with rounded bottoms that look to be cut-off double-enders.[32] (The Gulf shrimpers have beautiful transoms, too, but they rake outward and adjoin quite different bottoms.) Broad, angular transoms usually finish off a V-shaped bottom.

Excepting those that take after double-enders (mostly the Norwegian or Finn types), these boats offer much more breadth to the stern, and along the entire length of the boat, than do double-enders; their bows do not come to such a point, and they are proportionately not as deep at the forefoot, mid-section, or stern as the round-bottomed Norwegian troller and halibut schooner types. Bow stem and sheer profiles vary widely. Their houses are usually more massive, more angular, and less old-fashioned (trim, proportions) in appearance; they sit at or forward of amidships above the engine, many pushed as far forward as possible to ensure greater deck space aft, and they may be lacking in comfort, space, and finish in the fo'c'sle quarters below (see figs. 35, 58, 59, 67).

The square stern, or the boat with a transom, appears to have developed later in Northwest Coast motorized fishing boat design than the round- or canoe-stern varieties. Nonmotorized boats with transoms, both small and large, with aged antecedents, had been built in the region throughout the first 60 years of white settlement there, coinciding with the early implantation of gas engines in fishing boats.[33] But square-sterned fishing boats seem to have

Figure 34. Dory-Based Transomed Fishboat.
This boat was built in Astoria in 1958. Its measurements are 33.6′ × 12.0′ × 4.8′.

Figure 35. Variety of Transoms on Port Orford Fishboats, February 6, 1978.

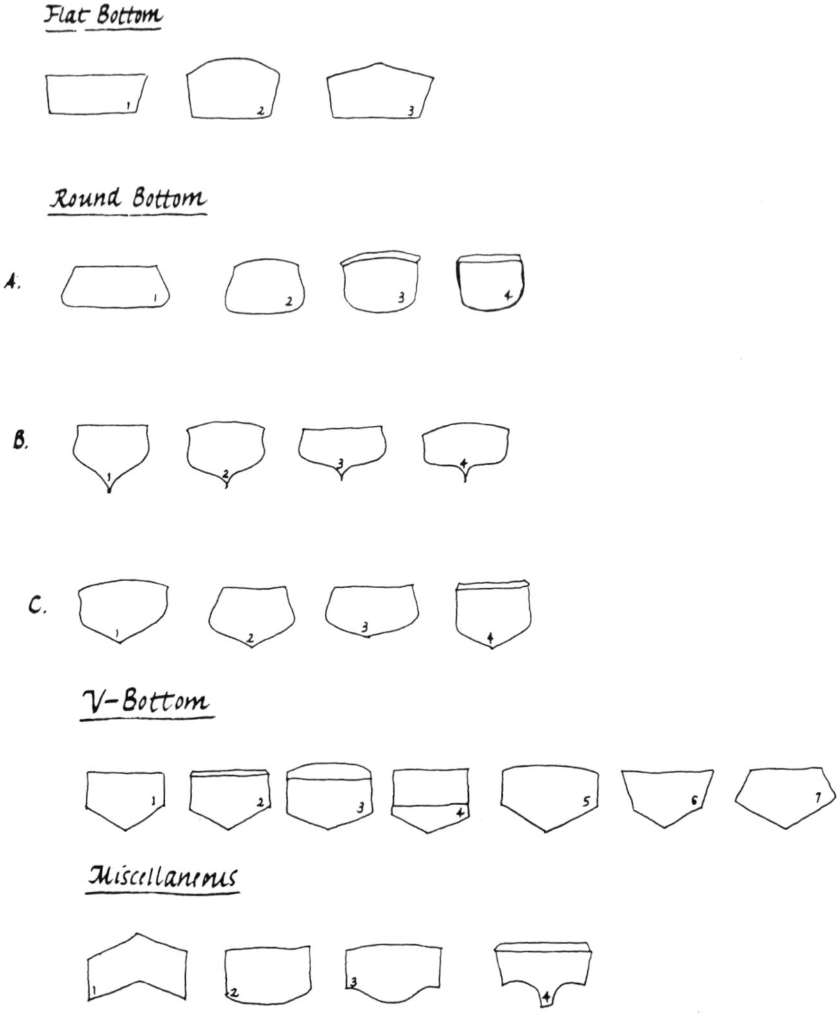

Flat Bottom

Round Bottom

A.

B.

C.

V–Bottom

Miscellaneous

emerged from cutting off the extreme stern-end of a double-ender troller type, retaining the rest of the troller dimensions and arrangements of components in initial stages (see fig. 63). As time went by, many of the double-ender features were lost and the entire boat as well as the stern deck became broader and flatter, as it was found that such a boat could handle the ever-increasing power capabilities of automobile and marine engines.[34] The broader stern deck area could also more easily accommodate several fishing uses such as trolling and crab fishing, and in handling more power, it could provide greater speed and more safety.[35] Of course, several strains of development are possible. Transomed boats that retain the rounded bottom could have evolved from double-ended designs. Boats with V-bottoms could have emerged from the smaller transomed open boats that were used to fish commercially in the coastal rivers and bays through the 1940s and 1950s, at first without power and then with outboard gas engines, and finally with inboard engines. (Many of these boats are still used for river sports fishing and some even for offshore commercial fishing.)

This boat shape clearly provided a solution to the material needs of the fisheries between the late 1930s and 1950s. Salmon trolling and the building of double-enders had declined, and it behooved commercial fishermen to take an interest in more than one fishery (especially in the newly developing crab and tuna fisheries) and in boats with more flexibility and power capability. Even so, square-sterned designs tend to be less seaworthy. Because of their transom construction, they are inherently weaker and more susceptible to damage than are double-enders, which do not have a flat surface for waves to pound against. Further, square-sterned boats have more of a tendency to broach, and to be jolted to the right and left when waves pound against the stern, than do double-enders—conditions that are most discomfitting when making the dangerous bar crossing.[36]

The round stern. Rounded sterns are precisely that—the sides of the boat bend continuously around the end of the boat, uninterrupted by the stern post of the canoe stern or the angular framing of the flat stern. (During construction of a wooden, round-sterned boat, the planking and rails have been steamed to curve thus; planking interlocks in various ways; see fig. 45.) Round-sterned boats comprise the smallest group of commercial fishboats in Charleston. Few of them (6) are small, most (43) are medium-range, but an almost equal number (36) are larger than 50 feet. In fact, round-sterned boats make up the greatest portion of the area's large-size vessels, 36 of 40. While most of them participate in the troll-only fisheries (38), a good number (23) are drag boats only, and another 24 are combination boats (13 salmon and crab, 11 drag and crab); basically they outstrip other boat stern-types in the crab or drag fisheries, combination or not.

Figure 36.   The *Frank F*, Trap Tender Turned Dragger-Crabber.
Note "net in tow" "basket" (black hourglass shape) in the rigging. Measurements
for the boat are 65.2' × 17.0' × 7.3'.

There appear to be many varieties of rounded sterns present among
Charleston's boats. One type strongly resembles a cross between Lunt's steamboat stern and washtub stern, or what Chapelle calls a "rounded fantail tugboat
stern with tumblehome in the bulwarks."[37] It can be found on some of the
oldest and largest fishing boats in the port, specifically the *Frank F*, built in a
Seattle shipyard in 1917 to be a fish trap tender (fig. 36), the *Amak*, built in a
Seattle shipyard in 1915 to be a cannery tender (fig. 69), and the *Zebra*, built
in 1921 by an eccentric Coos Bay boat builder, John Swing, to run the bar at
Gold Beach. Whether developed along halibut schooner lines (*Amak*, *Frank
F*), or tugboat lines (*Zebra*), these boats show the influence of designs worked
out by master carpenters in large shipyards (cf. also fig. 61). The halibut
schooner types are apparently quite deep, narrow, and round-bottomed; their
bow stems are vertical with a very slight inward curvature, and the forefoot is
deep and curved (see also fig. 71). Characteristically, the house sits aft over the
engine, that is, on the stern, leaving some deck space between it and the
extreme stern-end. High in the bow, low at the stern, these boats have very
beautiful lines and a graceful sloping and curved sheer. The sleeping quarters
frequently rest in the fo'c'sle; the main work space is abaft the fo'c'sle and

forward of the house.[38] (The *Zebra*, however, resembles the tug that she was intended to be, and the house sits forward.)

There are a number of boats in the area that were built as halibut schooners or along those lines, which show more fullness, height, and curve to the counter (the stern profile around and below the waterline), and the house and engine sit forward of amidships, troller fashion (see figs. 55 and 71). The sweep of the sheer is not quite as remarkable, though still graceful. It is possible that these more recent composite designs are based as much on purse seiner types as halibut schooner types. Purse seiner designs emerged, too, in large shipyards, but all along the West Coast during the early decades of this century (see figs. 8 and 57).[39] They were built as medium- to large-size boats to accommodate a crew of as many as six to eight men to haul a huge, heavy net by hand over the stern of the boat.[40] Deck space was at a premium, so the house sat well forward of amidships, and the hull was built broad and round at the stern (a round stern presumably because it not only is sturdier than a square stern, but it does not leave any edges for a net to hang up on). These boats were operated mostly by Yugoslavs (Dalmatians) in the Puget Sound area, and by Italian and Portuguese in the Monterey and San Francisco Bay areas (and on south); I have not yet found a source that discusses whether these ethnics were instrumental in developing and building these boats.[41]

Some old trollers bear round sterns without giving up any of the features that mark double-enders (see figs. 26 and 27). These sterns are fairly narrow, some quite curvacious (the Alaskan variation to the double-ender, according to Damron), and others somewhat squarish, with high, well-rounded counters—according to Lunt's proposition, these forms might represent transitions from double-ended to square or cut-off sterns.[42]

Then there are boats of more modern creation, mostly of steel, and some of wood (Humbert's boats), that feature high bulwarks with tumblehome at the stern, squarish in looks, but rounded at the corners and structurally continuous whatever the material. These rounded squared bulwarks may rest atop a deep, high, rounded counter, or one that is rounded to the sides, edged at the juncture of the transom with the boat bottom (see figs. 38, 39, 41, 46, 72, 73). Indeed these rounded-square sterns seem to predominate on the wooden rounded V-hull (Humbert's specialty; fig. 37), or on the steel hard chine hull type. These boats are very broad at the stern and similarly at amidships, drawing to a beamy point at the bow. The bow stem, or bow profile, while straight, flares slightly away from the boat; the forward sides may also be built up with bulwarks that slope in a pair of curves to the top rail just forward of amidships. The stern and sides are built up with high bulwarks of slight or marked tumblehome. The sheer is moderate on well-designed boats, and fairly flat on those less skillfully composed. The large house sits above the engine well forward of amidships, with the fo'c'sle to the fore, and the wide and spacious deck to the

Figure 37.   *Betty Jean*, a Humbert Boat.
Measurements are 34.3′ × 10.8′ × 4.6′.

Figure 38. *Betty Jean*: Stern View.

Figure 39.   Humbert's Last Boat, *Quasar*.
The *Quasar*'s measurements are 36.1' × 11.8' × 6.8'.

Figure 40. *Quasar*: Side View.

Figure 41.   Humbert's *Westerly*: Bow View.
Measurements for the *Westerly* are 34.3′ × 10.8′ × 4.6′.

rear, interrupted by one or two hold openings. These newer boats incorporate the breadth of the later square-sterned boats with the strength of a round stern; bottoms are rounded V's or modified rounds to give the boat less roll, more stability, greater hold and fuel-carrying capacity, as well as more gracious living accommodations (mostly above deck).

Charleston's round-sterned boats thus show what seem to be three separate developments. The adaptation of a tugboat/powerboat stern to early-powered large fishing boats during the first two decades of this century sparked one trend from which emerged later large fishboat designs such as purse seiners and the Western combination boat. Increased power capabilities and the desire for more stern deck space prompted yet another development, the adaptation of round sterns to canoe-sterned trollers during the late 1920s and early 1930s. Round sterns on these small boats may represent transitional forms between canoe and square sterns, but in some cases they may mimic the sterns of older, larger fishing boats, either halibut schooners or purse seiners. Finally, in the last 15 years, a composite form has emerged, probably based on both square-sterned troller/crab boats and evolved purse seiner designs. This design demonstrates an application of round-stern technology to the square-stern idea to accompany a composite rounded V-hull (which combines the deep round hull with the V-shaped hull). Incidentally, the rounded stern and the rounded V-hull are much easier to accomplish in steel than in wood, and may represent contributions from the developing steel fishboat "school of design."

Construction

Charleston fishermen take great interest in the material makeup of a boat's hull. Most of Charleston's fishing boats (220 of 286, or 77 percent) are "wood boats"; wood is the traditional material out of which fishing boats have been made for centuries, including the past 130 years of white settlement on the West Coast. Boats of newer materials, "iron boats," or "steel boats," fiberglass, aluminum, or ferro-cement boats, have been making their appearances on the Oregon Coast for the past 40 or so years. Charleston did not have any working aluminum or ferro-cement fishing boats in 1977–78, but she did have (in ever-increasing numbers) 52 (18 percent) steel or iron commercial fishing vessels, and 14 (5) fiberglass fishboats.

The wood boats were mostly small- or medium-size (112 medium, 90 small, 18 large); the majority of them were used for trolling only (176), fewer for crab combinations (28 salmon/crab, 9 drag/crab), and least for drag fishing only (7); most of them are square-sterned (92, or 42 percent), followed closely by double-enders (80, or 36 percent), and fewer of them are round-sterned (48, or 22 percent).

Steel boats are generally medium- or large-size (21 large, 20 medium, 11 small); most of them are used only for trolling (26), but they are followed closely by drag fishers (17), and few are crab combinations (4 salmon/crab, 4 drag/crab). By far, most of them are round-sterned (33, or 58 percent), with the remainder falling fairly evenly into the other two stern categories (10 square, 10 double-enders, double-enders being the smallest steel boats, square-sterners mostly medium-size steel boats, round-sterners being mostly large or medium).

Most of the fiberglass boats are medium-range in size, many fall into the small-size class, and only one is a large boat. They are used mostly for trolling only, some both trolling and crabbing, and they are pretty evenly distributed among the three major stern types (the small boats are double-enders, the large boats round-sterned, medium-size boats either round or square).

There is quite a bit of controversy among Charleston's fishermen about the benefits of one material over another.[43] Most fishermen, out of habit, are partial to wooden boats, even if they presently own a boat made of another material or even if they plan to build their next boats in another material. Fred Anderson, who owns a newly built steel trawler, reflects the feelings of a lot of fishermen:

> . . . a wood boat is still nicer than a steel boat, I don't care what anybody says. . . . they're prettier, it's awful hard to build a pretty steel boat, believe me, without going into tuna clippers or something. . . . Wood boats are prettier, they're warmer, they're easier to keep up . . . you're not fighting the rust and stuff all the time, you know. And, they're just better boats, I think. But a steel boat is much more practical, it's more tougher, you can bang it around, but just about every two or three years it gets looking so bad you got to go in and just spend seven, eight thousand bucks getting it sandblasted and painted. And then if you hit something, you got less chance of sinking, but really that's about the only advantage, is you can bang it around a little more.[44]

Though fishermen are fond of wooden boats, good wooden boat builders are getting increasingly hard to find on the West Coast. Even if one finds such a builder, the builder may not be able to build the boat of quality materials, or the boat is likely to cost $60,000 to $80,000 (1977–78 figures) outright. Fred Anderson continued:

> . . . the main reason switching to steel boats is there's very few people left that can work on wood boats, and wood's hard to find. You know, like you want to get a timber out of a piece of wood for marine use, you have to be what they call outside the heart and inside the sap. So if you want say a six by six timber to put in there, it takes a hell of a big tree to get inside the sap and outside the heart. You know most trees, you've only got a little spot about like that [gestures]. Well through the years as the old growth timber was used up and whatnot, there's one wood builder left, and he threatens to quit all the time because he can't get good wood, you know. He's always threatening to quit 'cause he can't get any good wood. Then he'll find some at some little mill up in the hills here some place or something, build another boat. . . .[45]

So new fishing boats — at least the large varieties — are increasingly of steel, an inexpensive, abundant material that makes a strong boat, even though it may be "noisy" and "cold" without much of the "personality" of the owner in it, may cost as much or more in time and money to maintain, and will demand more specialized labor to keep up.[46]

Some new boats (mostly smaller ones) are being constructed of fiberglass, which is high in initial cost — thus prohibitive — although likewise high in resale value. Some fishermen view it skeptically because they think it not as strong and impact resistant as steel or as reliable as wood; others however, value it for its lightness and speed in the water, and the small amount of maintenance it requires, compared to the other two materials.[47]

All three materials necessitate different construction techniques. In principle, wood and steel boat construction are similar: wooden planking, or recently, sheets of marine plywood, or steel plates, are placed edge to edge and attached to a rigid frame, or skeleton, which gives the shape to the boat. The main difference between steel and wood plank construction is that the edges of the steel plates are welded to each other, whereas wooden planks are only placed tightly together and attached to the frame, the lengthwise seams not joined together but filled with caulking. In wooden boatbuilding, this process is known as "carvel construction," or more correctly, "non-edge joined construction on a pre-erected skeleton," where the form "had to be conceived as a whole before she could be built."[48] This type of construction differs from the so-called "clinker" or "clench-lap" type constructions which create a shell composed of lapstrake or flush planks that have been joined together, to which frames may or may not be added later for strengthening.[49] Carvel construction, or skeleton construction, is a much more modern development than shell construction, which is ancient. Basil Greenhill suggests that this latter-day way of building boats developed at least by the late fifteenth century in European yards with the advent of widespread literacy and the use of half-models, precursors of ship drawings: its advantage lay in allowing the construction of very large boats.[50] Originally used only on ships, or the large boats of the times, it is now used widely for boats that are small compared to what we now know as ships, but which are large compared to the small sail- and oar-powered varieties made according to the other construction method, which once proliferated for local transportation and small-time fishing. As Greenhill puts it, "the small boats of today represent big vessels now vanished."[51]

Small steel boat construction, probably a recent transmutation of wooden skeleton boatbuilding, is likewise an adaptation of the big steel shipbuilding industry.[52] The advantage of steel skeleton over wood skeleton construction is that the edges of the "planking" can be welded together, thus forming a tougher skin.

Fiberglass boat construction, on the other hand, involves creating a hull

Figure 42. Humbert's Boat Shop with *Quasar* under Construction. *(Photo courtesy of Joe Parker)*

Figure 43. *Quasar* under Construction.
(Photo courtesy of Joe Parker)

shell composed of layers of fiberglass cloth and polyester resin that conforms to the shape of a mould modeled after an already existing, highly successful, probably wooden boat.[53] In larger boats, a fiberglass sheathing may be applied to a wooden frame of marine plywood or regular ribbing and planking. This method of construction resembles the more ancient shell-type of boatbuilding, yet it clearly depends on the pre-existence of skeleton-type constructions for models. Hence, all of Charleston's commercial fishboat constructions come to us from what we might call today nonfolk traditions, rather highly sophisticated technological advances, which occurred, however, in increments over the past 500 years in large and small shipyards, and probably also in small boat shops and in fishermen's backyards and garages.

My grandfather, the late H. C. Hanson, a self-made naval architect and marine engineer, designed hundreds of wooden fishboats that were built in large Seattle-area yards. He claimed, however, that the overwhelming majority of wooden trollers were made in small boat shops and backyards all along the West Coast.[54] Hanson also pioneered adapting large steel shipbuilding practices to the construction of smaller-scale fishing boats. He designed hundreds of steel fishboats that were built in yards in Seattle and all over the world; he inspired many West Coast shipyards to follow suit, especially in the Seattle area. Now not only most shipyards construct all fishboats of steel, but so do independent builders and fishermen in small boat shops and backyards all along the coast.

While some of Charleston's boats were designed by professional marine architects and built in the larger West Coast yards, others were developed in large yards by experienced shipwrights and old hands in the boatbuilding trades. More perhaps have come from the small shops of independently employed boat builders such as George Calkins of Three Rocks, Oregon; Andrew Pakonen of Aberdeen, Washington; Matt Tolonen of Astoria's Columbia Boat Building Company; the Yosts of Eureka's Build A Boat Shop; Joe Sanfilippo of San Diego; F. Pasquinucci of Sausalito Boatbuilding Works; and Coos Bay's own "Slim" Brown (who the last I knew was building his "last" boat at the age of 78), the late, great Wilbur Humbert, and a host of other old-timers, now deceased (fig. 42). Many Coos Bay fishermen have at one time or another built their own boats, too. In fact I have heard that to fly over the Charleston area is to see a boat hull in the works in every other yard. Several steel boats have been homemade recently, as have some of the wooden boats made with a marine plywood skin.[55] For large fiberglass boats, however, fishermen usually have to leave the port to go to specialized firms elsewhere on the coast.

Unlike the barns that Henry Glassie studied in upper New York State, completed boats in their stalls at the boat basin do not readily admit characteristics of their constructions, exposing their frames and joinery.[56] On the outside they have been smoothed and coated with layers of paint, and their bottoms are under water; on the inside, their frames are frequently hemmed in further by finish work. If a boat is wood, however, most fishermen will know the kinds of wood of which it is made, and they will know something of the characteristics of the framing—the size, number, and placement of the ribs.

Paul Heikkila says each craftsman has his own wood preferences—some like yellow fir, some like cedar, and some Alaska spruce. He said his father, an Astoria boat builder, used fir on the bottom, cedar around the waterline, and yew wood for the "bones."[57] Some boats, like the *Amak* and *Maria E*, have been made entirely of Douglas fir, ribs and planking.[58] Local fisherman Cyrus Little, Sr., built himself a 36-foot round-sterned salmon-crab boat entirely of Douglas fir except for a one-piece keel-bow stem which he adzed from a curved cedar that grew behind his house. Orville Wikes of Newport, Oregon, prefers clear fir framing with top-grade waterproof plywood for the sides, bottom, deck, and cabin of his small boats.[59] One fisherman recently built himself a boat with Port Orford cedar framing and marine plywood planking.[60] Wilbur Humbert liked to build his boats with frames of Port Orford white cedar, since it bends better than any other wood (and is also lightweight and rot resistant), and with planking of Douglas fir, because it is more durable than cedar and will not scuff as easily when rubbed along the docks (fig. 43). "Slim" Brown also built at least one of his boats with Port Orford cedar ribbing and fir planking and decking.[61] Humbert was also exceedingly concerned about the quality of wood:

> Humbert is very choosy about the quality of cedar and fir he selects from Tucker's Saw Mill in Bandon. It is not uncommon for him to send half a load of wood back to Tucker's with complaints about the wood not being clear, or having weak fibers . . . . One man told me that when Humbert gets annoyed at Tucker's Saw Mill, Humbert goes down there himself and walks around the stacks of wood, and with a piece of chalk, makes X's on the boards that he wants. He does all this without saying a word. He comes to the Mill, makes his X's, gets back into his truck, and comes back to his shop.
>
> Humbert definitely prefers old growth wood to new growth. Reasoning for this is because old growth is a more tightly fibered wood, therefore it holds screws and bolts more securely than new growth wood. Just where the cedars and firs are located also makes a difference to Humbert. He does not want the lumber from a tree that has been down in the meadow or valley all its life, somewhat protected from the sun and wind. Having lumber from that location is like a little boy who sleeps all his life and gets no exercise. However a tree that stands on top of a hill and gets too much sunlight and wind is not preferred either. Trees that get just the right amount of sunlight and wind are the trees that Humbert seeks. Still once the tree is cut down and sawed, Humbert does not like to use the wood for several months.[62]

The size and spacing of the ribs appear to be characteristics that locals feel determine the strength of the boat (figs. 44 and 45). One fellow told me that the *Zebra* was built exceptionally strong with ribs 6 inches square and placed on 12-inch centers, so that it could endure bumping the bar as it entered the

Figure 44. *Quasar*'s Ribs and Engine Mount, Looking Bowward.
(Photo courtesy of Joe Parker)

. *Quasar*'s Ribs and Stern.
Note especially the interlocking steam-bent plank stern construction.
(Photo courtesy of Joe Parker)

mouth of the Rogue River at Gold Beach. A crewman of the *Husky* especially went to the trouble of showing me the tough double-ribbed framing of that boat.[63]

Overall excellence in construction is attributed to Humbert's boats. In 50 years, none of his boats has sunk, and each is still fishing, even though one rolled over, self-righting itself; another was squeezed against a dock by an uncontrolled barge, which knocked the dock ajar but did nothing to the boat; and another crashed into a jetty, which dislodged the bow stem, but did not split it.[64] "Humbert builds his boats strong" (see figs. 37–45).

Color Scheme

While fishermen will pass judgment readily on the overall looks of a particular boat—it may be "pretty," "ugly," or a "big mess"—they are not very outspoken about why fishboats are painted the colors they are. I often drew some surprise and hesitation upon questioning a fisherman about the colors he paints his own boat, and I received a wide range of answers.

Usually there was no particular reason for painting a boat certain colors. Fisherman Leonard Hall said he just continued painting his boat the green (hull) and white (house) she was when he first bought her, while he had heard that "the Scandinavians all think that a green hull fishes better than a white one."[65] Fred Anderson had also heard that Swedes liked green-hulled boats, and he felt personally that it was traditional to have a dark hull, usually black with white uppers and trim, or the reverse, an all-white boat with black trim.[66] Charlie Ells gave no reason for changing his boat's hull color from black to grey, but he claimed that boats painted bright blue, both hull and house, are Portuguese.[67] Some people commented that certain colors were easier on the eyes while fishing on the ocean—mast buff trim on a white boat according to Wilbur Humbert, and a green hull according to Fred Anderson.[68] Fish processor Ruth Hallmark Day had heard that white, she thought, was safer because it could be seen more easily on the ocean from a distance.[69]

According to Damron, specific hull and trim colors of trollers were once identifiable with particular coastal areas and ports.[70] Generally in all areas the topsides (house) were white for visibility at night. In California, hulls, too, were white, and a favorite trim color was blue, while black or several colors combined were also popular. In the north, hulls were white, green, or sometimes grey, with black, green, brown, or red trim—blue was considered bad luck.

Chapelle suggests, on the other hand, that boat colors are highly subject to trends rather than tradition.[71] And Ruth Hallmark Day claimed, "Well, course some of them [fishermen] are very, very individual. I think most of them, they just pick a nice color scheme, something that's pleasant to them, and painted it that way, and once in a while one of them wants to be pretty different. . . ."[72] So perhaps color scheme today is more a matter of individual preference and a sign of the times than cultural imperative. However, I included color schemes in my boat survey to see if there were any correlations between color and shape, size, material, or use categories.

Below the waterline, the bottoms of all wooden hulls must be painted with protective anti-fouling paint, usually a dark brick red. Out of tradition, both steel and fiberglass bottoms may also be painted another color than what appears above the waterline, although the fiberglass boats do not actually have to be painted, and steel does not need the brick red copper paint. Above the waterline, exclusive of trim, the hull and house of any type of boat are generally each painted one solid color. Wooden boats, with their protective rub rails and often detailed finish-carpentry work, show the most detail in trim colorings. Often colored distinctively are: one sturdy rub rail that runs partly or entirely around the hull well above the waterline and at or just below deck level; rails that top the sides or bulwarks of the hull and additional rails that may demarcate and finish off the juncture of bulwarks and sides; on the house, trim around the windows, portholes, roof top, and door of the house; sometimes the house door (see figs. 57, 63, 65, 67, 71). Sometimes the entire lower half of the house will be painted one color—often grey—to match the deck, hatch, and cockpit paint. Sometimes the bulwarks will be painted a color distinct from the hull, house, or trim (see figs. 55 and 61). Between the main rub rail and top rails, usually on the older larger wooden boats, sometimes a colored horizontal stripe appears that does not extend the entire length of the side (see figs. 55, 57, and 69). Mostly on smaller boats, usually trollers, sometimes a one-inch high stripe is painted just above the waterline, ringing the bottom (one young fisherman had heard that certain stripe colors identify the boat's skipper with a particular gang of fishermen—he thought it was a tradition among Italian fishermen in the San Francisco Bay area—while an older fisherman pooh-poohed the idea). Sometimes the paint of the bottom has been extended up the sides to the main rub rail from the stern to about midships, whence it then angles down to the waterline (a north coast tradition?; one fisherman claimed the practice keeps barnacles from attaching to the sides of the boat which may be submerged when the boat is loaded with its catch; see figs. 57, 69, and 71). Protective stripping, often unpainted, often of ironwood, occurs sometimes on the hull to one side of the bow to protect the hull from damage that the anchor can wreak (see fig. 28), and on one midships side of a crab boat to protect the hull from swinging crab pots. Fiberglass and steel boats bear trim mostly in the form of decorative stripes, some ringing the boat around the waterline or where various rails might be located on a wooden boat; some are more flamboyant and bear little relation to the shape of the boat (diagonal stripes).

The majority of Charleston boats were all white with colored trim (207 of

286), including most of the wooden boats (178), most of the fiberglass boats (10), and only 19 of the steel boats. All of the Monterey clippers and Finnish-style trollers were white. White boats also included most of all varieties of stern types, most of the troll, troll/crab, half of the drag/crab, and only one-third of the drag-only operations. Most of the white boats sported only one trim color, mostly black, then light blue, blue, or turquoise, followed by brown, green, or grey, then red, red-brown, beige, or light green, or dark red, orange, light brown, or natural wood. The Monterey clippers bore trim of a variety of light colors (turquoise, blue, light green, as well as brown, black, and orange), and the Finn boats mostly black and some grey. About one-fourth of the white boats wore two trim colors, one black and the others usually turquoise, green, blue, light blue, or grey, followed by the other colors (reds, beige, natural wood, orange). Only a few of the white boats showed two trim colors, neither of which was black, and these included combinations mostly of blues, greys, turquoises, browns, reds, and greens, in descending order.

Forty-seven boats featured a dark hull with a white house. Most of the hulls were black, followed by green or grey (then light blue, blue, turquoise, light green, yellow, orange, red, natural wood). Most of these featured black or brown trim on the hull, with black and/or another color like brown, green, grey, or turquoise on the house. Most of these boats were wood (28), a good number were steel (18), and only one was fiberglass. More were round-sterned (21) than square (15), and fewest were double-ended (11). Most were trollers-only (26), or draggers (9), with 7 troll/crab and 5 drag/crab operations.

Twenty-one boats were of solid colors — 11 all one color, and 10 several colors. Those that were all one color were mostly light blue, turquoise, grey, pale green, yellow, green, or blue. The multi-colored varieties were mostly blue or black of hull, light blue, grey, or red on the top. Trim colors varied tremendously, but often were blue or light blue. Most of these boats were steel (12, wood 7, fiberglass 2); most had round sterns (10, double-enders 6, square sterns 5), and most were trollers (14, plus 1 salmon-crab), or draggers (5, plus 1 drag/crab).

A small contingent of boats, 11, were colored white on the hull, and a darker color on the house. These house colors were mostly quite bright — yellow, orange, or red, then light blue, light turquoise, and green and black. Trim mostly was black and/or another dark color. Most were wood (8, steel 2, fiberglass 1), square-sterned (8, round 2, double-ended 1), and troll/crab operations (6, troll 3, drag 2).

In sum, color categories appear to vary mostly according to size and hull material, hence probably age, too. The fiberglass boats were generally entirely white; if they varied from the norm, they might be a light pastel color such as light blue. Steel boats of all sizes, shapes, and fisheries were as likely to be all white as they were dark of hull and white of house (figs. 55 and 72), or of all one or two nonwhite colors (figs. 46 and 73); they edged out boats of other materials in the solid nonwhite color category. Wooden boat colors varied more according to fishery, size, shape, and perhaps age. Wooden trollers (including troll/crab boats), usually small- or medium-size, were mostly white. If a colored double-ender, however, the boat was most likely to have a dark hull (mostly green, black, or grey) with a white house, or secondly, to be all one color (probably a light blue). Very, very few round-sterned wooden trollers were anything but white in color; those that varied followed the dark hull, light house pattern. Trollers with square sterns that were not white, however, showed an interesting breakdown: about half followed the dark hull, white house strategy, but significantly, half had white hulls and dark houses mostly of flashy, bright colors (a recent color fad, I presume, interestingly, applied to newer troller types). Whatever their shapes, larger wooden fishing boats, those used for dragging or dragging and crabbing, were either all white (more recent boats), or dark of hull (usually green or grey) and white of house (older boats). Old purse seiners or recently arrived Gulf shrimpers were usually all white, while boats of the halibut schooner strain tended to be dark hulled (see figs. 33, 36, 55, 57, and 69).

Summary

In sum, then, most Coos Bay fishboats can be found in the Charleston vicinity, harbored usually at the boat basin. The great majority of boats are equipped only with salmon trolling gear. They are small boats, less than 35 feet in length, usually built of wood and painted white with a dark-colored trim. Roughly, there are as many double-enders among these boats as there are round- and square-sterned varieties, pointing to a continued demand for small wooden salmon trollers since the 1920s (and earlier). The double-enders and round-sterned boats represent the oldest of trollers, built usually before the 1950s, and they show the most diverse origins, from southern California ports to Alaska, from shipyard to backyard. The square-sterned varieties indicate more recent, local, and "home-grown" origins (1950s to the present; ports from northern California to southern Washington; small boat shops and fishermen's backyards). For the most part, the older boats are deeper and narrower than the more recent ones, and the older bottoms are usually rounder. Development of a regional small fishboat design can be seen in the southern Oregon coast proliferation of newer, square-sterned, decked-over troller-crabbers, which have been constructed of marine plywood and modeled after square-sterned boat types like the small open dory and evolved gillnetter types of the northern ports of Newport, Cape Kiwanda, and Astoria.

To describe solely the majority of Charleston boats, or the average or representative Charleston fishboat, leaves out the important constituency of larger Charleston fishing vessels, the draggers and combination boats. These boats range from 35 to 80 feet, the smaller ones (less than 50 feet) being used mostly for combined trolling, crabbing, and shrimping, and the larger ones for bottomfishing alone or combined with shrimping. Most of them are wood, but this group includes the majority of local steel boats; round or rounded-square sterns are most prevalent, while square sterns and double-enders are scarce; color schemes are quite diverse, but darker colors seem to outweigh lighter ones. Most of the large boats built before the 1940s were not constructed for their present purposes, whereas the boats built during and since the 1940s were; and pre-forties boats generally have Puget Sound shipyard origins, whereas post-1940 boats have humbler (boat shops, fishermen's backyards, as well as shipyards), more local (Oregon) origins. While initially modeled on these pre-forties types, the later boats have become increasingly broader and more capacious overall, without becoming longer or shallower. Those constructed since the 1960s are mostly steel-built; by the 1990s probably all but an exceptional few new West Coast fishboats over 35 feet in length will be built of steel. The death of Wilbur Humbert in 1977, his youngest son's hesitance to continue the business full steam ahead, the absence of any other apprentices to fill the void, and local acceptance of steel construction, have cast a pall on the evolution of a local specialized builder-based large fishboat design in wood. Since most locally built steel boats incorporate many of the features that Humbert included in his fishboats, the articulation of regional fishboat design preferences and the evolution(s) of large regional boat types continue. Since steel fishboat design and technology have hardly matured, a body of locally or regionally acceptable building practices may flower in the years ahead.

The Individual Nature of Fishboats

While Charleston fishermen identify their boats with a variety of broad classes of fishboats, they also often talk of a specific boat as an individual, as if it were a person. In much the same manner as a farmer treats his workhorses, Charleston fishermen endow their boats with human traits and personality, in fact according to them the status of ships rather than mere boats, as befits their sizes and constructions.[73] Indeed, Charleston fishboats are fully personified by local custom. Skippers often refer to their boats as female beings who have some measure of self-initiated behavior: "that old girl's been so good to us for 31 years, and still a good boat" or "she's been going up there to Bill's for how many years. . . . so he knows her inside and out."[74]

With careful ceremony, each boat receives a name, and symbolically the breath of life, at its launching.[75] I witnessed the launching of the *Sleep Robber*, a 78-foot steel dragger, in Coos Bay on Wednesday, May 3, 1978, around 11:00 a.m. (fig. 46). The date and hour had been set according to the tide only a

Figure 46. Launching of the *Sleep Robber.* Hillstrom Shipbuilding, May 3, 1978.

couple of days in advance, after the boat had reached the appropriate stage of completion. A large crowd gathered to watch the ceremony, even though it was not announced to the public until afterwards. Fred Anderson, the skipper, and yard workers had invited many of the guests—friends, family, notable members of the waterfront community, the press—but many of those in attendance had only heard of the event through the grapevine and, curious (and thirsty), had come uninvited. Anderson had hired a priest to read the appropriate passages from the Bible and throw holy water on the bow; though he was of a different faith, he felt that only an authentic Catholic priest would do to preside over the ceremony (even though this particular priest had never blessed a boat before). Following the priest's opening formulae, Anderson's wife, Betty, broke a bottle of champagne over the bow, as is the custom, and yard workers promptly ushered the boat into the water and its life, to the tune of the yard whistle. After the "big splash," a small tug rescued the new boat and brought her back to the dock. Thereupon, in celebration of the successful birthing, the crowd could mill around the yard, tour the boat, and water itself freely at the makeshift bar that had been erected at the site, courtesy of the skipper.[76]

Most Charleston commercial fishboats have been similarly launched and named. While the fisherman may be obliged to name a large boat under centuries-old government stipulations, he certainly is not so bound in his choice of names.[77] Rather, Charleston fishermen appear to select names for their boats according to coastal folk tradition.[78] Thus, a good third of the local fishboats are named after women, mainly fishermen's wives, a custom that long-time fish plant manager Ruth Hallmark Day deplores:

> Oh, I waged a one-woman campaign for years to try to keep them from naming their boats for women. Hurricanes are great, but not naming their boats for women, for their wives. I like names like, oh, *Intrepid*, and *South Wind*, and *Rambler*, and even *Old Dry Rot*.
> . . . I remember talking to a bunch of fishermen one day, and we were talking about boat names, and I said, "Well, our brand name I thought was such a pretty name, and I've never seen a boat named that, *The Wave King*, and I just thought that would be a beautiful name for a boat, and I didn't know why anybody didn't name it that instead of naming their boat for their wife." And this one fellow says, "Well, that is nice," he says, "I'll name my boat that." And it was the worst old junker in the fleet. It was just horrible looking, never painted, and in the back on the stern it had an old back seat of a car . . . that he sat on when he trolled, upholstery coming out of it. So I just dropped the subject, I never mentioned it again. I thought, boy, that'd be my luck.[79]

Typically, the boat gets the woman's first name (*Anita, Joyce, Lilly, Almae, Karla, Cleora, Naomi,* . . .), or both her first and middle names (*Kelly Jo, Kathy Jo, Jana Jo, Shirley Lynn, Tammy Lynne, Cheri Lynn, Christina Marie, Ann Marie, Metta Marie, Ella Mae, Dora May, Florence May, Betty Rose, Betty Lou, Betty Jean,* . . .), or her first name and the initial of her last name (*Wendy R, Pearl M, Zillah B, Ardis C, Georgia K*, . . .). Sometimes the boat is given two female names (*Ginny and Jill*) or a first or last name following Lady (*Lady Ann*), Miss (*Miss Everett, Miss Larene*), or Ms. (*Ms. Mills*).

A few boats, however, are named after particular men (*George, Edgar A, John Allen*), after particular places (*Pacific, Capistrano, Artic Sea II*) including stars and constellations (*Arcturus, Polaris, Pisces*), or after famous or legendary persons, places, or things often having some association with the sea (*Lincoln, Simon Peter, Odysseus, Barbary Coast, Arundel, Flying Cloud*). Some fishermen have combined two or more family names to come up with a name for their boats (*Faymar*), and some designate their boats only with the initials of someone's name (*RVA*), sometimes spelled out (*Cee Cee, Triple D*).

In short, most Charleston boat names (two-thirds of them) are proper nouns, primarily the names of women. The remaining minority (one-third) are overwhelmingly nouns, too, but common nouns. These nouns refer to classes of persons, places, or things that often possess certain characteristics that the fisherman imagines or wishes himself or his boat to have; not surprisingly, many reflect aspects of the fisherman's working environment. Of this group, about a third refers to classes of persons (*Ranger, Hustler, Dreamer, Vixen, Viking, Mermaid, Peasant, Pacific Belle*). Another third refers to classes of nonhuman, but mostly animate things such as fish, fowl, the sea, the heavens, and the elements (*Chickadee, Albatross, Eagle; Coho, Sockeye, Sea Trout, King Fish; Morning Star, Evening Star; Fog, Oregon Mist, Westerly, Pacific Breeze*). And another third refers to inanimate objects and abstract things (*Garnet, Brandywine, Mojo, Habitat; Conquest, Bounty, Ocean Pride, Renown, Legend, Moral, Quintessence, Wanderlust*).

Nouns and proper nouns aside, almost two-thirds of the local boat names refer to people, either to specific individuals, or to characters who possess particular qualities. Moreover, a boat's name, like a person's, is used repeatedly in the multiple legal and business transactions that attend the boat during its lifetime. At some of the local marine-related shops, a fisherman's account is kept in the name of his boat (probably so that shop owners can make easier claim against the fisherman's most valuable asset, should he fail to make good on long-unpaid debts). Also ordered according to boat name at local documentation offices and in government publications is certain information available to the public regarding each federally registered vessel. A change of boat name, further, requires legal procedures, and according to one person, must be announced in local newspapers, probably to notify would-be creditors.[80]

Notably, however, a local fishing boat is known and discussed by name and not simply as so-and-so's boat. She has an identity of her own, irrespective of specific skippers and crew members. In fact, a skipper is likely to be identified by the boat he owns: "I don't know if you know Gordon or not, that has the *Metta Marie*."[81] Similarly, crew members are often said to work on a specific boat rather than to work for a particular skipper: "Joe was a boat puller on the *Frank F* when we were buying shrimp" or "One of our sons used to fish on the *Lou-R.*"[82] (Perhaps to distinguish the boats from the humans after whom they are frequently named, in everyday parlance a boat's name is commonly preceded by "the." Thus, a boat named *Joyce* would be called "the *Joyce.*" This practice is so much the rule that occasionally the officially registered name of a boat may include the "the.")

Locals who have not necessarily worked a particular boat frequently know a boat by name, know its location and usually its present owner and possibly past owners, and know something of its physical makeup, general condition, handling characteristics, and present and original uses. At the slightest provocation they can rattle off some of the more idiosyncratic or striking features of a specific boat and its history, or they may offer an opinion regarding how well it is kept up, or whether it is a pretty, ugly, strongly built, or a ludicrous example of a commercial fishing vessel.[83] The oral lore that circulates in the community about these boats, and the personality accorded to them, are undoubtedly rooted in the fact that no two boats can be identical, even when built according to the same model in the same yard by the same people under very similar conditions. According to fishermen, traditional boat builders, and marine architects alike, each boat behaves and fishes a little differently than the next; even the marine architect's sophisticated formulae cannot guarantee identical results.[84]

The builder's lack of absolute control over uniformity in the materials out of which he constructs his boats accounts partially for variance across boats of the same build. Further, the process of fastening wooden planking or steel plates to a fixed frame tends to warp the entire structure as it is being built. With care, the boat builder can minimize the amount of twist that construction can give to the form, but the end result will still be warped ever so slightly, such that a given boat deviates from the ideal and other boats of the same ilk in ways peculiar to its specific construction and the specific qualities of the material components of which the boat is made. Addition of varied mechanical and hydraulic components can further widen the gap between boats of the same plan and build.

Fishboats are usually built to the order of a specific individual, however. Hence, the builder will incorporate individual desires in exact form and type of components into a boat for a particular person so that boats of the same basic plan will be built to vary from one another in the first place. Take the case of the Cyrus Littles, father and son. In 1972, Cyrus, Jr., decided to have a new fiberglass boat built for himself at a yard in Brookings, Oregon. The hull was fashioned after a Canadian model, but the Littles demanded that the bulwarks be built up 12 inches higher than the base model, and they paid an extra

$1,000 to have the deed done. Then they had the cabin, deck, and interior fashioned after their boat *Maria E*, which Cyrus, Sr., had helped complete when it was under construction. Even then the Littles left out the cockpit that is present in *Maria E*'s stern decking, and they built the cabin shorter than *Maria E*'s so that the new boat would have more deck space. The two Cyruses finally had to rewire the boat and replace some fittings, as well as install the engine, drive shaft, and fuel tanks. As Cyrus, Sr., put it, finally there is no boat quite like the *Silver Wave* (see figs. 58, 59).[85] Similarly, Fred Anderson, who recruited the same Coos Bay shipyard to build a second boat for him, requested changes desired in the first to be incorporated into the second, even though the second was to be built on the same basic theme (cf. figs. 46, 72, 73).[86]

Wilbur Humbert, traditional fishboat builder, basically built the same boat — rather the same model — each time he filled an order (see figs. 37–41).[87] Over the years he had developed a specific boat form, and he constructed his boats in a particular way with very special kinds of materials. But each time he built a boat, he built it to the length desired by the client, and he constructed the house, fo'c'sle, deck, hold, and engine room volumes somewhat to the client's specifications. In addition, from boat to boat he sought to solve a number of his own design problems. While he appeared to have his basic fishboat form worked out, he constantly tried to refine it and make it even more nearly perfect. For each boat he would prepare a half-model fashioned on his basic boat theme, which he would contemplate for weeks and pare down here and there from time to time, prior to the actual construction of the boat.[88] Hence, from boat to boat, the base model differed in more than scale, if only slightly.

Humbert further concentrated a lot of imaginative energy on developing a compact and efficient interlocking system of mechanical, hydraulic, and refrigeration equipment for his boats. His intent here, apparently, was to create more space within the boat for the hold, house, and fo'c'sle without simply creating a much larger boat. Simultaneously, he hoped to lessen the weight of heavy components by reducing their bulk. He also endeavored to position heavy, bulky components in the boat in such a way as to enhance the overall stability of the boat (even further than he already had with his basic boat design). In particular, he positioned the anchor, its weighty chain, and the winch about which the chain is wrapped, down in the engine room, rather than perching it traditionally above deck, forward of the house, just back of the bow stem. Further, he was careful to buffer and arrange noise-making elements in ways that would cut down on the overall noise of the boat, within and without, whenever it was operating.

Humbert also designed and welded the fuel tanks for the boat, put together the engine, fabricated smoke stacks, designed and assembled his own compact refrigeration and hydraulics systems (building some of the individual parts), and he positioned them tightly together with enough room still to get at the parts for maintenance and repairs (see figs. 52 and 53). He often worked with scrap parts and materials from a variety of sources, putting them together to make highly individualized components, which he then interlaced compactly and idiosyncratically within a specific boat. Clearly the complete boat was a Humbert creation, but a unique one nevertheless, that differed from any other boat, Humbert-built or not. Of course, Humbert's boats, regardless of their idiosyncrasies, all demonstrate excellent handling characteristics; they are particularly strong and stable; and those that were built to fish tuna can do so. Humbert more than most coastal boat builders seems to have been able to produce a predictably reliable boat, time after time.

Other builders are not nearly so successful in constructing boats that are uniformly stable from one to another; in particular, most builders, no matter how sophisticated, cannot predict the exact kind of roll that a boat may have.[89] How a boat rolls is especially important to a fisherman for fishing comfort and a sense of stability and security at sea. One local fisherman preferred what he called a "slow roll," the kind he associated with deep, heavy, older wooden vessels.[90] In contrast, he did not like the "quick roll" typical of steel boats. Another fisherman explained the difference in roll on the basis of the kind of bottom a boat might have. The round bottom typical of older wooden vessels gives a boat what he calls a slow, long roll, whereas the hard chine characteristic of a steel boat gives a boat the less preferable faster roll, but "you can use stuff to slow that roll down to where you get a pretty comfortable boat." Also, the hard chine varieties "don't roll near as far."[91]

Not only are certain rolling motions preferred over others for fishing comfort, but only a certain amount of roll, coupled with adequate self-righting capability, is desired for safety and stability. A boat that rolls too far to one side or another is not only a difficult one on which to work comfortably, but it seems to worry the skipper that the boat may just roll on over some time and not come back up. Both some of the older heavier wooden vessels and some of the newer steel boats have acquired reputations for their dreadful rolls — too much roll in the case of the *Frank F*, and too quick and jumpy a roll in the case of the *Betty A*. One local boat builder claimed that the Betty A in fact could not keep a crew, she rolled so disturbingly.

Another feature contributing to the individuality of boats, over which boat builders appear to have little control, is the ability of a boat to fish tuna. Not all boats can fish tuna successfully, even those built specifically for that purpose. The *Washington*, for instance, was built in 1939 in Ilwaco, Washington, allegedly to fish tuna, but she never did too well as a tuna boat, and eventually she was converted into a dragger.[92] One local builder attributes hull form to the inability of some boats to catch tuna:

> . . . there's good tuna trollers and good salmon trollers, and a lot of boats that make good
> salmon trollers don't make damn tuna trollers. That's what the fishermen claim, and I know
> the reason that they claim it, it might be real, but I don't know. . . . the canoe stern, or
> double-ender type salmon troller, they don't fish tuna worth a damn because they don't have
> enough weight coming off the stern, enough cheek wake that'll get the water boiling, and
> the tuna like that boiling water, it attracts them to the jig, and they . . . bite like crazy. But if
> you take a salmon troller out there, in the same grounds, it won't catch tuna. And I guess it's
> fairly well substantiated. So, it's a rule of thumb that double-enders don't make good tuna
> trollers.[93]

But even among boats that are not double-ended, but still of the same shape,
some will catch tuna and some will not.[94] According to Ruth Hallmark Day,
several other variables may play a role:

> . . . [fishermen] feel that the sound that an engine makes has a great deal to do with how well
> it fishes tuna, that certain boats give off vibrations that scare away the tuna schools, and some
> of them they think give off sort of an electric shock, too. . . . for tuna fishing particularly,
> some boats fish tuna well, and some boats just don't.[95]

Since Mr. Humbert liked to build tuna combination boats, one can partly see
why he took such pains with boat form, the composition and arrangement of
components, and with noise reduction. Further, a well-tuned boat — trued
propellor and drive shaft, tuned engine, and well-kept, grounded wiring —
might have a better chance of catching tuna.[96]

While salmon trolling success is not as crucially dependent on the individual boat, still some boats seem to do better than others. Fisherman Arnold
Hockema claimed, for instance, that he fished salmon more successfully with
his first fishing boat without much experience as a fisherman than he did with
his last boat and years of experience.[97] Of course, not all year-round fishermen
need the kind of boat that can fish tuna or salmon successfully. Dragging and
crabbing can be done with almost any kind of vessel as long as it is sturdy and
steady enough to withstand rough winter weather and handle a powerful
engine, and large enough to carry both bulky fishing equipment and huge
quantities of fish.

One further feature accounts for boat individuality that cannot be determined solely in the boat builder's shop. The quality of the materials and
workmanship that go into the creation of a boat can carry a boat only so far if it
is not treated well during its lifetime. From the day a boat leaves the builder's
shop, the quality of care she receives over the years determines in large measure
her longevity and her general condition, hence in many ways her value and
reputation. As Arnold Hockema said of one boat, "she would be a good boat if
she'd been kept up."[98] In explaining why another boat had sunk while the
Coast Guard attempted to tow it into port, he remarked that it had not been in
good condition anyway.

A boat's condition is usually at the mercy of several skippers and owners during its existence. While many former owners may be responsible for letting a particular boat become run down, the condition of the boat reflects very strongly on the present owner/operator, and he will be held accountable for allowing the boat to stay in bad shape. Several fishermen expressed dismay at not being able to keep their boats looking their best during the winter months when boats take a real beating and the weather mitigates against keeping them well-painted.[99] Others, who had bought boats that were in bad shape, complained of the years and the hard work it had taken them to put the boat back in shape, cleaning, fixing, and replacing parts; yet still there was much more work that needed to be done before they would be satisfied that the boat finally was in good shape (and reflected positively upon their fishermanliness).[100]

Keeping a boat in good shape involves maintaining her outward appearance: keeping the boat looking clean and well-painted, and the equipment above deck clean and ordered, relatively rust-free, and in good unbroken condition. Keeping the boat up means, further, that planks, decking, internal woodwork, caulking, and hull fittings have been regularly replaced and repaired, and that mechanical components have not been left to rust and ruin.

In keeping a boat in good condition, however, a fisherman does more than preserve the status quo. Otherwise, Charleston would be a genuine living maritime museum with extant examples of bar-runners, halibut schooners, Alaskan cannery tenders, Puget Sound purse seiners, Monterey clippers, trollers, and general purpose boats, representing the unsullied works of numerous West Coast builders. Fishermen try to keep a boat workable in the face of and in partial response to ever-fluctuating current fishing practices. It is true, some boats show that their run of skippers has been slow to keep them updated. In 1961–62, for instance, the *Frank F* was still fitted out with its original fish trap tending equipment of many years past. Also, some of the shrimpers that are brought to Charleston from the Gulf continue to retain their shrimping equipment—unfamiliar rigging (see fig. 33) and especially the wooden doors (which look like shipping pallets, and are built to fish the shallower waters of the Gulf). But others come to Charleston already fully converted to present-day fisheries—all of their original equipment gone, some bunks and the galley already removed from the fo'c'sle, a new galley or house installed on deck, and bulwarks added to the bow or stern.

In sum, then, the idiosyncratic character of a particular fishboat is guaranteed by the very nature of boatbuilding and the subsequent measures of outfitting a boat and keeping it in operating condition. Some of a fishboat's idiosyncratic qualities are determined in the boat builder's shop, but more interestingly, a boat can acquire additional character once it leaves the builder's shop through the kind of treatment it gets over the years. Thus, although a boat may have some inherent traits irrespective of her handlers, those who work her over the years finally have a lot to do with her endurance, her quality as a fishing machine, and the precise composition of her spaces and components. And through their experiences with a boat, and the stories they tell about her, a boat's handlers give her both a personality and a history, and they broadcast her reputation, confirming her individuality and making her a local character of sorts.

Maintenance and Repair Practices and the Parts of the Charleston Fishboat

For every three days of fishing, the average Oregon fisherman spends one day ashore maintaining and repairing his boat and gear.[1] This upkeep not only constitutes a significant portion of the fisherman's work effort, but like predicting the weather, locating fishing grounds, piloting a fishboat, setting out and retrieving fishing gear, and handling the catch, it is occupational behavior that every Oregon fisherman learns traditionally—first, by working for and observing experienced fishermen, and later by operating his own equipment and talking to colleagues about problems he may have with it. Importantly, as detailed below, this customary practice involves even the least handy fisherman intimately with boat mechanics, predisposing him to change the composition and arrangement of boat parts as a matter of course.

Today's typical Charleston commercial fishing vessel is composed of a number of divergent, complex, and highly mechanized components which must all be fitted together and tuned with respect to each other. Both boat and gear, complicated networks of parts themselves, are powered by gas- and diesel-fueled engines and driven with hydraulic equipment. With the aid of sophisticated electronics, today's fisherman guides his boat and searches for fish. Electrical wiring, run off an auxiliary engine and battery, laces the structure and provides the fisherman with juice to operate electric lights, appliances, and electronic equipment.

With so many complicated, interdependent systems at stake, breakdowns of equipment prove quite common and always upsetting. Occurring at sea, they can jeopardize the fisherman's chances for survival on the job by increasing the risks of losing his boat and his life with it. They can also keep a fisherman from deriving income to make a living and meet expenses. Indeed, Charleston fishermen often spice up discussions involving their boats with narratives detailing one kind of equipment failure or another. As veteran fisherman Leonard Hall put it, if fishermen share any occupational information with anyone, they:

usually talk about their problems with boats. I was talking to a fellow this morning . . . he's got a four-cylinder diesel engine in his boat and he was grease from head to foot. And I said, "Looks like you've been holding engine room drill," and he said, "Yeah." He was getting water down in his crankcase and he was pretty worried about it.[2]

Regular checking, cleaning, and tuning of parts help minimize breakdowns, as does prompt repair of damaged parts: says fisherman Arnold Hockema, "If you kind of do your stuff as it needs to be done, as it comes along, it isn't often you have a big project."[3] Consistent upkeep not only guarantees a safer, more efficient fishing operation, but it also helps the fisherman eke as much life as he can from very expensive equipment. At today's prices, a medium-size boat often compares with a small- to medium-size house in value, and the money that has gone into fishing gear and the mechanical and electronic equipment could easily buy a small fleet of prestigious late-model automobiles. Upkeep runs into more money still: as one Coos Bay shipyard manager remarked, "There's not a piece of machinery that operates without spending some money on it."[4]

Much boat upkeep is cyclical, involving the preparation of the boat and fishing gear during the weeks preceding the openings of shrimp or salmon seasons in the spring, and crab season in the fall, as Leonard Hall explains:

Well, for example, I would fish crab all winter and then bring the crab gear in, oh, by the first of June usually, and silver season opens June 15th so I'd spend that 15 days there getting the boat cleaned up and painted. . . . in the fall then, salmon fishing ends the last of October, then crab season would open either the fifteenth of November or the first of December, so you had a little time in there, but usually your're working on gear then, getting it ready.[5]

Local marine repair and maintenance specialists claim spring and fall as their busiest seasons. They may get some slack during hunting season in October, when many fisherman take off for the woods and forget their boats entirely. Periods of intense fishing activity in the summer bring local repair shops some respite, but a spate of bad fishing or several days of bad weather find them deluged with work. The winter season, too, tends to be slow. Fewer fishermen are fishing then, stretches of bad weather are longer, and weather conditions often are not conducive to maintenance or repair work anyway.

Even if the skipper does not change gear with the season, "there's always something to do," grumbled one fisherman who had just completed a fishing trip. "You just have to keep working at it."[6] "Boat upkeep is constant," acknowledged one fisherman's wife; from her experience painting the boat, by the time she had gotten to one end of it, it was time to start at the other end again.[7] Indeed, boat and gear do not necessarily wait for the preseason preparation period to break down, and frequent bad coastal weather guarantees many days spaced throughout the year when fishermen can turn to problems of checking, tuning, and repairing equipment. Further, there is always the routine upkeep that accompanies the daily use of the fishing machine, such as adjusting and patching gear during a fishing trip, and cleaning and ordering the deck and hold upon unloading a trip's catch.

The major boat components—hull (including fittings and all internal structures), engine(s) and cooperating mechanical and electrical apparatus, hydraulics equipment, and electronics—require different kinds of maintenance and repair at differing rates.[8]

The Hull

Most maintenance ritual revolves around the hull, the most essential of boat parts, with the greatest potential longevity. A wooden hull built of quality materials by a good builder can remain serviceable almost as long as it does not meet with disaster and it is carefully tended; some of Charleston's wooden boats have lasted 70 to 75 years and are still in operation. Steel boats, on the other hand, stand a chance of enduring only one-third as long, from 15 to 20 years. (The federal government in 1978 gave a new hull of whatever material 20 years to depreciate.)

According to tradition, at least once a year, and maybe twice, a fisherman will have his boat hauled out of water at a local shipyard to have the hull bottom serviced (fig. 47). The bottom of the hull will be thoroughly cleaned: "They take a pressure hose and wash it all down, soon as they pull it out while it's still wet."[9] Then usually the skipper and his crew check the planking carefully for rot or the deleterious effects of a variety of sea worms: "We check the hull completely. You can't do that very darned easy unless you hire divers, so we go over it real good."[10] Planks may have to be replaced at this time—a job usually relegated to the yard's expert ship carpenters—and seams between planking recaulked (see fig. 48). Finally, just before the boat is to be lowered back into the water, the bottom will be painted with the brick-red copper antifouling paint that has become so poisonous in recent years that many fishermen will leave its application to yard workers.

Fittings that fasten to the hull below the waterline will also be examined for wear and tear and proper adjustment. While the boat is on the ways, yard workers will check the drive shaft for balance, and if need be, remove it from the boat and turn it on a large lathe. The propellor, or wheel, is usually removed and taken to the local propellor repairman to be checked and balanced, or "blessed," as the "blesser" puts it, since often there is nothing wrong with it and fishermen are superstitious enough to insist on having their wheels blessed each year, regardless (fig. 49).[11] Sometimes, however, the prop has met up with some kind of trouble, and chewed up, needs to be bent back in shape,

Figure 47. Boats "On the Ways" at Hillstrom's for Their Annual Hull Checkups.

Figure 48.   Replacing Planks at Kelley Boat Works.
(Photo courtesy of Joe Parker)

Figure 49.   Art Horton, the Propellor "Blesser."

built up, and rebalanced. Sometimes, too, the prop needs to be built up or sanded down due to electrolytic damage that can occur because of faulty wiring within the boat, or more likely, because of highly charged waters surrounding poorly grounded moorage facilities. Zincs placed on the rudder to attract some of the potential damage from electrolysis are also checked at this time and replaced if necessary. Also the captain checks the sea-cock: "there're screens over the water outlet or intakes to keep moss and shells and junk and seaweed from going into them, and we pull those and take a flashlight and check all the piping to make sure there's no electrolysis in them."[12] Buildup from electrolysis on the rudder, piping, or elsewhere must be scraped off. Fishermen will also have the stern bearing changed and the stuffing box repacked at the yard, if necessary.

This annual event normally is part of spring, pre-salmon/shrimp season preparations, but some year-round fishermen will pull their boats out at other times of the year instead, frequently in the fall, toward the end of salmon season. A boat owner can expect to haul out for two to three days, although he may get stuck at the yard waiting to go up on the ways for as long as a week. Some fishermen simply plan to put in a week at the yard, using the waiting time to spruce up their boats, giving them their annual complete painting (except for the bottom), doing a little carpentry work, repairing rails, switching gear on the boat, and making other physical adjustments:

> Usually we're out of the water two to three days. We like to spend about a week up there cleaning and painting and fixing things up. And we sort of half-way enjoy it, I think. We work like the dickens, but it's a little different.[13]

Some fishermen, though, begrudge the time this yearly ritual takes, unless the fishing has not been very good, since it keeps them away from fishing and making money while they can.

At other times of the year, sometimes in the heat of a fishing season (to his dismay), a fisherman may need to haul his boat out of water again to repair damage to the hull or its fittings, or, as in Arnold Hockema's case, when his engine has died and needs to be replaced:

> I bought another engine—[Doris Hockema:] Cummins, wasn't it?—Yeah—and I got up to Hillstrom's to take it out. He said, "Oh"—whole yard was full of boats—"O.K.," said, "pull it out and get it in the hold," and he said, "As soon as we get room here, we'll pull you up and take it out." My new engine, setting on the dock. So I unholded that son of a gun—it's hard work, just for one guy—I got it back in there [hold], took me a couple of days. I got it clear back in [the hold], and they pulled me up, took the shaft and the wheel out, and somebody come in sinking, so they plugged the hole in my boat and sent me back in the water. And I think it took me *three weeks* before I could get it in place. And the guys was catching fish. Geez, I was up there over a month. Every time they'd put me on the ways,

somebody'd come in, and they'd [plug] the boat and down I'd go. . . . Never has happened to me since. Just when I really needed it.14

Steel boat maintenance requires additional, time-consuming measures. A steel boat does not have planking to be checked for rot or worm damage, but its skin does have to be treated for rust and electrolysis (and its plates sometimes have to be examined for cracks). Once every two years or so such a boat must be completely sandblasted inside and out, and then repainted with several coats each of primer and exterior paint; the biennial sandblasting is what makes short shrift of steel boats. This procedure takes up a tremendous amount of the fisherman's time, and it costs him a pretty penny. One fellow took nine days to sandblast and paint his steel boat, and altogether spent three weeks at the yard.15

Like this steel boat owner, many fishermen advocate doing as much yard work as they can for financial reasons:

> You do everything you can, because the shipyard charges $18 an hour—including their coffee breaks. And you can't even haul out from the shipyard for usually less than a thousand dollars, if you have anything done at all.16

Others participate in yard work depending on their abilities:

> We sort of figure out all the work, things that need to be fixed up for the year, and then we give a list to them and they do that part that we're not skilled enough to do. . . . we have the shipyard do just the heavy stuff. . . .17

And fishermen who have attained a certain amount of financial security and do not consider themselves particularly handy anyway prefer to let the yard take care of the majority of the work.

Fishing Gear

Fishing gear, another essential fishboat ingredient, has changed little in basic design over the years, according to some experts.18 The materials out of which the various kinds of gear are made, however, have become stronger, more durable, and more maintenance-free. For example, nets, now composed of nylon or polyester "web," and trolling lines, now of top-grade stainless steel wire (salmon) or of nylon (tuna), previously were made of cotton or linen, which not only were not as tough or lasting, but had to be tanned periodically to cleanse them. Old-style bait boxes used for crab fishing also required more maintenance than do new types, as Leonard Hall explains:

> I always used stainless bait boxes, but a lot of them use glass jars. Up around Grays Harbor they still use wooden bait boxes, but that's what I started out with, that was the only thing

that was available. But, trouble is you have to have two sets of them because they foul up pretty badly, you know, absorb the bait. So you have to have one set of boxes out airing out and drying while you were fishing the other. And they weren't too durable either. Fellow in Portland started building stainless bait boxes, you throw them around or anything, you know, they're always clean. So I was the first one around here started using them. And I was out fishing with some of the other guys and so they would look at my [gear] to see what it was, and they thought it was that bright stainless in there, so they didn't have any bait boxes or anything, but they put flashers in there, think that was what was doing it. I just had my pots in the right place is all, in the right depth.[19]

Use of stronger materials than wooden slats and chickenwire, and development of reliable designs has also helped crab pots last longer.[20] And otter boards or doors are now constructed of steel rather than wood, and they are rarely built flat anymore, but rather in a variety of V shapes.[21]

The use of highly sophisticated materials of the industrial age has resulted in some standardization in gear, especially in small items like bait boxes and most salmon gear. Some of the experimentation in gear design that once permeated West Coast fishing communities has diminished to periodic and regional trends in the popularity of different brands and styles of manufacture.[22] Nevertheless, despite the inroads of standardized, industrialized products and materials, and the alleged stasis in much gear design, experts claim there is more variation in gear across boats in the same fisheries than there is in any other major fishboat component.[23] Each fisherman assembles and rigs gear in his own inimitable way, and the components of each man's gear, while the same in kind, differ in brand, style, and material makeup. Some experienced fishermen still carefully protect the exact makeup of some of their gear from the scrutiny of other fishermen.[24]

Without the aid of the shoreside community of skilled marine technologists, fishermen spend most of their maintenance and repair time switching gear with the seasons, repairing damage to this equipment, and replacing gear that is lost, worn out, or irreparably damaged. To get ready for crab season in the fall, a trollerman will remove salmon gurdies and possibly the poles (and lines), too, which can catch a lot of wind in the winter.[25] A shrimper likewise will remove his net, net reel, and doors to prepare the back deck for stacking pots, but seldom will he remove the overhead boom and blocks, nor the stanchions to which the doors are fastened. To complete the change, the crabber will install his crab gurdy and its boom, and perhaps a live tank. Drag fishermen who lack double-rigging, sometimes will change nets depending on the market and season to fish for different kinds of bottomfish, or to switch from bottomfish to shrimp gear and vice versa. Salmon trollers likewise will rerig to fish tuna during the summer, if the tuna fishing looks promising, only to rerig again for salmon trolling in the fall.

Fishing gear is perhaps the least durable and most easily damaged of fishboat components. Crab fishermen and trollermen can expect to lost out-right a certain amount of gear each season. Trollermen often lose sinkers, lures, floats, and even fishing lines in encounters with fish, rocks, snags, and other boats. Replacement of this equipment usually involves purchasing new components, and rerigging and resetting them (mainly, fitting the lines with straps, eyes, and slings). "Snapping off" a pole, not a frequent occurrence, is cause for greater to-do. Most fishermen have not adopted purchasable aluminum poles but continue to fashion theirs from straight, tall trees of white cedar, fir, pine, or spruce with a good taper.[26] Length of the poles is determined by the specific boat length and the fisherman's individual taste. The fisherman must "find some place where there're some good poles growing, and cut them down and peel them."[27] Then he must drill holes through the base of each, and finally fasten the poles to the boat and guy them with lines. Infrequently, some fishermen will season and treat the poles before installing them.[28] Transporting the long poles from source to shop to boat requires the use of a small trailer hitched behind the fisherman's pickup truck (and a thrilling ride around sharp curves).

Crab fishermen annually lose from 15 to 30 percent of their pots along with the attached ropes and buoys, and the bait boxes enclosed inside, not only from rough weather, but from:

> . . . boats running over your gear and cutting it off. Other crab boats. They're your worst enemy. And then once in a while a tug and barge would go down through your gear and that chain and bridle would really cut a swath.[29]

In replacing their equipment, most crab fishermen make from 30 to 50 new pots each year, and purchase new rope, buoys, and bait boxes to go along with them.[30] In recent years, however, one fisherman has been buying completed pots from a fellow who custom builds them for several local fishermen. Many fishermen mentioned that they purchase the frame members (uprights and rings of 3/4-inch steel reinforcing rod) already cut to order, and in the case of the rings, already "rolled." They then weld the frame members together, the weights to the bottoms, sometimes adding identifying marks, and the escape rings to upper frame members (see fig. 19). At times some of the fishermen have either hired people to weld the frames for them, or they have bought prewelded frames. After welding the frames, fishermen then wrap all of the steel rodding with rubber strips cut from inner tubes (these used to be abundant at no price, but with the advent of the tubeless tire, they have become scarcer and thus costly). And finally, they will weave a stainless steel wire mesh around the pot frame, building entry tunnels and a door for access into the mesh. After a few seasons, the steel wire mesh becomes brittle; thus in addition to making new pots to replace lost ones, the fisherman must patch and eventually entirely replace the mesh of veteran pots every year.

Pot making is associated usually with the fall precrab season. Fisherman Floyd Green said he starts building his pots in September, he takes off October to go hunting, and when he returns he finishes up. Sometimes, however, he might start building frames in the spring, so they would be ready to wrap and knit by the fall.[31]

For each new pot, also, a new buoy must be painted according to the color scheme that each fisherman chooses to represent himself.[32] Since buoys attract a growth of seaweed that obscures their color scheme and hinders their visibility, the crab fisherman must clean them at sea by immersing each in a bucket of bleach. Initially it takes about three months of use before the buoys need to be cleaned. But after the first cleansing, regrowth occurs more often, so, as the season progresses, bleaching becomes a more frequent duty. Indeed, during crab season it is common to see fishermen lugging gallons of bleach down the docks to their boats.

Drag fishermen do not suffer the seasonal losses of gear with the regularity that crab fishermen and trollermen do. Instead they are beset with the perennial mending and patching of net and net assembly (see fig. 50); and they occasionally lose their nets, doors, and cable to nasty underwater hang-ups or to skippers of large (foreign) sea-going vessels belligerently running over their gear when it is in tow, despite adequate, internationally recognized, "net in tow" signs posted in the rigging (see figs. 36, 56).[33] Most often, however, the net suffers reparable damage from hanging up on the bottom or from capturing an incredible array of unwieldy refuse from the bottom. During my inquest, drag fishermen reported bringing up a sleeper shark, a dead whale, a dead sea lion; detritus from inland flooding such as an entire tree, a dead and bloated cow, bales of hay, lengths of barbed wire and post fencing, a washing machine, and a refrigerator; ship garbage thrown overboard such as chamber pots, and fuel tanks from big Russian trawlers; refuse chunks of wood and bark from sawmills and the water storage of logs; boat parts and sometimes entire fishing boats.[34] Fishercouple Richard and Verna Lilienthal were particularly loquacious on this account:

> *R*: We've had airplanes and we've had one, two, three trollers in the last two years in the net and every one of them rolled out luckily. The one was a steel troller and we knew it was around somewhere, but we hung up on it and we couldn't move it, the net just slipped off of it. But we've had two up where we could see them, and they just rolled out, they were smaller ones.
>
> *V*: And [an] anchor.
>
> *R*: We had big anchors, yeah, with chains on them.

Figure 50. Mending an "Eastern 400" Trawl Net.
Note groundline weights cut from truck tires.

V: It's at the Western Bank up there, in front of the Western Bank, it's one off an old sailing ship. And I met the boat and everyone's face was a mile long, you know, and the kids, they were tiny then, they said, "Oh, look what Daddy got." Days of patching. He was unhappy.

R: But anyway, we got our first nylon shrimp net in June or something like that, and I rigged it all up 'cause we were going to take the kids to Yellowstone the first time and my brother was going to work the boat in my place. So I got all rigged out and I went out and fished it a couple of days, to make sure it was fishing good, and we went down to Yellowstone. We come back and put the trailer away and came down, here was my nylon net in a little bitty pile about this tall [gestures about a foot and a half off the floor]. They picked up one of those Ford motor planes going from Portland to Hawaii. They ditched one out here about, they said they were twenty miles offshore where they hooked this with that shrimp net. That's the only thing I can think of that would be heavy enough and sharp enough to cut that net in two like that. They got it up where they could see the wing shimmering down there, and then it cut the net in two. And, about two months later, friend came along, and the net had drifted off and he scooped the rest of the net up and then I sewed it back together that winter, so it worked fine from there on.

V: The biggest thing you caught, tell her what the biggest thing you caught was.

R: You mean the outfall from the pulp mill?

V: That was the biggest and the best.

R: We didn't get loose of that, we left the net there.

V: Someone had moved the markers on the beach.

R: By law they were supposed to put two markers as a range so that when you're crabbing or fishing you knew where you were. But the outfall went out into the ocean, and you picture an outfall as a pipe coming out and a little flapper valve with, the pulp mill goop comes out of it. Well, not so, that's what we thought it was, but anyway. . . . It was just a beautiful smooth day, and we were sitting cleaning a bunch of scallops we'd got the day before, and I could see this piling coming that we thought was the marker, and what it was, it was the northward marker and we were towing from the south and they'd let the other three fall down. And boy we stopped just ka-bang and we thought it was just a crab pot, 'cause we weren't near where that thing was supposed to be. So I just hooked it on, I told Rick I'd pull that pot out of the sand. We didn't move for a while and we finally just backed over the gear and got everything back but our tow. I got our doors aboard and then we had the tow lines all tangled around the, as it turned out it was a great big pipe . . . that went out to a big divider that stood 14 feet tall, and then two pipes come out of that, and then it had 26 big valves that come up like a goose neck and then out, come up 6 feet, then out. . . . We had that all tangled up around all those. . . . We were really pulling on that, we had that old black goop just a-boiling around the boat. And anyway, they hired divers and went out and got our net off.[35]

Draggers who fish for both shrimp and bottomfish and maybe also for crab, tuna, and/or salmon are most likely to prepare and replace gear as the seasons change, mainly in the spring before shrimp season begins, or in the fall when it ends. But full-time, year-round bottomfishermen pretty much replace gear aseasonally, as they need or want to, preferably whenever there are a few days of weather that is good for repairs but not for fishing.

Unlike crab fishermen, drag fishermen participate unevenly in the creation of their gear. Some get together and order in bulk the materials they need to fabricate the gear, in particular, cable and special polyester webbing with which to make nets. They also help each other fashion and put together their own nets and floatline-groundline components, and fabricate (design, cut, and weld) doors and net reels. Others, mainly shrimp fishermen, will purchase ready-made nets, doors, reels, and groundline and floatline components from firms in the South or the Puget Sound area, or through local marine supply stores. Many fishermen, however, have their winches and sets of doors custom built by local marine fabricators and welders. All drag fishermen, however, will assemble this gear, rig it to the boat, and adjust it to make sure that it is working properly.

The Engine and Hydraulics

With each new engine, fishermen have gone to greater horsepowers, made possible by continuous improvements in marine engines (fig. 51). Originally slow-turning, low in horsepower, and heavy (with high displacement), marine engines have become higher turning, with higher speed capabilities.[36] Now made of lighter weight metals, marine engines can command greater horsepower without the previous proportionate gain in weight. The old-style engines evidently could last longer than today's quick-turning variety, but still a good, well-kept engine can last more than 10 years (in 1978 the federal government allowed a fisherman to depreciate his boat's engine over a period of 10 years). In some 50 years, the *Kodiak* had been served by four engines (fig. 57); during the 40 to 45 years that Norman Walker and Charlie Ells had known their boats (*Rambler*, fig. 63, and *Amak*, fig. 69), they each had gone through three to four engines, and one engine lasted Ells 22 years; and then in 25 years, Floyd Green had utilized four engines (*Oregon*, fig. 65).[37]

Today's fishboats are not only powered by engines, but so is much of their fishing gear and auxiliary equipment. Since the 1940s most trolling lines, crab pots, and the various kinds of large nets have been hauled by machine instead of by hand. Winches, hand-operated at first, have acquired their own engines. With inexpensive materials on hand, fishermen frequently created networks of chains, pulleys, and gears to run the steering, iron mike, and trolling gurdies directly off the main engine. A breakdown in one of these older systems could prove harrowing both to experience and to repair, as Arnold Hockema reports:

> Oh God, we broke the steering, Jesus, in the surf. . . . I was running pots in about four fathom of water, and just outside the breaks, and my steering cable, steering broke. I remember that very plainly. Well, I backed up and the darned boat backed off out in the ocean. So I stopped and — it was a complicated deal anyway, the pulleys and cables went back and forth — the courses was broke, so I patched it up. By eliminating one cross, I could do it

Figure 51.   A Gray Marine Diesel Engine.
(Photo courtesy of Joe Parker)

quick, you know, the only thing, it made the steering wheel turn the wrong way. I thought, well hell, I can handle that for the rest of what we got to do. But I couldn't. And that's hard. . . . I went and tried it, and I had to give up and back off and go fix it right. . . . I took the chain out and just hooked the cables directly together, but . . . when I turned the steering wheel to the left, instead of the boat going that way, why it goes this way. Why heck, I knew it was going to do that. I thought, well, you know, running them pots, I'll get done, I can handle it, only had 50 pots or so to go. By God, I could not come up there. And everybody was worried, and we was right on the edge of the breaks, I turned the wrong goddamn [direction], oh Jesus! . . . later on in years . . . I put a hydraulic steering on it. I think that cost me three thousand dollars, but it was worth every penny.38

Since the 1950s, fishermen have increasingly adapted hydraulic systems to replace or work in conjunction with these earlier means of mechanizing the boat and gear (figs. 52, 53). Now the steering, iron mike, trolling gurdies, winches, net reels, and crab and drag power blocks on most boats are fully hydraulically operated. Still, some fishermen have clung to their old systems of chains, pulleys, and gears, or older nonhydraulically powered machinery— partly because of inertia and being used to the operation of gear already in hand, partly because of the expense of replacing it or financing new stuff, partly for extracting their full use, and partly, too, for sentimental reasons:

We don't have a high-speed winch, no. We have the same old winch that's been clunking away for 29 years, hasn't given us a minute's trouble. It's slower, but it's so powerful it'll pull the boat under if you really wanted to. . . . Most fellows have the hydraulic winches now. . . . We are, I think, going to put a new winch on this next year. Not that the old one is, it'd last 3 or 4 more years yet.39

According to Charleston marine mechanic and fabricator Keith Ott, these older systems, while bulky, are basically simpler than the hydraulics systems that could replace them; he found no fault with fishermen for making and using such equipment if it cost them less and it worked.40

Most fishermen are fair mechanics, even if they claim they lack mechanical skills, capable of dismantling and replacing worn parts or assembling parts to make a "new" machine (but generally not of fabricating the parts they need to replace). In fact, one marine machine shop manager contended that a lot of the machine repair business they get from fishermen comes from the inexperienced, younger types who have not been able yet to acquire both the know-how and the tools to do as much of their own work as they can.41 About half the fishermen surveyed regularly tuned their engines themselves, and when the time came, overhauled and rebuilt them, often with the help of crew members, relatives, or friends. The Cyrus Littles, father and son, additionally built the 100-horsepower hydraulic motors for the winches they use on their boats.42 But another half typically referred most engine maintenance and repair to dealers who usually send a man out to work on an engine in the boat itself. But even

Figure 52.   Humbert's Hydraulics System for the *Quasar*.
Humbert fabricated the tank for holding the fluid.

Figure 53.   Humbert's Hydraulics System (contd.).
He also designed the valve arrangement, as well as fitted and assembled the parts.

those who prefer to give major routine engine maintenance to dealers will still often install new engines in their boats themselves.

Fewer fishermen are as handy with hydraulic systems as they are with engines and other machines. Here again, some few have gone so far as to thread and fit the pipes that make up these systems and otherwise to fashion and assemble the hydraulic gear. But most can only do very minor work, like replace seals, Ott said.[43] Hence, in this realm, most fishermen rely more heavily on the few local marine hydraulics specialists who work with specific fishermen to work out their systems for them. Even so, as Arnold Hockema tells:

Well, I have to work on that [hydraulics] sometimes. You have to put in new parts, hoses. And you have explosions, you know, you blow the hoses off, get an oil bath. Boy, we really got a bath. This guy I had working for me, was a big man, he was pulling pots, you know, and I was stacking on the back and we was moving, just the two of us on there. I picked up this pot, I carried it to the back, and something hit me in the back of the head, you know, it felt kind of warm. And Puckett . . . I heard him, you know, and I turned around and looked, and there he was, that hose had broke, and it shot right in his mouth, and in his face, in his eyes, and he was nearly blind. It hit me in the back of the head clear on the back of the boat.

God, it just drownded him. He couldn't get his breath for a long time. Oil. Hot oil. It didn't burn him, but it sure stopped him for a minute.[44]

Electronics

In spite of the mechanical and material advances made in fishboat technology, some members of the Charleston-Coos Bay fishing community claim the greatest changes in local fishing have occurred in the adaptation of highly sophisticated electronic devices to boats.[45] Most fishboats now are fully equipped with two radios (a shortwave or VHF, and a ship-to-shore or "Mickey Mouse"), one or two fathometers (depth finders, depth sounders, fish finders), a Loran receiver, direction finder, and a radar (fig. 54).

Most Charleston fishermen between the ages of 50 and 70, who are fast becoming the old-timers, started out fishing only with a compass, a watch, and a sounding iron or lead line. One younger fisherman, brought up occupationally under the wing of one of Charleston's older old-timers, says he can locate himself anywhere on the local ocean grounds even in the densest fog, simply with the use of such equipment.[46] But some fishermen have come to rely so heavily on their electronics that they lose days of fishing when any of them malfunction.[47] Similarly, some have become fondly dependent on their iron mikes, mechanisms which lock the steering into a particular compass bearing, keeping the boat on a specific course without the skipper having to stand at the wheel and steer constantly:

> First thing I ordered was an iron mike. After standing up from the Columbia River down here, I, first thing, I didn't even come home first, I just ordered one for it. I was tired of standing there steering. That's about the most important thing. . . . That's better than any man. . . . Oh, they're like anything else, they go haywire, you know, once in a while, but not too often. Gee, I've had this one now for a long time, and last summer's the first time I ever had anything go haywire with it, and just switches is all it is that wore out. . . . I use the iron mike so much, I can hardly steer by hand anymore. It's hard, boy, if you're used to an iron mike, you know, especially at night. You forget about looking at the compass. And if that iron mike goes haywire in the dark, God that's terrible, got to stand there and look at the compass all the time. Gee, that's horrible. . . . This I can set there and kind of doze off.[48]

Most of the newly old-timers spurn the use of radios almost entirely, except, of course, in the event of an emergency. They cite overuse of radios as one reason — "it's so busy you wouldn't be able to hear anything [important] anyway."[49] Another reason given is that a fisherman who talks on the radio is likely to give away his position; if he's a good fisherman, or one who has met with numerous recent successes, within minutes he may have lost his fishing grounds to competitors eager to get in on the good deal.[50] And some of these crusty folks have resisted acquiring radars until recently:

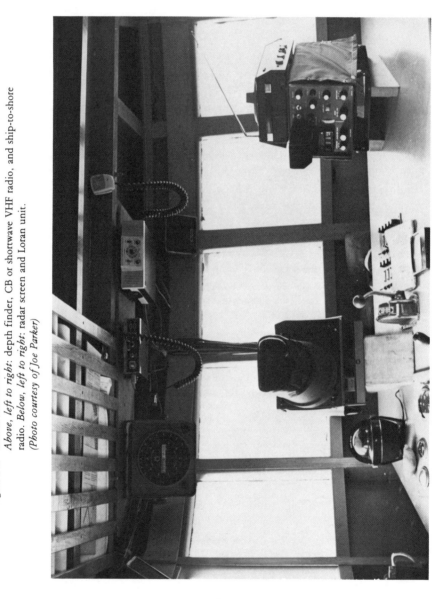

Figure 54.   Marine Electronics.
Above, left to right: depth finder, CB or shortwave VHF radio, and ship-to-shore radio. *Below, left to right:* radar screen and Loran unit.
(Photo courtesy of Joe Parker)

I never got a radar until four, five, six, years ago. . . . Oh, I almost run underneath a tow boat. That convinced me. We was day-fishing shrimp. Gee, you know, we run east and west to go to shrimp grounds. Dark, dark in the morning and dark at night, and in the fog. God, I almost got hit a couple times. I was so close to one . . . underneath, the first thing I saw was the chain from that barge that come down — you know, what the tow cable hooks on to, the big chain links. God, I put it in reverse and I backed up as hard as it'd go and I hollered, the boys was asleep. God, I thought we was going to hit, you know. . . . I was almost underneath the front of it there, right in between the tug and the tow. God, it was rough, the ocean was rough. By God, that was the second time. The first time Fred . . . he was pretty close to me, he told me he was watching on the radar, he said there was a tug and barge out there. Said, "looks like you and him might get pretty close." Pretty soon he said, "You better stop," he said, "looks to me like you're almost together." And I kicked it out of gear and opened the door and Geez, the noise come right in, you know. . . . It was foggy, you can't see nothing. . . . So I turned around and come back and got one. I couldn't keep counting on the other guys. What had happened, there was three of us going out, there was Fred, and Orville, and me. Everybody'd come back, it was rough, foggier than hell and northwester blowing. Said, I thought we'll go out and drag a few tows anyway, Orville and Fred's going to go, and they both have radar. And I heard them talking about it, they was ahead of me, when we started. Evidently they stopped, you know, and I heard them talk about the tug and barge. But hell, I said, "Well heck, we're O.K., because they're ahead of us, so we're alright." I was running under a full speed, that's when I run into him. And they'd stopped evidently, you know, and I kept on going. Boy, that was the closest one I think I've ever had. You couldn't get any closer. Puckett, he reared up in bed, he was about half asleep, said, "Geez, red isn't it?" and I said, "It wasn't red, it was a black barge." We was so close, all he could see was the bottom paint, painted up high.[51]

The varying kinds of electronics for fishboat use last for different amounts of time, but to many fishermen, none last long enough to justify their exorbitant costs. The government lets fishermen depreciate such gear in three to five years on the average; one man said the equipment is usually ready to throw overboard in three years, but some can last years longer.[52] Indeed the inhospitable environment (moist and salty air) in which they must function, plus the driving use that fishermen give them, do not guarantee much life expectancy for marine electronics apparatus. Sometimes too, one must change equipment to pick up new regulation frequencies before the old gear has worn out. In 1978 fishermen had to purchase new Loran C receivers to pick up the new signal (that the U.S. Coast Guard, et al., had so generously decided to adopt), thus dispensing with their old invalid Loran A and B receivers. A new receiver was going to cost one man $12,000, while the previous one had cost him $5,000.

Most fishermen do not even try to learn how to repair electronics when they could, since most problems are minor (faulty connections), according to one electronics shop manager.[53] Most fishermen are just happy to find a reliable marine electronics expert who does quality work, who will show up at the boat when he says he will, and who will help out the fisherman when he finds himself in the middle of fishing season, perhaps in some other port with malfunctioning equipment.

In sum, then, fishermen are very well acquainted with the annual procedures of inspecting and repairing the hull, but here, most of them tend to the more humdrum tasks of diagnosing the hull and cleaning and painting the boat, leaving most hull bottom repair, or the "heavy work" that demands specialized expertise and equipment, to yard workers. Fishermen are very much involved, however, in creating, rigging, and maintaining their fishing gear independently of shoreside specialists. Of necessity, most fishers are experienced mechanics, good at diagnosing and repairing, even if temporarily, mechanical problems on board. But here again, most fishermen occasionally rely on the expertise of experts, and some gladly pass off mechanical problems, no matter how minor, to the area's mechanics and engine dealers. While fishermen are becoming increasingly knowledgeable about hydraulics systems and more proficient in putting them together and repairing them, they still mainly tend to only minor matters, relying on experts to solve most problems. With even greater deference, fishermen refer almost all electronics problems to specialists, and thus far have not ventured to dabble with such equipment.

Regardless of how much maintenance and repair work a fisherman prefers to do himself, he still must become acquainted generally with the workings of every part of his boat, and he must be capable of fixing and patching everything on his own, for, as Leonard Hall says, "You've go to learn to manage your own things, because something happens out at sea, just you there to fix it."[54] Ship builder Bill Hillstrom, Jr., concurred that a fisherman is very versatile in his skills because he has to be:[55] the diversified state of present boat technology demands that he be so, given the size of his crew and fishing operation, and the nature of the environment in which he must work the tools of his trade.

Fishboat Alterations: Eleven Charleston Fishermen and Their Boats

The most routine maintenance and repair tasks involve fishermen in part replacements that do not generally result in readily apparent, significant changes in fishboat structure or function. In time, the replacement of planks and fittings, for example, may gradually weaken the integrity of a wooden hull; or some brands and makes of hydraulic, engine, or gear components, being less durable than others, may cause greater wear to entire complexes of equipment, decreasing their longevities and increasing their upkeep requirements accordingly. In participating in the less frequent maintenance and repair chores, however, the fisherman can often institute dramatic changes in the makeup or use of his fishing boat. For instance, when faced with the dying gasp of an aged engine, he may opt to replace it with an engine of greater horsepower. To take advantage of the more powerful engine, he in turn may increase the capacities and thus the composition of other equipment on board, and accordingly, he may use the boat in a more strenuous fashion than in the past. This heightened activity may in turn cause structural strains that force additional modifications. The fisherman's ongoing experimentation with gear—trying out different kinds of components or adapting an entire complex of gear to a boat not intended for it—can result similarly in altered patterns of use that compel further structural changes.

Without necessarily waiting for an opportunity to make replacements, the following 11 fishermen have all made changes in their boats over the years. Very roughly, the extent to which these fishermen have involved themselves in boat upkeep correlates with the amount of significant changes they have made. Since these fishermen are difficult to cast into hard and fast categories of any kind, I have chosen to present each man as an individual case, and have ordered them according to the extensiveness of their involvement in boat work. The first four fishermen, Cecil Crockett, Carl Harrington, Cyrus Little, Sr., and Leonard Hall, were very active in the routine maintenance and repair of most boat components, and made the most dramatic boat modifications. The following three, Norman Walker, Jake Harlan, and Floyd Green engaged in some but not all aspects of maintenance and repair, and they had other people modify their boats or had no significant alterations made at all. The last four men, Arnold Hockema, Charlie Ells, Dick Lilienthal, and Fred Anderson, left most maintenance and repair chores to experts, and if they had any alterations made, they also had someone else do the work.

Cecil Crockett and the *Lou-R*

From watching his father rebuild a 28-foot troller when he went into fishing in the 1940s, and from working for old-timers on several veteran wood boats during his apprentice years, Cecil Crockett knows well what kind of work needs to go into an older boat, and he has not been reluctant to make whatever changes a boat might demand for more than adequate operation.[1] "We do everything we can ourselves," he said. Bottomfisherman and owner of a steel boat in 1978, Crockett had recently built a new net reel and rebuilt both of the boat's engines. He can do some welding, as can his son, who at 18 had been helping his father fish during summers; a few years back, Cecil had hired a hand just to do welding on the boat. He maintains a shop at his home in the garage, he owns sophisticated tools including drill presses, and he sometimes uses expensive specialized equipment himself at a couple of local machine shops. When Cecil recently had to have his boat sandblasted, he had taken her to a yard where he could participate in the procedures himself, sandblasting, painting, and helping the welders. He says it used to be more economically feasible to take work to the yard to have it done more quickly so the fisherman could get back to fishing sooner, but now he is of the mind that it pays to lose the fishing time and do the stuff himself. Increasingly he joins with several other bottomfishermen to buy equipment in common (like a lathe and sandblaster), to purchase quality materials in bulk, and to trade off labor in building each other's gear in order to afford high quality, long lasting, custom-made equipment (which they could not afford if they relied on local experts and suppliers).

In 1974 Cecil was able to buy the *Lou-R*, his first boat, at a decent price ($30,000) from a trusted, experienced fisherman who had purchased the boat because he could get such a good deal on it (figs. 55 and 56). The steel boat had been built in 1968 at Friday Harbor, Washington, to be a Coast Guard icebreaker. Before she was completed, a fire at the shipyard warped her, making her unsuitable for her intended purpose; but an enterprising fellow who was able to buy her and a twin survivor cheap, converted her into a fishboat and the twin into a tug. When Cecil acquired her, she was still incomplete and not in very good shape, for, as he puts it, the "bunch of hippies" who had been running the boat had let it fill up with water in port and had almost sunk it.

Figure 55. The *Lou-R*, Converted Icebreaker, and the *Puget*, Converted Halibut Schooner,
Docked at Peterson Seafoods.
Left, the *Lou-R*; *right*, the *Puget*.

Figure 56.   The *Puget* and the *Lou-R*.
   Left, note Jake Harlan's steel stern bulwarks on the *Puget*; and *right*, Cecil
   Crockett's steel stern ramp and bulwarks on the *Lou-R*. A "net in tow" basket, in
   this case a plastic laundry basket, is just barely visible high in the *Lou-R*'s rigging.

Just to make the boat workable, Crockett cleaned her up by sandblasting and painting her, and made her more seaworthy by adding ballast, putting on stabilizers, and fashioning and welding new bulwarks to the hull. He also tried to complete the boat by building a new house of wood on her. To enhance the boat's ability as a dragger, he repowered the boat, installing new twin engines with more horsepower; he also refashioned the stern, incorporating a stern ramp into it (see fig. 56). In four years, Cecil felt he had been able to make the boat "pretty decent," but he also felt that it was a losing battle to keep and fix up the boat, especially since she is steel. Besides, he did not like the shallowness of her icebreaker hull nor her quick roll. At the time I spoke with him, he was sprucing up the boat to sell, hoping to buy a large older wooden vessel, preferably a halibut schooner, which he believed would last longer, be easier to tend, and be more seaworthy (deeper hull) and comfortable (slower roll) than a newer steel vessel. As of 1981, Crockett had indeed succeeded in purchasing such a vessel, not a halibut schooner, but an East Coast boat built in Maine, presumably "descended" from the same evolutionary parent, the Gloucester schooner.[2]

Carl Harrington and the *Kodiak*

Carl Harrington, a shrimp and bottomfisherman in 1978, feels that most specialists take their own time getting a project done, so the fisherman cannot have his equipment when he wants it.[3] He also finds it too expensive to have someone else do most boat work for him at $26 an hour, claiming that a project might cost only $500 in materials, but $3,000 in labor. So Carl has taught himself how to do a lot of specialized boat work—engine work, welding, and electrical wiring. He also put together the hydraulic network and built the doors for his boat, and he then was making a net reel. He has a very well-equipped shop at home and was planning to buy a lathe. He gets help occasionally with his welding from his step-brother, the expert welder of the local bottomfisherman cooperative. Carl participates in this group to a certain extent, mostly because of family connections, but he also has maintained his independence from it, probably because he then fished for shrimp in addition to bottomfish, and now fishes for crab, taking specialized work to a different range of experts, and buying materials and parts more locally and on his own.

From 1972 to 1983, Carl operated the *Kodiak*, a wooden vessel built in 1926 in Tacoma, Washington, to purse-seine for herring and sardines in Puget Sound, according to Harrington (fig. 57). In 1974 he was able to purchase this boat, his first large one, from the previous owner's widow. When he began working the boat in 1972, as he put it, she was a big mess, all black and filthy inside; previous owners had let the boat become increasingly run down. Past owners had also removed two bunks to give the fo'c'sle more space, and had

Figure 57.   The *Kodiak*, Converted Puget Sound Purse Seiner.

moved the galley from the fo'c'sle to the deck, adding it to the after end of the house and finishing it in mahogany (which had since been painted over with light blue enamel paint). The boat had also been repowered several times, most recently in 1972.

Since Harrington bought the boat, he had replaced the entire hull bottom to the waterline with new planking and caulking, exchanged the extensive system of chains and pulleys for steering with a hydraulic system, and remodelled the fo'c'sle by removing the water tank from its horizontal position under the floor boards and setting it vertically next to the bow stem, between two pair of bunks. He was planning then to close off the four bunks and the tank with paneling and to panel the remaining space, leaving only two bunks usable. He had already paneled the stateroom above, but he had plans to replace the entire house and galley, making it a little larger. A little downhearted in 1978 after six years of working on the boat, he said it still was going to take a lot to get her in shape; he had dreams of buying a better boat. Apparently in partial response to some exceptionally bad shrimp years, Harrington has since sold the *Kodiak*, replacing it with a much smaller, newer, Bandon-built, wooden crab boat, the *Pioneer Lady*, which is similar, I believe, to the *Halco* (see fig. 34).

Figure 58.   The *Maria E* and the *Silver Wave* next to Her.
(Photo courtesy of Joe Parker)

Cyrus Little, Sr. and the *Maria E* (among others)

Cyrus Little, Sr., fished for salmon, tuna, crab, and shrimp out of Charleston from the early 1940s until his retirement in 1966.[4] Together with his son, in 1978 he was still actively keeping up both his old boat, the *Maria E* (which they leased until it sank in 1981), and his son's boat, the *Silver Wave*. They tried to do as much of their own work as they possibly could without relying on specialists — machine work, gear construction (crab pots, net reel), and assembly of hydraulics equipment and fishing gear (nets, cork lines, chains). Recently when a Seattle firm had so many back orders that it could not readily furnish the Littles with a custom set of "China doors," they returned home from inspecting the firm's products and made their own. They also had recently built the 100-horsepower hydraulic motors for their winches. Together they maintained a large workshop behind the elder Little's house, complete with two lathes (15 inch and 12 inch), acetylene torches, and electric welders. They bought tons of steel each year from different places in Eugene and locally.

A lot of Cyrus, Sr.'s, participation in maintaining these boats came from his remarkable handiness. Before moving to Charleston, he had built an 18-foot dory-shaped rowboat from which to ring for crabs and gillnet for salmon in

Figure 59.   The *Maria E* and the *Silver Wave*.
Both are general purpose boats.

Alsea Bay during the 1930s. Soon after arriving in Charleston, he built himself a larger 36-foot boat for offshore salmon and crab fishing. Wanting still a larger boat, in 1948 he bought the 50-foot, 6-inch *Maria E* — a general purpose wooden fishboat — before the Winchester Bay builder had completed her (figs. 58 and 59). Little then finished her himself, installing the engine, fastening the gas tanks, connecting the engine to the prop shaft, putting on the mast, and lining the cabin. Later he adapted her to fish shrimp in addition to the salmon, tuna, and crab for which she was built.

The *Maria E* almost lost the house once when a surprise wave broke over the bow, breaking the windows and pushing the cabin back several inches. Little faulted the builders for not constructing the bow high enough, so he built up the bulwarks 16 to 20 inches higher, and he reinforced the house with heavier timbers and bolts. In supervising the construction of the fiberglass *Silver Wave* for his son in 1972, he required the bow to be similarly heightened.

Because of recurring health problems, Little had given his son major responsibility for fishing the *Maria E* since the mid-1950s. Deprived of his boat and undaunted by age and health, the elder man built himself a steel fishboat in 1970. Unfortunately a steamer ran into the boat the same year she was built and sank it. After that, Little "retired."

Leonard Hall and the *M. S. Electron*

Leonard Hall (fig. 60) retired from crab and salmon fishing in 1977, selling his boat of 31 years, the *Electron*, "washing his hands" of boat work, and handing down his gear-building equipment to a fisherman-son.[5] But he still maintains a workshop in his spacious garage not only for both fisherman-sons to use, but for himself to keep up a miniature railroad which he operates around his house on Sundays, offering rides to passersby. Indeed, he can be easily spotted in public by the railroad engineer's cap he wears.

Hall's fascination for well-running machines made him a natural at fishboat maintenance and repair. He did as much of his own upkeep as he could (for, as he says, "You've got to learn to manage your own things, because something happens out at sea, just you there to fix it"). He made crab pots, cut and replaced trolling poles, and rigged his gear. He said he never had much mechanical trouble; he kept the engine tuned, and three years before he sold his boat, he overhauled the engine:

> Well, when I sold the *Electron*, that Cummins diesel that's in there is about either 18 or 19 years old. Runs like a Swiss watch. Course, I had to give it a major overhaul about 3 years ago. The sleeves are wet, they just have overring seals at the top and bottom, and one of the overrings started leaking, so, it had a lot of years on it, so, figured while I had to tear it down to find out which overring was leaking, why, we just replaced it, give it a major overhaul, new

Figure 60. Commercial Fisherman Leonard Hall and the *M. S. Electron* in 1976.
(Photo courtesy of Holly Hall)

Figure 61.   The *M. S. Electron*, Converted Radio Phone Service Boat. Note Leonard Hall's flying bridge and his style of davits and blocks for trolling.

sleeves, and pistons, and rings. And the main bearings showed absolutely no wear, in about sixteen years, still the original main bearings, but gee they're three and seven-eighths in diameter, about that big around.

He also advocated doing as much annual yard work as he could himself because the yard charges so dearly per hour.

Unlike most bottomfishermen, Hall procured all of the materials and components he needed for his boat from local suppliers. And like most crab and salmon fishermen, he did not cooperate particularly with other fishermen in creating gear, although his brother, an expert welder, helped him weld crab pot frames for a few years, and when Hall was just starting out, he recruited an experienced fisherman, John Walker (Norman Walker and Doris Hockema's father), to help him learn how to fish and make gear.

When he was called up for Coast Guard duty during World War II, Hall sold the small double-ended troller he had owned since entering the fisheries in 1940. After the war he was able to procure the *Electron* (fig. 61). Constructed of wood in a Seattle shipyard in 1935, according to Hall:

> . . . it was built by some radio technicians. They built it to install service radio phones in Alaska, but they laid it out on fishboat lines because they didn't know how that venture was going to turn out. When the war came along they sealed all the phones, so that put them out of business, so they converted it over to a salmon boat then.
>
> . . . Because the boat was built to install and service radio phones, there's no iron on the hull, it's all brass. Cast brass rudder, brass shoes, brass stem piece, even the tie-up shocks are brass—cleats. . . . That cast brass rudder, takes two men to lift it. You buy that kind of brass today, you're talking money.

Then only 10 years old, bought from a man who would not have given her up except for recurring health problems, the boat came to Hall in good condition. Besides, says Hall, "I sure was happy, because at that time it was one of the larger boats in the port. Now it's one of the small ones!" Further, since all of her fittings were brass, she never would require as much upkeep as other wooden vessels whose fittings were mostly iron. Pleased and lucky as Hall was with the *Electron*, he still made some changes in her, mainly for his own fishing ease and safety:

> I changed from gasoline engine to diesel. Added a flying bridge to it. Basically the rest of it's just the same. . . . I renewed the well deck. Of course, I had to put new fuel tanks in. I took the tanks out of the engine room when they started getting leaky, and put the new tanks in the stern. Left plenty of room in the engine fuselage. When I had to overhaul that diesel engine, I didn't have to take it out of the boat, just right in the engine room. Course I've added electronics, and radar, and all that other stuff. . . . The only thing that was on the boat when I bought it was a radio receiver with a direction finder on it.

Under Hall's care, the *Electron* gave him very little trouble, and she fulfilled his expectations admirably.

Norman Walker and the *Rambler*

Norman Walker, a crab-salmon-tuna fisherman (fig. 62), is one of the few local fishermen who braved the difficult journey to Humbert's remote boat shop for his boat's annual check-up.[6] He preferred Humbert's because he could do the work on his boat himself, and the old man would let him use his tools. Walker himself tests for rot, removes planks for replacement, packs the stuffing box, puts in a new stern bearing, and, if the wheel, shaft, or engine need specialized repairs, removes and transports them to appropriate shops. Over the year he does minor work on the hull, engine, and hydraulics. Working out of a "gear shed" adjacent to his home, he makes 100 crab pots every year; he used to make the pots in their entirety, but now he has another fisherman's brother weld the frames. Walker also cuts and replaces his poles and rigs his gear. Like most crab and salmon fishermen, he works independently of other fishermen (keeping them under close observation, however) and buys gear components and materials mostly from local suppliers.

In 1961–62, Walker took over the *Rambler* from his father who had fished the boat for salmon, tuna, and crab since he seriously entered the fishing business himself in 1940 (fig. 63). The boat was built of Port Orford cedar ribs and Douglas fir planking and decking in the Coos Bay area in 1938 by local builder M. E. "Slim" Brown. Walker had heard that Brown had put together the boat with several other people (including the eccentric local boat builder, John Swing) on Henderson Slough, a remote location "on the other side of the bay" (North Spit), where no one lives to this day. He figured they had a still over there, and that was why they built the boat way off where they did. Rumor has it that the bunch drank so much whiskey while building the boat that they could have floated her on it. Walker did not know what model Slim had in mind, but he thought he built the boat to sail: "these old boat builders had a notion of building a sailboat and sailing away on it."

In his youth, Norman had worked for his father on the *Rambler*, and after World War II he journeyed with his brother and father to San Francisco to buy a faster 671 Gray Marine engine to replace the boat's original two-cylinder German engine. From 1951 to 1961, Norman had struck out on his own with a 32-foot double-ended troller. Back with the *Rambler* in 1961–62, he immediately initiated changes in the boat, but unlike many fishermen who remodel their boats, he did not rebuild and refit the boat himself. Instead, he had Mr. Humbert put on a new cabin which was "about the same" as the former cabin except that it incorporated the galley, which formerly had rested in the fo'c'sle; raise the bow with 30-inch wooden bulwarks where there had only been an iron

Figure 62.   Commercial Fisherman Norman Walker and the *Rambler* in Recent Years. *(Photo courtesy of Norman and Virginia Walker)*

Figure 63.   The Locally Built *Rambler*.
This boat is a "Slim" Brown boat remodeled by Humbert. Note the crab pots and gurdy.

pipe railing; and install a new mast on the boat. Norman also had the engine overhauled at that time, new fuel tanks fabricated and put in, and a hydraulic power block installed. Soon he may have all the timbers in the hold replaced. He mused that the boat had fished just as well "the other way," before she was remodeled and refitted.

Jake Harlan and the *Puget*

Jake Harlan participated actively in the local bottomfisherman's cooperative in 1978, directing most of his imaginative powers to building fishing gear and upgrading its fishing potential.[7] He showed me some rollers that he had created to keep the net from hanging up on the ocean bottom. He tries to do all of the mechanical work he can himself, and he had just installed a new engine and hydraulics, threading and fitting the pipes with the help of the expert welder-bottomfisherman. When he lacks the tools at his shop at home, or the expertise to do a specific task, he turns to fellow bottomfishing friends, or, occasionally, to fishboat repair specialists like Keith Ott, who try to help the fisherman help himself. He defers his annual yard work to the experts, as he does most hull modifications and his electronics repairs; he takes his boat to one yard in particular because the yard employs the skilled woodworkers that his boat needs.

Harlan had had his eye on the *Puget*, his second drag boat, for some time before he was able to buy it in 1973 (see figs. 55 and 56). The boat was built of wood in 1928 in Tacoma, Washington, and according to Harlan, she was built to be a halibut schooner. Since at least the late 1960s until she sank without loss of life in 1982, she was used as a dragger off the Oregon Coast, and Harlan fished her only for bottomfish. Except for the replacement of two bunks in the fo'c'sle with a work bench, the galley and quarters in 1978 looked virtually unchanged since construction, and they had not been kept up exceptionally well in recent years. Also it looked as if someone in the boat's past replaced the more traditional rectangular windows in the house with smaller circular types, perhaps to keep them from being easily broken if a wave swept over the bow and dashed against the house. A few years before Jake bought the *Puget*, its owner had rebuilt the boat, replacing the hull bottom for $30,000 to $40,000. Harlan claimed, however, that the reconstruction did not alter the original shape.

After acquiring the boat, Harlan had the right half of the stern decking and internal members of the boat rebuilt and built up. In 1978, the left side was soon going to have to be rebuilt, for it, too, was buckling from the strain of the stanchions, which take a lot of stress from holding the doors and towing them along with the net and cable. I believe Harlan also fitted iron bulwarks to the stern. Otherwise, he had not altered the boat, nor did he confess any plans for reorganizing, remodeling, or restructuring it. At the time, he felt the boat was adequate for its bottomfishing job, unless markets changed to absorb more fish, and more of each kind of bottomfish. Then Harlan figured he would be tempted to sell the *Puget* rather than revamp her further, and go to a new, larger capacity, probably steel, boat. In seeking a replacement for the late *Puget*, he may indeed go this route, since the markets have changed somewhat in the direction he specified.

Floyd Green and the *Oregon*

Fisherman Floyd Green is very concerned about the economic constraints of his salmon-tuna-crab enterprise (fig. 64).[8] He says when he has not had enough money, he has tried to do all of the annual work at the yard he could, everything but cleaning the hull surface, working on the propellor, rudder, and drive shaft, and replacing planks. Eventually he got so he could afford to have the yard do all of the work, but now since labor has been getting so expensive, he does what he can again. Green maintains a workshop and tools in his garage at home, and he buys materials and supplies wherever he can get the best deal, independently or through a bulk order with other fishermen. Most of his boat work involves his fishing gear, and he builds about 50 crab pots a year. He does what work he can on his engine, taking what he cannot do to local marine mechanics. He loyally takes all of his electronics problems to one expert who greatly helped him once when he was in a pinch.

For the past 25 years, Green has skippered the *Oregon*, a classic wooden Finnish troller (double-ender) built in Astoria, Oregon, in 1926 by builder Matt Tolonen (fig. 65). Since acquiring the boat, Green has installed radios and other electronics, and he has had to replace the engine several times: when the gas engine that came with the boat gave him trouble, he replaced it with another; but when he had trouble with the new engine, including a fire on the boat because of it, he exchanged it for a diesel; soon after installing the new engine, however, the block cracked, so he had to procure and install yet another diesel, which, fortunately, has not given him significant trouble since.

Green says he has kept the woodwork and structural features of the boat the same as when he bought it, since there are no modifications he could make that would remedy its imperfections. He finds the boat too small, and the double-ended shape prohibitive, since he would like more deck space in which he could work and stack more pots. But since he says he cannot afford a larger boat, he is pretty much stuck with the *Oregon* as she is. (She must be a good boat.)

Figure 64.   Skipper Floyd Green Emerges from the Hold While Unloading His Crab Catch. *(Source: News clipping from the Empire Builder, December 6, 1962. Photo courtesy of Mr. and Mrs. Floyd C. Green)*

Figure 65.   The *Oregon*, Finnish-Style Double-Ended Troller.
The *Oregon* is now used for trolling and crabbing. Note trolling davits and blocks
and crab gurdy; note also the salmon gurdies.

Arnold Hockema and the *Elaine Dell*

Arnold Hockema, a crab-salmon-shrimp fisherman who retired in August
1983, in 1978 called himself lazy and confessed that he was not capable at
carpentry, mechanics, hydraulics, electronics, or even gear building (fig. 66).[9]
He said the most he could do was change a fuse! He did keep a gear shed
adjacent to his house where he made his own crab pots and trolling poles. But
since he did not weld too much, he frequently bought pot frames already
welded for him, and at times he had full pots made for him locally. Otherwise,
he bought most of his trolling and crab fishing equipment locally; he bought
his shrimp net ready-made from a firm in Biloxi, Mississippi (he said he never
did learn how to make a net, and he could barely patch one); and he bought his
net reel and doors locally, although he had his doors and winches custom-made
for him at local fabricators. Occasionally he would get one or both of his
fisherman-sons to help him with gear assembly (one son was building his own
iron fishboat in Hockema's backyard in 1978). He painted the upper portions
of his boat, but he let the yard do the majority of the annual hull checkup,
including painting the copper; in the past he did more of the yard work
himself. For any problems with his engine he prevailed upon the dealer to

Figure 66. Commercial Fisherman Arnold Hockema Shrimping on the *Elaine Dell*.
Fifteen miles off Coos Bay in 117 fathom, April 28, 1978. Catch: 1 tow of smelt
and 2 tows (2,968 lbs.) of shrimp.
(Photo courtesy of Doris Hockema)

Figure 67. The *Elaine Dell*, a General Purpose Boat.

come down to the boat; for any problems with hydraulics, likewise, he got help from local expert Keith Ott.

Hockema bought the *Elaine Dell*, his second boat, in 1959 from the man who had built her the year before, inland, in Corvallis, Oregon, of all places (figs. 67 and 74). As Hockema and his wife Doris jointly tell it:

A: It was built out south of town there on Lincoln Lane, and they drug it down to the gravel pit . . . and then when the [Willamette] River raised, why, it floated away. . . .

D: The man that built that boat was named Swin Carpenter, and he built it himself, and his family helped him, his wife and his children helped him build it. . . . He wasn't a boat builder, he was a carpenter.

A: He wanted to go to Alaska and fish. His wife was a schoolteacher and she said he can do *anything*. All he had to do was go to the library and get books and read them, and he was a carpenter, so that's what he done. . . . he done some kind of crude work on it.
It was at Warrenton [Astoria area] when I bought it. . . . that's the first year it had been in the water. He put it in the water in '58, the winter of 1958. They took it down there and they was fishing crabs on the Columbia when we bought it. . . . They was going to go to Alaska fishing, but his wife was sick, and he couldn't stand it, he got seasick. He wouldn't even go out with me and pick up his pots.

Hockema fished the boat out of Charleston until he sold it soon after retirement to a Morro Bay, California, fisherman. He took Mr. Humbert to Warrenton with him to assess the *Elaine Dell* before he bought the boat. Humbert told him that the boat was built strong but crude, and that though there would be a lot of work that needed to be done to her, Hockema could not go wrong for the price. In retrospect, Hockema thought it was a good deal, too—it had lasted him 20 years at that time and he had not had to change the boat that much.

Humbert did some initial work on the boat and later replaced the front deck and part of the bow stem. Hockema's son remodeled the house for him in some undisclosed fashion. Hockema himself put on new decking and recaulked it, replaced the engine, and exchanged the old steering system of pulleys and chains with hydraulics. The first thing he bought and installed when he brought the boat home initially was an iron mike. He had installed electronic gear—radar only a few years before he sold her—in addition to the radio and fathometer original with the boat. He never exchanged the *Elaine Dell* for another boat, but he did dream of getting a new, larger boat built of iron.

Charlie Ells and the *Amak*

Charlie Ells, now retired, once fished for tuna, shrimp, and bottomfish (fig. 68). He said he never did do too much on his boat but just paint her, work on the engines, make nets, and assemble and set the fishing gear.[10] He did not weld, and he took some engine problems to the dealer. He had pairs of doors built at shops in Eureka and Coos Bay, and claimed he was one of the first local bottomfishermen to adopt China V-doors, of which he learned from an article in one of the fishing magazines. He made sure to use better quality materials, better gear designs, and more efficient and powerful equipment as it became available. Thus in recent years he could get by with a crew of three or four rather than the four or five needed when he did not have the equipment to handle the gear.

Except for a brief period (1947–50) when he simultaneously owned the *Sunderlin*, the *Amak* was the only boat that Ells owned and operated in 40-some years of commercial fishing (fig. 69). Sturdily built of exceptionally fine quality Douglas fir, she is about the steadiest boat that he ever fished:

> Well, in the first place the *Amak* was built in 1915 in Seattle, and it was used as a cannery tender in the Bering Sea, in Alaska, picking up salmon in the rivers that come into the Bering Sea. And then every winter, why they'd put her up on dry dock in King Cove, Alaska, and that's right up there. And I was able to buy it in 1939, and fished out of Bellingham for a while, out to the Cape [Flattery], fishing fish. But it was such a long run, and I only had a 60-horsepower engine, that it took me too long to go back and forth. So I decided I better head closer to the ocean, so we moved to Astoria, and we fished there for 4 years, and then we fished out of Eureka, we came to Eureka, and we fished out of there [here?] for 25 years. And

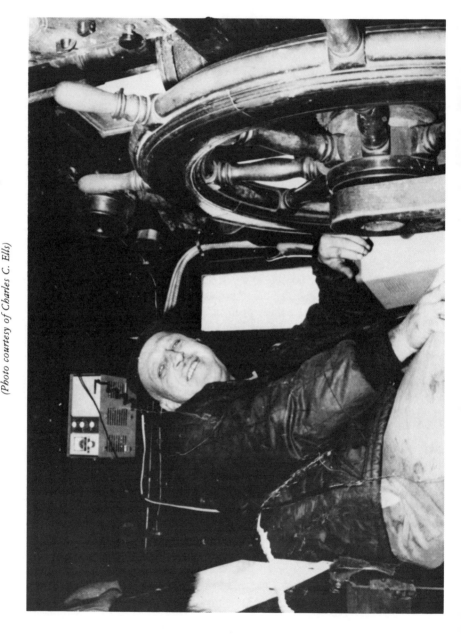

Figure 68.   Commercial Fisherman "Petrale Charlie" Ells at the Wheel.
This photo was probably taken sometime during the 1950s.
(Photo courtesy of Charles C. Ells)

Figure 69.   The *Amak*, Converted Cannery Tender.

we dragged with it for fish, and also fished tuna. We were in Mexico. So we've fished from Alaska to Mexico.

Ells fished the boat out of Coos Bay since the late 1950s, and beginning in the late 1960s, alternately out of Port Orford, mostly just for shrimp and bottom-fish. A son currently fishes her for shrimp and bottomfish out of Port Orford and Coos Bay.

Soon after Ells acquired the *Amak* and began fishing her out of Astoria:

> The house came off on the Columbia River bar. . . . we were coming in and it was a big storm. And we'd laid out there for two days 'til the bar looked like it might be better. And the pilot boat came on out and he signaled that the bar was fine, or it wasn't fine, but it was a lot better than it had been. So we started in and a big breaker caught us and broached the boat, and knocked the wheelhouse off with three of us in the wheelhouse. And the house floated because there was an oil tank underneath the house that kept the house afloat, and we crawled out on top of it. And there were two fellows on the boat, the boat was about 75 yards away, and they came out of the fo'c'sle and threw a heaving line to us, and we drifted down toward the boat. And about that time a mine sweeper came in, and he shot us a line, and towed us up the channel . . . the boat was about half full of water. So we took it to Portland and put a new wheelhouse on it. . . . Only difference is we put the galley on deck, whereas the galley before was in the fo'c'sle, forward.

Other than having the galley put on deck and removed from the fo'c'sle, Ells has not altered the structure of the boat. For no apparent reason, however, he did change the hull's color scheme from black to grey soon after he bought her. The *Amak* seems to be a very rare boat that deserves the praise that the Ells family and shipbuilder Hillstrom give her. With little structural change, she has been successfully fished for 70 years, for several different fisheries, in a variety of oceanographic settings.

Dick Lilienthal and the *Nel Ron Dic*

Dick Lilienthal is a combination fisherman of longstanding, as he puts it, "one of my first cradles was a net boat" (fig. 70).[11] Lilienthal and his crew "do quite a bit of our own work, repair work, all we can anyway. My deckhand's a fair mechanic, he does quite a bit of our work on the motor." They participate about half and half in the annual maintenance exercises at the yard, painting, doing a little carpentry work, and "stuff that isn't big," and leaving the heavy stuff and things they are not skilled enough to do to the yard. "We don't try any of the electronic gear. I'm one of these people, if something happens on the car or something, I just say it's broke and take it to the mechanic. Oh, I know a little bit, but darned if I'm going to ruin it myself." Otherwise, Lilienthal rigs his own gear and in the past has created his own from leftover gear he has had on hand:

Figure 70. Commercial Fisherman Dick Lilienthal Spinning a Yarn.
March 21, 1978.
(Photo courtesy of the Coos Bay World and Charles Kocher)

We willowed up an old beam trawl and then I took the old seine net we had left over from seining in the bay, cut it into four pieces and pulled together a, well we sent back to Mississippi, Louisiana, somewhere back there, and one of the states sent us a little booklet of shrimping and a picture and diagram of a net, and so I sort of whittled one out of that like it showed there.

But originally, when Lilienthal's father decided to go bottomfishing, through a friend's advice, he sent away to a Tacoma firm for a complete trawling outfit — net, doors, stanchions, winch, and reel, "the whole thing."

In recent years I believe Lilienthal has participated minimally in the creation of fishing gear components, buying most of it ready-made including his net, doors, stanchions, net reel, and possibly his crab pots. He does not weld; he does not go in with other drag fishermen to buy materials and components in bulk, nor does he consult closely with them about building and assembling gear.

Lilienthal inherited the *Nel Ron Dic* from his father several years ago, after working the boat with him since 1946, when the boat was built in North Bend (fig. 71):

. . . we got the big boat built at Hillstrom's. The war [WWII] was just over, they had just built their last mine sweeper, and they had a big crew and nothing to do, so they built our hull pretty cheap. Besides that, Dad's best friend was a good friend of the Hillstrom's and they sort of worked out a deal. . . .

. . . I was a senior in high school and the shipyard was only about, oh, a little over a quarter of a mile from the bus stop, so I could go over every evening after school and then catch the late bus home, and I could count every nail that they'd, every piece of wood they put in. It was real interesting to watch it go together.

Fred Holland that has the *Kangaroo*, his dad was the master shipwright, or foreman, whatever you want to call it, that laid out the templates and did all the overseeing. And they had quite a crew of shipwrights, old Scandinavian fellows, that's all they'd ever done. In fact, they worked on our boat at the shipyard for years and years. . . .

Dad's friend, an old Swede from the Columbia River that fished all the time he was a boy, designed the boat, and then he and Billy Hillstrom's dad worked together and put it down and got it pretty well set up. And then — ah, I can't forget, Cecil Holland — Cecil drilled the templates, he and Swede got together, got it all set up and cut out. Swede did it just for the fun of it, just to see it, what it'd look like when it was through.

Really, it's a strange model. It turned out pretty nice looking, but the hull is more like a schooner type. And it's real deep and narrower than it should be and rolls like a son of a gun — until we got stabilizers, and that stops that. It's so deep that once you put the stabilizers out, it doesn't roll anymore, thank goodness. . . .

The boat has not caused the owners much trouble and she has proved that she is built solid and stable:

We got a good test, we were hit by a steamer, at anchor. We were 20 miles out of the steamer lane, we were right along the beach, but they must have been moving between ports. And they hit us a glancing blow and it laid the boat clear down to where the mast was in the water.

Figure 71. The *Nel Ron Dic* Built along Halibut Schooner Lines at Hillstrom's.

And I just walked down the side of the cabin to look out the back door, and stood right by the galley window and once the steamer got by, quit pushing on it, well she righted herself as soon as the bow wake went by. And then of course it rubbed along the steamer all the way. That'd be a sensation for your tape recorder. Sound like you're inside of a tunnel with a freight train, all the rivets roaring down along the guard rails and stuff. . . . But other than that, didn't hurt any. The boat's built pretty solid. It just pushed the flying bridge and the rail over six inches where it rubbed along the hull, tore off a little paint and stuff. But it did give her a good test. It rolled the galley door clear into the water, and most boats, you know, would go on over. But she come right back up again.

Lilienthals have been able to fish the boat successfully for tuna, salmon, and crab, for which she was built, as well as shrimp and bottomfish, but they have not altered the boat much to perform well for its variant duties. They did have to put stabilizers on her, and:

As they get older the rust starts to bleed through. We've replaced all the iron we could with stainless, whenever we could swap or buy stainless. We've put all stainless rails and stainless ladders, but still thee's just enough iron it bleeds through and ruins your nice white paint invariably somewhere.

Thinking about the *Nel Ron Dic*, Lilienthal mused:

> . . . sometimes I think it'd be nice to have a new one and then that old girl's been so good to
> us for 31 years, and still a good boat, hull's in fine shape. We're at the place where we can
> take 3 or 4 months a year off and such things, and I hate to go borrow a bunch of money and
> go back in that nose on the grindstone bit again. . . . But, so far we've been extremely lucky
> and haven't had too much trouble.

But he has also not felt compelled to keep pace with the latest in fishing technology. While he has adopted some hydraulic gear—a crab block and net reel—he still had not exchanged the original winch and steering gear for newer models in 1978. Besides, according to his way of thinking, adopting all the new technology would make fishing too easy.

Fred Anderson, the *Sleep Robber,* and the *Betty A*

Bottomfisherman Fred Anderson (fig. 22) attributes his success to fishing very hard with good gear:

> If you don't put good gear on it [the boat], you're not going to make it. You've got to put
> good gear on it, and all it is is hard work, you know, that's all it is. You put the best gear on it
> you can, not the best gear you can afford. You go borrow money to put the best gear you can
> get on it, the best gear that the boat'll handle, even if you have to go borrow money, and go
> fishing and pay it back.12

Not surprisingly, in 1978 he was the "web" buyer and acknowledged net-building expert of the local bottomfisherman's cooperative, and he was heavily involved in creating and building his own gear, saying:

> I do it myself, strictly myself. In fact, I help a lot of my friends do gear. . . . I can't weld, but
> we do manufacture a lot of stuff, like, there's one guy here, in Charleston, that has a drag
> boat, that's a excellent welder, but he doesn't know anything about web. So we trade off
> labor. I'll help him build a net, you know, or help him on his gear some place and then he'll
> weld for me. We do quite a bit of that, trade off, you know.

He does not dabble with any of the mechanical or hydraulic systems aboard, or the hull work and modifications, but instead he fishes enough to pay to have them taken care of by experts—another reason for his fishing success, according to some. Rather than keep an older boat and try to make it work for Charleston commercial fishing, he has preferred to have a new steel boat built for him in Coos Bay incorporating the latest in bottomfishing design and technology:

> . . . in 1970 for what I wanted, you couldn't buy used, in good shape. Now don't get the idea
> there wasn't any of them around, it's just there wasn't any for sale, you know. And I wanted a
> good boat in the 70-foot class with, well at that time what was considered quite a bit of
> power, and, course now that's all changed, but we're talking about 1970 now. I wanted a
> boat that would pack some fish. I didn't want to run out of room like we did with the *Trego*
> and the *Washington*, and I wanted a little more comfort for myself and for my crew. And we
> got all that on the *Betty A*, you know.

Figure 72.   The *Betty A*, a Hillstrom-Built Bottomfisher.

Figure 73.   The *Sleep Robber*, a Hillstrom-Built Bottomfisher.
This photo was taken when the *Sleep Robber* was fishing in the Bering Sea sometime in the past few years.
(Photo courtesy of Betty Anderson)

But seven years later, the *Betty A* (fig. 72) was:

> . . . outmoded, you know, it's under-horsepower and our gear is, well, see what we do we're dragging a certain size gear, you know, and then we get a bigger boat with more horsepower and we're right back with the same problem, we up the gear, and here we are again, we need more horsepower again. And it's just a vicious circle, I don't think there's any end to it. Really, I don't. I think the bigger the boat, the bigger the gear you put on it. And then, here's somebody that's bigger that's doing better and so you try to use that gear and you don't have the horsepower to use it, so, you know, it just don't work. . . .

So in 1977, Fred contracted the same local shipyard to begin building him another boat, 1¹/₂ feet longer and 110 horsepower more (fig. 73; also see fig. 46):

> . . . it's going to be bigger, more horsepower . . . but I'm not interested in putting more people on it. I can put more fish on it. The *Betty A* has accommodations for the same amount of crew that we'll use on this. Good accommodations above deck, nice staterooms, big galley, refrigerator, freezers, it's got good living conditions on it. This will be maybe a little better, but not that much, there ain't that much difference, as far as living, you know. We're adding a few things on this one, like washers and dryers and stuff like that, and fancier stoves . . . electric stove with built-in french frier, built-in charcoal grill and that kind of stuff, you know. . . .
> And we're putting reasonably nice quarters in so you can live on it like a home, you know, and the only thing we're leaving out is a dishwasher . . . 'cause they don't work too good on a boat. The only time you can use them is when you're in port.

At the time, Anderson had pooled assets with his eldest son and a colleague to finance construction of yet a third new boat so that each of them eventually would have a relatively new steel dragger; at this writing, the third boat has still not materialized. In building such new-fangled boats, Anderson and his cohorts have had to leave the local fishing scene for more lucrative fishing enterprises off Alaska in the Bering Sea. Pacific Northwest waters cannot offer up, and the markets cannot absorb, the quantities of fish these men must bring in regularly to pay off the boats and justify their expense.

Beyond routine upkeep, much of the work that these fishermen have put into their boats has been (felt to be) obligatory to ensure the boat's proper functioning: on the one hand, to improve its seaworthiness and safety to increase the fisherman's physical odds against nature; on the other, to bring the boat up to certain standards of completion and appearance to increase the fisherman's psychological odds against nature; and on the third hand, to outfit the boat with fishing equipment appropriate to local custom, to enter the fisherman in the local competition for shared resources. In several cases, fishermen could not confidently operate newly acquired boats until certain structural imperatives had been met: Crockett and Little had to complete the *Lou-R* and *Maria E*; Harrington and Crockett had to give the neglected *Kodiak* and *Lou-R* major structural overhauls; Hockema had to have some clumsily executed construction details on the *Elaine Dell* reworked; the Littles refitted the *Silver Wave*'s house; and Hall, Hockema, Crockett, and possibly Ells had to convert their boats to fisheries for which they were not outfitted.

Many structural inadequacies which fishermen had to remedy surfaced only with local use, however. The discomfort experienced from the rolling habits of the *Lou-R*, *Nel Ron Dic*, and *Betty A* hastened their skippers to add ballast or stabilizers. Encounters with hard weather prompted Little to bolster the *Maria E*'s house with timbers and bolts and her bow with bulwarks, Ells to replace the *Amak*'s house with one better anchored, and a past owner to improve protection of the *Puget*'s windows. Damage caused by use of specific kinds of components also instructed changes such as Green's switch to a diesel engine and Harlan's reconstruction and reinforcement of the *Puget*'s back deck and bulwarks. Some fishermen changed the makeup of their fishing machines because of a close brush with disaster (Hockema adopted radar and exchanged mechanical steering with a hydraulics system), or simply because of the potential for disaster (Crockett built up the *Lou-R*'s topsides, Little and Walker the bows of the *Silver Wave* and *Rambler*, respectively, and Hall replaced his gas engine for a diesel).

On the other hand, many boat modifications were made for enhanced personal use: to improve efficiency, thus the fisherman's odds against other fishermen, or to improve on-the-job comfort, thus relationships among crew members and the fisherman's overall satisfaction with his operation (with self). Several fishermen had created roomier, more accessible or generally more pleasant living spaces by removing the galley from the fo'c'sle and either adding it to the back of the cabin or incorporating it into a rebuilt house (Harrington; Ells, Walker), by refinishing or remodeling the house and fo'c'sle (Harrington, Hockema, Littles), or by building an entirely new house (Crockett; Harrington had plans to do so). Littles, on the contrary, had shortened the length of the *Silver Wave*'s cabin, favoring greater working space on deck. Similarly to improve working conditions, Hall and Anderson had created ample work space around their engines, which maneuver additionally saved Hall the pain and time, and Anderson the repairman's expense, of removing the engine from the boat for necessary repairs. A concern for an easier, more effective (and competitive) fishing operation also motivated additions of a flying bridge which gives the crab fisherman better visibility (Hall, Walker), and installations of a stern ramp (Crockett), hydraulics, electronics, and higher-powered engines (Harlan, Ells, Harrington, Walker, Crockett, Anderson).

With several of the apparently obligatory modifications, fishermen have attempted to bring their boats up to performance standards that they must have abstracted from their experiences with fishboats in general. Anderson, Crockett, Ells, and Lilienthal, for example, had acquired a feel for comfortable and safe boat movements, the lack of which prompted each man quickly to add ballast or stabilizers to bring their boats up to code. Charlie Ell's boat the *Sunderlin* continued to feel so worrisome that he eventually sold it, as he and his wife Jessie explained:

> *J:*   Well, the *Sunderlin*, you were always afraid of her . . . he was always afraid she was, she wasn't seaworthy . . . it was a tuna boat, and we had quite a crew.
>
> *C:*   We had tuna tanks on it.
>
> *J:*   And he was always afraid of her. . . . Yes, we were making a turn into Bodega Bay, and I was just on for the, a little cruise, and engineer was in the engine room and I don't know who all was on deck, and I was in the stateroom with Charlie, or the wheelhouse, and he made the turn into Bodega Bay in this northwest wind, and she went over, and you just wondered if she was going to come back. And he said, "Look, quick, look out and see if Peter and somebody's on the after deck," thought they might have gotten washed overboard. And then the engineer was coming up out of the engine room and got a wall of water on him, on his head, didn't he?
>
> *C:*   Yeah.
>
> *J:*   She, they sold her to the Mexicans and I think she was sunk after that, didn't she?
>
> *C:*   Yeah.
>
> *J:*   Down off Mexico, so I'm sure . . . and she had nice accommodations, but she wasn't. . . .
>
> *C:*   She wasn't a schooner, she was kind of a sardine boat.
>
> *J:*   But you had that feeling, I know he always had that feeling that she wasn't seaworthy.
>
> *C:*   She was alright if she had plenty of ballast in her, and you see those tuna tanks hold a lot of water on deck and they're dangerous, especially on that boat, you just didn't have too much stability. So, when it'd get rough, why we'd have to dump our bait, which we didn't like to do very well either, 'cause we fished with live bait.[13]

Additionally, Crockett, Harrington, Hockema, and the Littles were loathe to operate their boats until they had met detailed standards of appearance down to secondary features like well-paintedness, overall cleanliness, and appropriate quality house fittings and interior finish carpentry.

Other obligatory practices such as building up the topsides or deck, bolstering house fastenings, and protecting the wheelhouse windows, are widespread, common-sense responses to boats battered by use. Varying the height of bulwarks on the stern and aftersides of a boat according to fishing use has been a very common and visible practice at least since the post-World War I development of the combination boat (post-1930s for the southern Oregon coast).[14] West Coast fishermen had also been exposed for a long time to variability in bow height and performance, since builders have expressed a wide range of bow flairs, sheers, and heights to deflect water and to give them a look that reflects the builder's individual stamp as well as his community's ethnic standards.[15]

By their alterations, however, Charleston fishermen indicate a preference for tall topsides and sturdily-built or reinforced boats, features which fishermen praise in existing boats not necessarily of local origin, and which local builders and fishers have jointly expressed in new boats. Most Coos Bay builders, undoubtedly in response to their clients' urgings, have also given tall, sturdy bulwarks to bows since at least the mid-1940s (*Nel Ron Dic*), as well as a good flair since the 1950s and 1960s (Humbert's and Mattson's boats, exclusive of bulwarks; Hillstrom's and Nelson's steel fishboats since the 1970s). Slim Brown, however, (and some of his cohorts) consistently turned out boats with graceful sheers but lowlying topsides in the Finnish troller vein, but at least since the 1940s, boats such as his which have been converted for hard winter fishing use (crab or bottomfish) have generally received additional bow bulwarks.

Additionally, like the "improvements" made in the English houses of the Banbury region during the seventeenth and eighteenth centuries, many of the more optional modifications (efficiency and personal use) mirror trends of the times.[16] Recent refinishings of house and fo'c'sle interiors with wood-grain paneling echo current preferences in home interiors, particularly in those of the working class. Similarly, West Coast fishermen have generally adopted engines, hydraulics, electronics, and new materials (stainless steel, aluminum, and synthetics) as they have been developed for automobiles, airplanes, and ships. While some individual fishermen have innovated revolutionary equipment specifically for the fishing industry like the iron mike and the Puretic block, for the most part Charleston's fishermen have adopted new devices after other West Coast fishermen have already tested them.[17]

While Charleston fishermen did not invent the stern ramp, flying bridge, on-deck galley, high-powered marine engines, hydraulics, and electronics, some certainly have initiated incorporation of the features into both new and existing local boats—especially in the cases of engines, hydraulics, and electronics—following examples set by nonlocal and nonregional fishboats and nonfishboats such as tugs. Stern ramps, flying bridges, and on-deck galleys, however—features that affect the structural integrity of the boat more visibly than do advanced engines, hydraulics, and electronics—appear to have been implemented first in newly built rather than already existing local boats.

Stern ramps, for instance, have been common to North Atlantic trawlers for years; only in the past decade have West Coast fishermen begun to accept them, probably spurred on by the examples of Soviet and Polish trawlers fishing West Coast waters.[18] The first Coos Bay trawler built locally that incorporated a stern ramp was initiator Fred Anderson's boat, the *Betty A*, completed in 1971. Cecil Crockett built a ramp into the *Lou-R* after that, and local shipbuilders have since turned out several more stern-ramped trawlers.

Another adopted feature, the flying bridge, seems to have been adapted to West Coast trollers and crab combination boats in the 1940s and 1950s, following the precedent of Puget Sound purse seiners, which had probably borne the bridges since the 1920s when the houses for these boats became positioned forward. By the 1950s, flying bridges were extremely common on all newly built large Puget Sound combination boats.[19] Lilienthals had one worked into the *Nel Ron Dic* when she was built at Hillstrom's in 1946 to fish tuna and crab, and Hall and Walker each added one to his troller-turned-crabber after that.

There are also ample precedents in large pre-World War II West Coast vessels (including some halibut schooners, cannery tenders, and purse seiners) for the galley to be positioned on deck aback of the house. Well before Walker had the galley of his boat moved above deck, both Lilienthal's and Little's boats were built with the galley on deck in the late 1940s, and Ells had an on-deck galley incorporated into the *Amak's* new house when he was working out of Astoria in the 1940s.

Importantly, it appears that Charleston's fishermen not only routinely change their boats according to their experiences with a particular boat and with boats in general, but they also change them in predictable ways, conforming to changes that other fishermen and boat builders have made in the past. Thus, collectively, these fishermen's modifications are imitative and traditional rather than pioneering, and they confirm the local acceptability of certain fishboat characteristics, both old and new, in much the same way that regionally evolved traditional boat designs would.

However, while all fishermen modified their boats to improve their odds against nature, indicating that they share a concern for meeting specific boat performance standards (appropriate roll and feel of boat, appropriate response of boat to stresses of use, proper condition and selection of boat parts), they differentially enforced alterations. Some men waited for disasters to occur before remedying boat parts. Others took measures to avoid such problems before they occurred, perhaps based on the experiences of the disaster-struck. In preparing used boats for safe fishing, some fishermen went beyond absolute necessity and the examples of peers in insisting that various secondary features such as interior fittings and finish work meet certain qualifications. Similarly, the fishermen differentially modified their boats to improve working conditions on board for themselves or their crews, or to improve their odds against other fishermen. Differing personal motivations—ambitions, skills, experiences, and ages—and identification with other fishermen through pedagogical, familial, and professional affiliations account for these dissimilarities.

All of the bottomfishermen have adopted higher-powered engines, new net materials, hydraulics, and accordingly, in most cases, larger nets and heavier, V-shaped doors. But Ells and Lilienthal have not so greatly increased the capacities of this interdependent equipment that they have had to reinforce and rebuild strained boat structures like Harlan did, or raise the stern bulwarks substantially and reinvent them in steel (or in the form of a stern ramp) as

Harlan and Crockett did, or outgrow boats like Harlan and Anderson did. Indeed, Ells and Lilienthal have remained aloof from other bottomfishermen, not entering into the cooperative in which the other four fishermen participate, instead working closely with their crews, which in both cases include a son. Involved with bottomfishing well before any of the other men, both put an old-fashioned emphasis traditionally associated with north coast Scandinavian and Finnish fishermen on the quality of fish caught as opposed to the fish quantity and better money that the other bottomfishermen condone. Neither man, at least in his golden years of fishing, wanted to sacrifice home and family life to work hard for quantity of produce in order to pay off expensive and more efficient fishing paraphernalia which would have required boat modifications or a new boat. "We don't keep up so much, we don't care now. We just try to make a decent living and go play," says Lilienthal.[20] Not particularly inclined to handiwork either, both men appear to be most interested in the art of fishing, making the most out of what equipment they already have, having other people improve it if need be, but not involving themselves concertedly and ambitiously in significantly upgrading it. Lilienthal states his philosophy this way:

> Well most of the new fishermen are in it strictly for the money. And I'm out there just trying to make a living at it. But I enjoy just guessing right, or whatever you call it, just like steelhead fishing, it's just the thrill of going some place and setting the net and getting what you went after. So I don't even pay much attention to the other guys. If they get a big catch, sometimes I just go the other way and do my own thing. Find them sooner or later.
>
> . . . We do bottomfish quite a bit, 'cause it's real interesting. . . . It's every man for himself, you got to be a fisherman to catch them, you just can't throw the net out and follow somebody else. . . .[21]

Further, by earning reputations for quality produce, each has developed a close relationship with his fish processor, thus guaranteeing a market for his catch, and to some extent, a steady income with which he can pay to have boat work done for him. Of course, these men have also been blessed with some extraordinarily sturdy and versatile boats.

Anderson, Harlan, Harrington, and Crockett, on the other hand, all ambitious men, foster a "big producer" strategy among themselves. They aim to catch tremendous quantities of fish in order to make lots of money in order to afford the finest gear available in turn to make their fishing operations more efficient so they can catch more fish, make more money, and keep up with new technological developments ad infinitum. Since the right gear cannot be procured locally or ready-made, adherence to this philosophy depends on the rather extraordinary willingness of highly competitive fishermen to cooperate with each other in designing, building, and rigging the equipment. The interpretation of these commonly and openly shared ideas varies with the individual, however.

In his eagerness to succeed even more than he already has, and keep up with the latest in West Coast dragfishing technology (hence, with "big producers" in other ports), Anderson, who calls himself greedy, has carried the strategy to extremes by using modern-day business skills, going deeply into debt, and having new boats built that can handle the equipment he wishes to run. Acknowledging that he would have to go to more lucrative fishing grounds in order to pay for this technology, he had his latest boat designed so that his wife, son, and daughter-in-law could accompany him and live on the boat "like a home." Unwilling to give up hard work as he ages (he is in his fifties), Anderson is also clearly reticent to continue to sacrifice his family life and the comforts of home.

Preferring to keep working out of Coos Bay, Harlan, however, also a successful, maturing big producer, had settled down with his second drag boat, an older vessel, which with adequate reinforcement allowed him to fish it to full capacity and maintain his competitive edge locally. Having "made it," he could afford to have specialists repair and rebuild the boat superstructure to his specifications as he punished it. Inclined to work with his hands, yet a driving worker fascinated with the problems of fishing competitively and locally, he concentrated only on what boat work directly influenced his fishing capability. He cared little to improve the boat's living spaces for a comfort which he seldom sought (or expected his crew to seek), or for an appearance to which he seemed to be oblivious.

Crockett and Harrington, on the other hand, are both relatively new to the big producer game, having acquired their first drag boats in 1974. For them, the selection of a drag boat was partly a matter of their self-confidence in their own abilities to upgrade boats and partly a matter of expedience, or as Fred Anderson would put it:

> . . . that's the reason a person buys a boat, don't think there's any other reason. They buy it because they can get into it. They don't buy it for no big love affair or anything like that. Boat that they've seen for years, you might . . . say it's a nice boat and you'd like to have it, but when it comes to buying a boat, you buy what you can get into, what you've got money for.22

Crockett and Harrington's energetic involvement in improving the fishing capability of their boats as well as their obsessions with boat comfort and appearance has as much to do with their youthfulness and their inclinations toward handiwork as it does with their desires to prove themselves successful drag fishermen. Indeed, they seem goaded into energetic and competitive performance because they are younger men bound into occupational and (unlike Harlan and Anderson) family networks filled with senior expert fishermen, most of whom espouse some sort of dynamic interaction with fishing boats.

While Crockett has sought to incorporate many of the features that Anderson had built into the *Betty A* (stern ramp and fancy accommodations), Cecil admittedly favors Harlan's stance of using an old wooden halibut schooner for local bottomfishing. But he prefers a wood boat more because he trusts and likes the feel of wood and deeply respects fishing and boatbuilding traditions of the past (emulating his teacher, a Norwegian master fisherman to whom Cecil attributes most of his knowledge) than because, like Harlan, a good used (wood) boat is more economically feasible than a new (steel) boat within the limitations of Coos Bay.

Harrington, on the other hand, is not as enamored of the older wooden vessels. I imagine he really would like to have a new steel boat like Anderson's, but for the time being, he is confined to a second-hand boat. His strategy was to continue to improve the *Kodiak*'s image and work up to buying another used drag boat (probably of steel), and then lease out the *Kodiak*, at once signifying his "own wrinkle" among bottomfishermen and solidarity with several peer shrimpfishers who had recently made such moves.[23]

In comparison to the bottomfishermen, the five crab fishermen show a conservative streak in not graduating to bottomfishing, in loyally maintaining the same boat for the past 20 to 30 years even though several would prefer a larger one, and in not expecting so much out of their fishboats that they have forced substantial modifications. While competitive, the crab fishermen are not as overweeningly ambitious as the big producer types, nor as interested as Ells and Lilienthal in proving their skills at the most demanding kind of local fishing. In general, their challenge is figuring out how to make a decent living from a kind of fishing they like to do—a kind of fishing to which they are also accustomed and for which the technology and fish stocks have remained fairly stable since each man entered the fisheries (unlike bottom- and shrimpfishing). Further, I get the impression that they like the smaller scale of operation, and the greater opportunity to work alone when salmon fishing or with only one other person when crabbing. While basically conservative in fishboat taste, each crabber has adopted new ideas or modern conveniences idiosyncratically.

Leonard Hall and Cyrus Little, Sr., for instance, took particularly fresh and active approaches to their boats because they liked handiwork and efficient, well-running machines, and because they came from highly diversified occupational backgrounds. Both men also converted to fishing later in life, entering the fisheries atypically, without the usual youthful steeping in fishing traditions. While Hall hired an experienced fisherman (Norman Walker's father) to teach him the basics, he remained free-thinking, selectively absorbing crab/salmon fishing traditions, readily implementing new ideas if they proved more effective or efficient (less because other fishermen had or had not done so themselves), and assuming the role of an initiator, somewhat like Anderson. As he reached the age of retirement, however, he grew increasingly pessimistic about his chances of making a decent living with a boat he liked. I think he was relieved to retire, for he could avoid choosing between changing his ways or persisting in them and facing a decreased standard of living. His son's choice of boat—a 49-foot Humbert-built crabber-troller, "probably the best looking boat in the port," according to Hall—perhaps reflects the direction in which he would have gone had he been a younger man facing the problems of the late 1970s.

Little and two younger brothers, on the other hand, not only followed their elder brother Paul into the fisheries, but each married one of four sisters, supporting a kind of competitive conformity among themselves which additionally accounts for Cyrus, Sr.'s, dynamic attitude toward boats. Thus, while Cyrus had built a rowboat modeled on his elder brother's after following him to the Alsea, Cyrus was the first to build an oceangoing fishboat (a troller in size but notably with a broader, rounder stern for crabfishing) after joining Paul in Charleston. Shortly thereafter, Paul had a boat built larger and broader than Cyrus's but, so Cyrus says, modeled on it. Not to be outdone, but also impressed with the possibilities of a larger boat such as his brother's, Cyrus got hold of a boat of similar size a few years later. Both men later adapted these boats to fish shrimp at about the same time in the early 1960s.

Restricted in his fishing activity by recurring illness, the conversion to shrimpfishing gave Cyrus, Sr., a welcome opportunity to apply his handiness to the creation of gear in a way resembling the most active bottomfisherman's involvement. But unlike the bottomfisher, once he had acquired the *Maria E*, he was subsequently not motivated to outgrow her. Rather, he turned over the boat to his son, and using his welding skills, built himself a small steel troller for occasional "retirement" fishing. (Many fishermen find they cannot retire upon retirement, and after handing on their boats, procure another, usually smaller, which they can fish on their own whenever they feel like it.) Further, reflecting his father's orientation, when Cyrus, Jr., had a new boat built like some of the activists have, it deviated little from the *Maria E*, mainly in construction material and hardly in size, shape, spatial allocations within the boat, or the arrangement of parts. Slight changes made in the new boat were pretty clearly derived from both men's experiences with the older boat. And Littles did not sell the older boat, reserving it probably for Cyrus, Jr.'s, son. Except for the younger man wanting his own boat made of a material that is allegedly easier to maintain, both Littles had found a boat design that fit their formula for continued fishing success.

Hockema's boat behavior, in contrast, is probably most understandable in terms of his professed laziness and disinclination for handiwork. Thus he probably would not have had his house remodeled if his son had not been around to do the job, and he might not have bought the *Elaine Dell* if Wilbur Humbert had not been available to critique it and then to refinish its finish work. However, Hockema has not been as lazy as he says, for he clearly has been able to make enough money to have specialists do most boat work for him, and further, to purchase a relatively new boat with a fair amount of work space and generous accommodations. He also demonstrated some business acumen in converting his boat to fish shrimp whenever salmon season did not pan out. While the size of his boat allowed him to convert to shrimp more easily than would his brother-in-law's (Norman Walker), Hockema's conversion, as well as the number of crab pots he runs, is probably related to his identification and friendship with several local crab fishermen who preceded him in converting their larger boats to fish shrimp. Unlike them, however, he has been slow to adapt modern conveniences like radar and he has resisted installing a flying bridge, reflecting his individuality in a kind of stubborn old-fashionedness.

Indeed, somewhat like the Little brothers, Hockema and his brother-in-law, Norman Walker, a die-hard troller-crabber, seem to have competed in resisting or accepting new ideas. Both brought up under the fishing tutelage of Norman's father, Norman preceded Arnold in leaving the nest, buying a small double-ended salmon troller. When Arnold subsequently struck out on his own, he purchased a troller of about the same length, only broader, and then a few years later acquired the *Elaine Dell*, an even larger, broader boat, fitted out better than either his first boat, Norman's, or his father-in-law's. When Norman took over this father's boat shortly thereafter, he promptly took it to Humbert as Arnold had done with the *Elaine Dell*, and had the old man enlarge the house to include the galley on deck like the *Elaine Dell*, and add a flying bridge, which Arnold never added, perhaps following the elder Walker's model more closely than Norman cared to. Both men persisted in not installing radar until Arnold finally gave in first, due to a near disaster. It appears that Norman will not convert to shrimpfishing even if he procures a larger boat, despite the increasing difficulty of making a living from crabbing and trolling.

Walker, like Floyd Green, is quick to suggest economic strictures for actively participating in boat maintenance and gear production, and for not going to a larger boat, but Walker made enough money at one time to have substantial alterations made to his boat. Rather, more like Hall than Hockema, he seems to enjoy boat work, even if somewhat grudgingly and even if not to the point of making his own alterations. However, a strong adherence to crab-salmon fishing tradition seems mostly to motivate both Walker's and Green's involvement in boat work, for both men so cling to conservative, traditional financing schemes that neither feels he can afford the larger boat which would enhance his economic circumstances. Further, despite the shortcomings of his boat, Green has not sought to make any changes in it which could mitigate his displeasure with the boat, like rebuilding or repositioning the house or adding a flying bridge (interestingly, Green is friends with Hockema and once worked for him; perhaps he identifies with him in not adding a flying bridge). If he were to acquire a larger boat, his main interest would be in greater work space and not necessarily in the possibility of more commodious, deluxe living quarters. By the later alterations Walker made, however, he clearly does not so wish to sacrifice comfort and fishing ease for work space, and keep faithful to the "true way" as Green does. Rather, he would like a large enough boat so that an enlarged cabin would not restrict work space as it does somewhat on the *Rambler*. On the other hand, Walker is torn between wanting a larger boat for crabfishing and a smaller one than the *Rambler* which he could man alone for salmon fishing, adhering thus to another old strategy for saving money by eliminating the cost of the puller he needs for the *Rambler*. If he were to go to a small troller, he would then willingly revert to the old-fashioned fishboat style, giving up the large house so that he could see through the cabin windows from the cockpit as he worked.

Faced with a pessimistic economic outlook for their choice of fisheries, both Walker and Green have fallen back on what they know best, nostalgically and ornerily wishing for the old days and the efficacy of old ways. Both men, of course, are in their fifties preferring to ease up on the amount of effort they have to put into their jobs, instead of working hard to persist in what they are doing or to learn new fishing ways and pay off loans to acquire larger boats.

Like the careful grooming of home exteriors and interiors, the custom outfitting of vans and low-riders, and like one's choice of automobile or clothing, fishboat alterations are highly visible, significant expressions of self and group identity.[24] Through boat upkeep and modification, a fisherman articulates an aesthetic of boats and equipment; he demonstrates artistry in his work and his capacity and maturity as a fisherman; and he communicates solidarity with specific like-minded fishermen, his "own wrinkle" among them, and his separateness from and opposition to other fishermen. Altogether he expresses his fishing philosophy, a unique vision balancing work effort and sense of gamesmanship; scale and sophistication of operations and equipment; type, quality, and quantity of produce; ways of doing business; and relationships with other fishermen, crew, and family.

Collectively, boat modifications show the fisherman's real frustration with the price of a new boat and the reliability of boatbuilding technology, basically, with risks inherent in changing financing ways and in giving up a known older boat for an untested new one; they demonstrate the viability and continued acceptability of converting used boats for local use; and they reflect a corpus of ideas which fishermen have found acceptable through their own experiences, networks of power and influence, and quests far afield for knowledge. While articulating preferred boat characteristics in much the same way that an evolved boat type does, yet operating so powerfully in expressive ways for fishermen, boat conversions set Charleston fishermen collectively in opposition to local boat builders. With their converted boats, fishermen force builders to give primary attention to the regeneration of existing boats, relegating the creation of new ones to the back burner. In taking boat work into their own hands, indeed fishermen extend towards boat builders and shoreside specialists the kind of distrust and competitiveness that they harbor among themselves.

Fishermen and Craftsmen: Cooperation and Conflict

Full-time, year-round Charleston fishermen typically set themselves apart from the rest of the world, geographically, occupationally, and socially. Proclaiming themselves professional fishermen, they distinguish themselves from part-time and sports fishermen. Further, they claim that their occupation differs from most other kinds of jobs, saying that fishing gives them more freedom than a regular eight-to-five job: they can set their own hours and they are not answerable to a boss or countless co-workers. Additionally, they characterize themselves as particularly independent people, strong individualists, who prefer to get off by themselves and work in peaceful isolation more than most people do. Finally, these fishermen identify themselves strongly with the Charleston vicinity, distinguishing it from "uptown," that is, the more populated districts of North Bend and Coos Bay on the upper bay which, historically, are the seats of local waterfront activity.

Distinctive and aloof as this varietal bunch of characters would have you believe they are, they still depend on a host of shoreside specialty shops and craftsmen in order to keep their boats in shape. This reliance associates fishermen with members of other water-oriented occupations with whom in fact they share many occupational characteristics and with whom they form a greater waterfront occupational community. The nature of this occupational network and the participation of fishermen within it explain partly why many Charleston fishermen do as much of their own boat work as they can.

Like Astoria and Newport, the Coos Bay area provides its fishermen with the entire range of maintenance and repair services, although it falls short in supplying complete lines of ready-made boat parts and fishing gear components. In fact, Coos Bay functions as a major marine maintenance and repair center for ports between Eureka, California, and Newport, Oregon, and it attracts customers from the entire West Coast, "from San Diego to Kodiak."

Charleston fishermen depend heavily on about a dozen local shops, which included in 1976–78, four boat/shipyards, five machine shops, three marine electronics firms, and two marine supply stores. Hillstrom Shipbuilding then was the largest operation, employing about forty people, including joiners, caulk specialists, welders, machinists, hydraulic specialists, electronics experts, a yard supervisor, an accountant, three secretary-receptionists, and Hillstrom himself, manager and self-taught designer.[1] Located on the Coos Bay waterfront (see fig. 7, no. 5), the facility could accommodate boats up to 120 feet in length, three at a time — one in the shed under construction, and two on the ways (see figs. 46, 47). Workboat repair constituted about a fourth of the business, and the remaining three-fourths was pretty evenly divided between fishboat construction and towboat construction. Local fishermen with larger-size boats usually took their vessels to Hillstrom's not only because the yard could more easily handle them, but, they claimed, because the facilities and equipment are the best in the area. Further, the yard still employed several expert ship carpenters whose skills are essential for wooden boat repair.

More and more, however, fishermen with large boats had been switching to Nelson Log Bronc (later known as Mid-Coast Marine), even though the facility was not as sophisticated as Hillstrom's and even though it hired only one ship carpenter. Located upstream from Hillstrom's on the Eastside waterfront (see fig. 7, no. 10), the firm then employed around twenty-five people, including two secretaries, a draughtsman, the manager (a trained marine architect and engineer), and mostly metal workers — welders, machinists, and mechanics.[2] Five craftsmen worked year-round on boat repair; another five tended solely to log bronc maintenance and repair through the year; and the remaining ten or so worked on the new construction of log broncs, towboats, and fishboats. The facility then could handle two boats under construction at once, but only one boat at a time out of water for repair; only one-fifth to one-fourth of the yard's work effort was devoted to repair. Nelson's had built boats up to 86 feet in length, but for repair it normally accommodated boats only up to 65 feet.

Kelley Boat Works in Charleston (see fig. 7, no. 20, and fig. 1) probably got the most fishboat maintenance and repair business in the area, from both local and transient fishermen. Moreover, unlike the two larger yards, which repaired and constructed a variety of workboats, Kelley's mostly only serviced fishboats. The yard hired only about ten people, all boatwrights, that is, woodworkers, all of whom could also weld with varying degrees of ability.[3] The facility could handle boats up to 70 feet in length, 8 feet in draft, and 30 feet in overall height; and six to seven boats at a time, two inside the building and five outside. However, Kelley's usually attracted only the small- and medium-size boats up to 50 feet in length, and usually no more (nor less) than four at a time, day after day (see figs. 25, 27, 28, 37, 38, 48). In 1978 the business had produced no new boats since 1968; the elder Kelley, who had designed them (and who was professionally trained), died in 1977. Maintenance and repair of boat superstructure constituted the major portion of the yard's work effort; needed welding, mechanical, and hydraulic repairs had to be referred elsewhere, usually to the adjacent Jerry's Machine Shop.

Unlike the other yards, Humbert's boat shop was pretty much a two-man operation. The elder man and one or both sons could handle two boats at a time, one in the shed (usually under construction), and one on the ways, up to 59 or 85 feet, depending (see figs. 39, 41, 42, 43, and 7, no. 1).[4] Since the shop was very inconveniently and inaccessibly located on a remote section of the upper bay, few fishermen actually took their boats there regularly for maintenance and repairs, and those who did generally owned smaller boats well under 50 feet. Nevertheless, most of Humbert's work was in fishboat repair, usually of woodwork; often times fishermen would remove defective planking themselves and take it to Mr. Humbert to make a replacement for it. While he was adept at blacksmithing, welding, machine work, and hydraulics as well as ship carpentry, ordinarily he only practiced his complete repertoire of skills in building a new boat.

None of the yards completely satisfied a fisherman's maintenance and repair requirements, however. The old standby for machine and metal work for years has been Koontz Machine Shop on the Coos Bay waterfront (see fig. 7, no. 7). In 1978 the firm employed a dozen craftsmen—two welders, eight machinists, a hydraulics specialist, and a propeller repairman—but only a few of them devoted any effort to fishboat mechanics.[5] In recent years, especially since John Koontz, the founder, and his son have passed away, fishermen rely on the shop solely for drive shaft and propellor repair. Koontz's is still one of the few firms on the Oregon Coast that houses a lathe large enough to turn fishboat drive shafts. Further, the shop provides space for the only propellor repairman between Newport and Eureka. Until his recent retirement, Horton, the prop man (see fig. 49), also custom designed and made the patterns for 10 to 12 pair of otter boards annually, leaving the actual fabrications to a couple of young shop workers.

Next door to Koontz's on the Coos Bay waterfront sits Knutson Diesel and Machine Shop (see fig. 7, no. 8), a smaller outfit that in 1977 employed four machinists, all of whom were versatile in their skills, and one of whom specialized in hydraulics.[6] These people mainly maintained and repaired Knutson's towboats, but they devoted a fourth of their work to fishboats, mainly maintaining and repairing their hydraulic systems and the G. M. C. engines, "jimmies," of those that have them.

Knutsons bought the shop several years ago from Keith Ott, who had operated it for many years previously. When Ott ran the shop, almost half of his business was for fishermen, building and repairing fishing equipment, maintaining and repairing engines.[7] At that time Kelley Boat Works referred all of its customers' machine, welding, and hydraulic work to Ott. Ott has since retired, but he started up another business near Charleston, away from the waterfront (see fig. 7, no. 18), working with an apprentice. Ninety percent of his work in 1978 was related to fishboats, mainly building and repairing a variety of fishing equipment only for former customers (many of the older, more experienced local fishermen who also owned the larger boats and took them to Hillstrom's or Nelson's for yard work). Since he has "retired," he no longer takes on work that Kelley's refers to him, so Kelley's recently hired Jerry to man a machine shop at the yard.

Fishermen with smaller boats, mostly salmon-only enterprises, who took their boats to Kelley's, generally would take their mechanical problems to Jerry's, Knutson's, or most likely, to Bill's Machine and Welding in Charleston (see fig. 7, no. 7; fig. 1). Bill's shop was devoted almost entirely to fishboat repair—welding, fabrication of metal parts and fittings, hydraulic repairs, engine work and rebuilding, and some prop and shaft straightening and balancing.[8] Bill Chard managed the shop, did most of the engine work himself, built crab pot frames to order, and sold parts and supplies for "the cheapest prices in the area." He was never quite sure who was working for him, but sometimes up to three other people, frequently from his family, would help him with managing the shop or fabricating and repairing fishboat components.

There were several marine electronics firms in the area in 1978, but I heard fishermen refer only to three, one of which worked in tandem with Hillstrom's (Roger Spaugh), and two of which are independent operations in Charleston (B and F Marine Electronics, and George's Marine Electronics [see figs. 1, and 7, no. 6]). George Hartley of George's Marine Electronics repeatedly received glowing praise from local fishermen. He then employed two electronics helpers, an office manager (his son), and a secretary.[9] He mainly serviced the equipment he sold to fishermen but whenever a customer bought another boat with different brands of electronics, he would continue to service that man's gear; he could repair any brand name. Ninety-five percent of his work was for fishermen, and he served customers from Crescent City, California, to Newport, including at least 100 Charleston fishermen.

Charleston fishermen also depended heavily on two marine supply stores in 1977–78: Hanson's in Charleston (fig. 7, no. 20; fig. 1), and Oregon-Pacific in North Bend (fig. 7, no. 3).[10] These stores provided a service to fishermen in much the same way that a hardware/old general store does for farmers and skilled workers in a rural community. For fairly high prices, fishermen could procure a variety of materials and ready-made parts in addition to complete gear outfits, clothing, and appliances for the galley. Crab and salmon fishermen bought a good lot of their fishing gear from these stores or they ordered components through them; fishermen who plan ahead and try to buy their materials and supplies elsewhere to get better prices still would rely on these stores for items they might need on the spot.

At first glance, a folklorist would reject these businesses from scrutiny, with their often formally trained personnel; their stocks of purchased, standardized fittings, parts, and materials of sophisticated manufacture (steel rods, plates, cable, wire); their shelves of trade manuals and supply catalogues; their wholesale adoption of factory-made tools and machines (lathes, drill presses, welding and sandblasting equipment) and the techniques that go along with using them; and finally, with their mechanized creations. But at least until very recently, they have exhibited characteristics common to the business of a folk craftsman.[11]

For one, in 1977–78 these shops were all small businesses, independently owned and operated. Significantly, most of them were family affairs, either operated by several members of one family, or handed down from family member to family member. Bill Hillstrom, Jr., Fred Humbert, and Jack and Dick Kelley ran their fathers' businesses, which they assumed respectively after working many of their younger years for their fathers. Similarly John Knutson managed the newly acquired machine shop for his father's towboat company; John's father in turn inherited the towboat business from his father, John's grandfather. Norm Anderson went to work at Oregon-Pacific for his brother shortly after World War II, and he worked there in partnership with him until recently, when he took over the business after his brother's death. For the thirty-some years that the Hanson family ran their supply business, they either lived immediately adjacent to or within the store, bringing up their children to participate readily in the business. Similarly, John Koontz brought his son up to work in his machine shop; in 1972 the family sold out, and shortly thereafter, both men died, the elder man being in his nineties. One of Koontz's nephews worked at the shop as a blacksmith for years until he retired recently.

Even in the more recently formed firms, family is an important element in the business. George employed his son to manage his marine electronics business; Bill's wife and daughter tended the books, and his son helped with repair work at his machine and welding shop; and Nelson Log Bronc started out as a family-run business until it ran into hard times and the family sold out to Jack Wilskey. Further, some of the longer-lived, larger shops such as Koontz's and Hillstrom's have hired members of certain local families for several generations.

While some shop workers have followed their relatives into their jobs directly, others, like Keith Ott and Art Horton, have attained their present positions through apprenticeships, working for one man for years and eventually acquiring his shop, in Ott's case, and in Horton's, working every job in Koontz's until by ability, experience, seniority, and predilection, he worked the job he pleased. Interestingly, Ott came from a family who was involved in the local water trades; his father and brother ran riverboats and towboats. Ott opted to work not in the same trade, but in a related one, thus entering the work force indirectly through family, a common occurrence on the waterfront.

Indeed acquaintance with one of the water-oriented trades, through family or apprenticeship, seems to breed familiarity with others. The nature of the fully mechanized, motor-powered workboats and the care they need brings together fishermen, towboat operators, managers of small sawmills, loggers, and a variety of craftsmen at local repair shops. In turn, numbers of disparate specialists rub shoulders to ensure complete boat care, cooperating under one roof as at Hillstrom's, Nelson's, or Koontz's, or between shops, as with Koontz's (Horton) and all of the boat/shipyards, Kelley's and Ott's or Jerry's, or Humbert's and George's. Further, as several of their managers averred, repair shops that are in competition with each other try to help each other out when they can. Shop employees know the kind and quality of work and equipment that each business can offer; when one shop runs short of supplies or acquires too much business, or encounters a particularly difficult repair problem, other shops and experts will pitch in to help, sharing needed supplies, equipment, or expertise, assuming some of the other shop's business, and gaining even more exposure to one another.

This interdependency of shops and trades has allowed waterworkers the mobility to obtain work in more than one area over the years, as it also has clearly exposed offspring to a variety of job opportunities. As a consequence, veteran waterworkers like Ott, Horton, and Humbert exhibit great versatility in their skills, mastery of several, and wide-ranging occupational experience. In fact, many of the men who originally established some of the more important contemporary waterfront businesses came into them from related trades with such diversified backgrounds and abilities. For instance, Bill Hillstrom, Jr., claims that his family has worked jobs involving the water for generations. His father got his early training as an apprentice shipwright at Kruse and Banks, one of the old-time area shipyards (fig. 7, no. 2). When the yard closed, he started a contracting business for waterfront work (pile driving, for example). Then in 1941, he opened his own shipyard to build mine sweepers for the government during the war, hiring many of the old shipwrights who had worked at Kruse and Banks. After the war, his business survived by switching to local workboat construction.

Similarly, Wilbur Humbert, coming from a family of carpenters and shipbuilders, apprenticed out as a blacksmith, later got work at Kruse and Banks doing finish carpentry in the captain's cabins, survived the Depression by fishing commercially, and later operated a small sawmill. When most of the small mills were put out of business by the big corporations in the 1950s, Humbert opened a boat shop on the site of his sawmill, and there productively combined all of his talents.

Oregon-Pacific had its origin in the fishing partnership of two locally born men who also worked together at local wood products mills.[12] Bill Chard, born into a family of local longstanding, worked on bay dredges before he opened his machine, welding, and supply shop. While Nelson, Hanson, and Kelley did not originate in the area, previous to opening shop on Coos Bay each had worked in a related water trade: Nelson had operated tugs and riverboats; Kelley had worked in Pacific Northwest shipyards; and Hanson had worked aboard seagoing ships.[13]

Additionally, waterfront firms such as Knutson's and Koontz's have diversified into several related trades over the years. Louis Knutson, for instance, came to Coos Bay to work for the C. A. Smith Lumber Company. He began operating towboats for the company and eventually established his own towboat business, which his son Harold now manages. Harold, working with his son, in turn has expanded into the marine machine shop field; recently they began constructing a new steel fishboat. Koontz started his shop as a motorcycle repair garage, but he soon "got busy as the devil" making and repairing engines for the area's multitude of boats.[14] Since then the firm has expanded into the fabrication and repair of logging equipment, fishing gear, and other mechanical features of fishboats, towboats, and Caterpillars (heavy equipment).

Clearly, in the face of rapidly fluctuating, often difficult economic circumstances, diversification in skills can guarantee a man a job within the work force, while diversification in a business can often likewise secure a shop's longevity and family continuity in its ownership. On the other hand, the tendency of those in the waterfront work force to involve their families in their businesses helps perpetuate existing shops and the network of trades. For these types of jobs it is common and fairly easy to involve children in one's business from a very early age. Fishermen and some of the more independent self-employed craftsmen often start their children working for them after school and during vacations when they are still in grade school, even when they are as young as four years old. The Hansons literally brought up their children, and then their grandchildren, in their marine supply store.

Exposed early to a family business and to a variety of interrelated jobs, perhaps as many offspring are likely to remain within the family's occupational community as to seek employment in another sphere. Daughters of fishermen are especially inclined to marry sons of fishermen, or men who are receptive to becoming fishermen and working for the wife's father or other male relatives. Friendships between tradesmen often involve the families of both men: a child brought up in his/her family business is a good candidate for a job/apprenticeship that might come open in a friend's business, whether it is the same kind of work as the child's family or not. So many local waterfront jobs are filled in this manner that it becomes extremely difficult for an outsider to enter the work force; this is especially true today of acquiring a job on a fishboat.

Patronage to certain shops or certain craftsmen again often follows family lines. Family participation guarantees a certain amount of continuity in a shop's service year after year. Customers, knowing that they can expect a certain kind of service reliably year after year in turn patronize the shop for years. Shopworkers thus come to know local customers and their individual requirements; similarly they become well acquainted with customers' families, and vice versa. In turn, children of customers often patronize the same shops that their parents do, out of friendship, loyalty, and familiarity. Some Coos Bay area families have patronized certain shops for several generations.

This intergenerational, interfamily intercourse gives many of the local shops a very comfortable, informal, familiar atmosphere. Hanson's and Bill's were downright homey, with regulars dropping in briefly, rummaging about the place and helping themselves to whatever they needed, chatting and joking comfortably with the store workers, calling each other by first names, and charging their procurances to their boats. Cars and trucks frequently flooded the parking lots of both places, while inside swarmed gossipy customers and a variety of local characters who had a few spare moments with nothing to do but hang around and talk. Interestingly, Jack Wilskey, professionally trained head of Nelson's, tried to encourage a "neighborhood service station" atmosphere in his shop:

> . . . it seems like each yard attracts its own clientele. You establish a relationship between the yard and the people working for you and the customer. And it's just like going back to your neighborhood service station; if you have a problem, you'll kind of go back to that area, unless you're caught in a different, a remote geographical area, but most of the coastal fishermen kind of orient around one harbor or port. And they seem to come back as long as they get a fair deal, and good work, well then they'll return for additional work. So normally you build up a clientele and it's like going back to the same doctor every time. He can kind of understand your boat and you, and gives you a little better service than the next guy, maybe. . . . that's good business, really. . . . we try to give a fisherman a fair break and make him realize that he's part of our business, too, and we care whether he goes away from here feeling, having a good feeling, and would come back, maybe send somebody else back.[15]

While many of these businesses are places of work, they are almost equally social centers. At the local shipyards, customers milled around the facilities waiting for work to be done or consulting yard workers about work that needed to be done. Whenever George was on the premises of his electronics shop, he was inevitably swamped by half a dozen fishermen waiting to ask him for advice about anticipated repairs or purchases. Humbert was oft beset by a small crowd of men watching him work or waiting to ask him advice about their own projects and dreams. Chard and Horton each attracted a constant flow of customers daily, asking the expert when he might be able to do some work for them, or when he might be likely to get work completed that they had already submitted. In Chard's case, many people hung around the shop waiting to ask him advice about how to put something together themselves, and some dissatisfied customers returned to question the specialist about past work that he had done for them: "You weren't interrupted when you rebuilt that engine?" queried one fisherman who knew that Bill rarely got much time to himself to work, he was so frequently besieged with advice-seekers and clients begging for their work to be completed first.

A man might visit a craftsman such as Horton, Chard, Ott, or Humbert several times to chat and eventually ask when a piece of work will be done before the expert will finally get it out. Taking work to an expert in the first place characteristically involves some discussion of the weather and recent occupational events of note. In fact, craftsmen are often excellent sources of information about the latest in the fishing or logging business, and, as well, in the vicissitudes of certain men's fortunes. Art Horton, a self-professed gossip and publicly acclaimed tall-tale teller, offered to tell me *anything* I wanted to know about any of the local fishermen (no doubt relishing the opportunity to make taller tales of scandalous local events). Chard related distinctive crab pot size and framing preferences of certain fishermen, telling how one fisherman had always requested a certain height pot until one year when he wanted pots of less height, thinking they would not roll quite so much on certain types of ocean bottom. Chard admitted that he had gossiped this information to another fisherman, who remarked that he had gone through that stage, too.

A trip to the craftsman's shop, consequently, provides an occasion to learn the secrets of other customers. But for fishermen, the availability of an expert is something of a mixed blessing. In order to get work done as well as get in on some tasty gossip, the fisherman must confide some of his own preciously guarded occupational habits, and risk having the craftsman spread knowledge of them to people whom he would rather not let in on his secrets. By relying on a craftsman, a fisherman not only gives up some of his highly valued privacy and independence, but he risks the proper functioning of his fishing tools, and thus his life, in the event that specialized work taken to a craftsman is not expertly done.

Thus the waterfront craftsman maintains a very powerful position within the greater occupational community. Like a shaman or a priest, he is the custodian of highly specialized information and skills that the fisherman cannot do without, and to whom the fisherman must pay homage, make the sacrifice of his independence, in order to receive the benefits of the craftsman's expertise. The craftsman wields his power by withholding or divulging information regarding customers' private affairs, and skills in accomplishing work. He can slander a man if he chooses, encourage the ruin of his reputation; similarly he can do a better or worse, more or less time-consuming job, depending on how he feels about a particular customer.

Verbally, Coos Bay craftsmen seek to establish themselves as the keepers of esoteric lore, to substantiate their authority and superiority over their fisherman clients, and clearly to keep themselves in work. Experts are quick to generalize about fishermen and their habits, especially judging what they should or should not do:

> Let me make one more comment there. The real top-line fishermen realize that they have to have a good yard, and they have to be good fishermen. When they have a problem, they take the damn boat to the yard, and they have them do it, and it's a bill to them, but it also means that when it's done, it'll, should be done right. If not the yard'll, should do it over again. And they can concentrate on being good fishermen. But a lot of them think that . . . the boat is their hobby, and . . . they're really slaves to the boat and . . . they're not very good fishermen.
>
> . . . most of the fishermen call themselves fishermen, but they're really kind of boat mechanics and do-alls, they spend more time fiddling with their boat than they do fishing, that's really their lot in life. Maybe . . . they like the sense of going to sea on the boat, and maintaining it, but . . . they just fish enough to pay for the bills. . . . But the good ones, they don't do very much on the boat themselves, but they maybe paint it, and clean the galley and make sure the internal quarters are in good shape. They're good fishermen, they're in the business to make money and to catch fish, and the boat is their tool to do it, and they recognize having professional help to maintain the tool.16

Some craftsmen are overtly contemptuous of fishermen as a group, branding them stupid and superstitious, while others aggressively spurn fisherman handiwork, especially that which might overlap with their own kind of work.

Explicit disdain for the work of nonexperts and competitors, and self-confidence in one's own judgments about what constitutes good handiwork, are classic characteristics of master craftsmen. "Craftsman arrogance," I call it. George Sturt, for example, noted the ridicule that the expert wheelwrights in his shop showered upon the less sophisticated wagons that regular carpenters and joiners occasionally put together.17 The Maine lobsterboat builders of whom Lunt speaks often refused to bend their aesthetics to the eccentric demands of their fisherman clients.18

Indeed, by virtue of their awesome abilities and experiences, and their overt self-confidence, the master waterfront craftsmen of Coos Bay command tremendous respect. And fishermen treat even the less accomplished with appropriate reverence.19 However, in witnessing several craftsman-fisherman interactions, it is interesting to see a funny mixture of respect and skepticism on the fisherman's face. On the one hand, the fisherman reveres the craftsman for his knowledge and skill and for fear of what the craftsman will or will not do for him. On the other hand, the fisherman worries that the craftsman is withholding information from him, that he will not give him the quality service or advice that he desires, that he is going to exact more money or more personal information out of him than he wants to give. In the end the fisherman may not know whether he has been swindled or not. And, of course, he just does not like giving up any of his independence.

Then every fisherman has had a bad experience with a craftsman or specialist somewhere along the line. Many men have had more bad experiences with experts than they have had good ones, or at least they expect outright to have bad experiences instead of good ones. As one shipyard manager puts it:

> . . . a lot of fishermen feel that going to the yard is the next thing to . . . going to the local pawnshop or something, or a local shyster. They really look on shipyards as being people that are out to get an awful lot out of them; they don't like their bills, and they don't like a mass of humanity working on their boat to get things done that they, so you're offering then to the person that is a real thorn in your side that you'd have to satisfy him, and there's no way in the world you're going to satisfy him, because he's just decided there's no good shipyards in the whole damn world, you know.[20]

Fishermen commonly complain about the cost of specialized services, the quality of specialized work, and the time away from fishing that such work takes. Indeed complaining and steering potential customers away from certain specialists is the major weapon a fisherman can use against craftsmen. On the other hand, when a fisherman repeatedly has good experiences with a craftsman, he makes a point of lauding him. Floyd Green, for instance, takes all of his electronics work to one man who seems to like him, who will get work out for him as soon as he can, and who does good work. This expert has also offered to help him whenever he needs it. To testify to his appreciation of his relationship with this man, Green told that once when he was tuna fishing out of Newport and his Loran was not working, he called up his electronics expert. The man told him to put the equipment on the bus and ship it down to him in Coos Bay, and he would fix it. So Green shipped it, and the electronics expert promptly fixed and returned it, earning Green's everlasting loyalty.[21]

Many Charleston fishermen are relieved and pleased to be able to take their electronics problems to another expert, George Hartley. Dick Lilienthal says of him:

> George is dependable . . . good at his job and dependable. . . . at least with me he always has been. He says he's going to be there at two o'clock, he's there at two o'clock. I've had a couple of fellows, I bought a radar from a drunk and he'd say he's going to be [there] at eight in the morning, and I'd sit there all day on the boat waiting for him, and he never would show up.[22]

Another Charleston fisherman flew George down to the Gulf to install reliably, reliable electronics equipment in the second-hand shrimper he had just purchased before he navigated it back to Charleston. Further, at one time, George planned to leave the area because he was not financially solvent enough to go into business on his own. Worried about losing such a good man, some local fishermen got together and encouraged him to stay, forming a company with him to get him started in his own business. George has gradually been able to buy out the fishermen's shares and he is now firmly ensconced in the Charleston fishing community.

Some men will develop such close and trusting relationships with their craftsmen that they can exchange goods for labor. Art Horton accepted a trip's catch of albacore tuna from a friend in exchange for a propellor "blessing"; he added that there were only 15 fish, but indicated that the exchange was a fair deal. Acknowledging the adversarial relationship between fishermen and craftsmen, however, Leonard Hall took great pleasure in relating the manner in which he was able to extort prompt work out of John Koontz, who he called, "a foxy old guy . . . good machinist, too":

> I went up there to see Johnny, and see if I could get it fixed, you know, so I could go fishing the next day. Johnny was there all by himself, Bud [his son] was off up in Portland, drunk, just sent his wife to the hospital, and he gave me a tale of woe. And he had jobs laid out all over the floor there, just him himself there, and I told him, said, "Johnny, you sound like a guy needs a drink." He said, "You got one, son?" I had a pint out in the pickup, so I went and got it. He got my job out right away.[23]

Unlike the rosy, idyllic picture of craftsman-client interaction that folklorists often paint, Coos Bay craftsman-fisherman relationships are not always neat, happy equations of complementary parts. Charleston fishermen generally have difficulty in establishing and maintaining good relationships with local craftsmen, in spite of family and occupational bonds; indeed, most fishermen appear to be reticent to negotiate such an interchange in the first place. Craftsmen, on the other hand, often view fishermen as problem clients, not easily satisfied, unwilling to submit work, "afraid to open up too much and tell you what's wrong with their boat for fear you'll find everything else wrong and really stick it to them, as far as the bill," capable with their complaints of discouraging potential clients, and frequently unable to pay bills without being reminded bluntly several times over.[24]

As Chiaramonte has shown, however, unsuccessful relationships do not necessarily invalidate the existence of sets of rules governing craftsman-client interactions to which both parties subscribe.[25] In the Coos Bay situation, it seems that there are several conflicting sets of rules in operation, rooted in variant occupational and craft traditions. In particular, while many veteran craftsmen are well diversified in their skills and experiences, and many have survived locally by diversifying in skills or services, they are specialists at heart—machinists or mechanics, welders, hydraulics or electronics experts, shipwrights, boatwrights or boat builders, or propellor repairmen—and they expect fishermen to be specialists, too. Charleston fishermen, on the other hand, are reluctant specialists. By insisting on participating in the maintenance, repair, and modification of their boats, they compete with craftsmen and hold on to a model of the diversified, self-sufficient fisher-crofter—a small-time seasonal fisherman who fishes alone or with only a few men, with a boat and gear that he might have built himself or procured from a neighbor.[26] These fishermen, however, use vessels which qualify as ships, require dependence on specialists, and force them to become more like deep-sea skippers of hull trawlers or San Diego tuna seiners—men who delegate the operation, maintenance, and repair of their vessels to crew and shoreside specialists.[27]

In general, the more the fisherman adheres to a specialized mode, the better relationships he may have with local craftsmen. This in fact seemed to be the case for Fred Anderson, Charlie Ells, Floyd Green, Jake Harlan, Arnold Hockema, Dick Lilienthal, and, to some extent, Norman Walker—notably, fishermen who themselves have not made major changes in their boats. Craftsmen complicate the picture, however, by fluctuating between two methods of transacting business. Several local craftsmen give certain fishermen a break in the cost of work (not charging by the hour or job); do extra careful or quick work for them; or accept goods from them for services rendered because they are relatives or long-time friends (insiders with a history of cooperative or interfamilial behavior).[28] This way of doing business is more personal and open, and it is usually associated with "traditional country craftsmen" and small rural towns where everyone knows everyone else.[29] Fishermen, operating from the frame of the self-sufficient farming community where people have known each other for generations, expect to be treated in this manner. Unfortunately for fishermen, craftsmen extend such treatment very selectively. Most of the time, craftsmen adhere to a specified, impersonal, seemingly urban and modern system.[30] They explicitly and uncompromisingly charge for work by the hour and job—unavoidably displayed signs stating terms hang in many shops—discouraging fishermen from spending time trying to articulate the kinds of esoteric work they might want to have done. This strategy is basically a means of self-preservation, for competition between shops is keen and large numbers of untrustworthy outsiders—transient boats, sports fishermen, and newcomers to the fishing world—enlist their services during the summertime.

Occupational specialization is often cast in impersonal tones and looked upon as the product of urbanization, hence industrialization, particularly characteristic of urban crafts and tradesmen as opposed to self-sufficient farming community crafts and folk craftsmen.[31] The traditional craftsman, usually found in a rural setting, frequently works alone, creating artifacts from beginning to end entirely by himself. He procures the raw materials, refines them for use, and completes the subsequent steps of manufacture himself that result in one complete work of art. He may employ himself solely in this pursuit, exchanging his wares with neighbors in return for labor or goods that they can offer him; or he may only practice his craft part time along with farming, fishing, or other rural and household pursuits. He may have learned his craft through an apprenticeship, but more than likely he picked it up from the habits of friends, neighbors, and/or family.

In contrast, the tradesman is a specialist who works with other specialists within a craft. Alone he may not be able to create the artifact from beginning to end, but only one part of it. He is a member of a guild who, through apprenticeship more than family and friends, acquires "professional training" and a standard set of occupational terminology. He is more likely to exchange his wares for cash instead of the goods and services of neighbors.

Many of the traditional country craftsmen of whom Jenkins and others have written fit neither of these two categories absolutely; rather, they fall somewhere in between.[32] In rural settings, besides the self-sufficient craftsman or farmer-craftsman, there are village craftsmen, men who specialize in the production of specific farm and household tools and implements. They often work independently to produce these goods; together they fulfill most of the major material needs of surrounding farmers and villagers. Often more than one craftsman may be found working at the same craft, in the same shop: "In the larger yards where two or more craftsmen work, it is customary for each one to specialize in a particular category of work."[33] In the case of George Sturt's wheelwright's shop, for example, not only did craftsmen specialize within the shop, but they cooperated with specialists outside the shop such as woodcutters and sawyers to gather and prepare their raw materials, and blacksmiths to produce wagon fixtures and the tyres. These interdependent traditional village craftsmen, specialists of one sort or another, thus resemble urban tradesmen to a certain degree.

Jenkins attributes the lack or presence of specialization, indeed of specialized craftsmen, to the economic circumstances of farmers.[34] The farmer of small holdings on inferior land with the consequent low yield and income could not afford elaborate tools and implements. The farmer himself thus would make his own tools and implements from materials he could find on his farm; Jenkins found the use of primitive agricultural vehicles, carts rather than wagons, concomitant with an upland farm of small holdings. Wagons abounded, however, in districts where farmers maintained larger holdings on richer, flatter land, which was easier to cultivate and which produced a better income than the small upland farm. Along with the larger, more prosperous farms, and the use of wagons, go specialized craftsmen to produce the elaborate and expensive tools and implements which the wealthy farmer can afford to purchase and use.

Thus, economic constraints and isolation seem to foster one kind of craftsman, while economic well-being and close proximity to other human beings seem to foster another. The complexity of an artifact, as well as specialization, seem to be functions of population density and economics. It seems plausible that the creation of more and more complicated artifacts such as wagons and pre-erected frame boats (ships), with their more complex production, is a result

of several craftsmen working together on the same problem, refining the artifact and its means of production at a much faster rate than a lone craftsman can
accomplish. Neither craftsman is necessarily less folk or less traditional than the
other, provided that each man maintain certain attitudes and habits regarding
his work, carefully cultivating and refining acceptable, long-tested designs,
learning his craft by watching his elders work and hearing them talk about it.
Further, as Chiaramonte's study has shown, even within small, rural communities where everyone knows everyone else, traditional craftsmen will employ
specified, impersonal methods of doing business to protect themselves from
clients who take advantage of their generosity when they have extended open,
personal contracts to them.[35]

Early settlement brought both urban and rural, specialized and diversified, impersonal and personal craft systems to Coos Bay. Wealthy entrepreneurs
opened up the area to settlement by starting logging and lumber operations,
offering jobs of a specialized, urban nature to newcomers. Moneyed interests
thus supported the creation both of shipyards and the larger varieties of local
workboats. Today's waterfront workers have inherited their specialist traditions
from men who worked in the early shipyards and manned the early workboats.[36] And in 1977–78 they still owed their jobs to the continued economic
well-being of the logging-lumber industry, in much the same way as specialized
village craftsmen owed their jobs to wealthy British lowland farmers.

On the other hand, once they had arrived in the area, most Coos Bay
settlers re-created the diversified, self-sufficient ways of life to which they were
accustomed, setting up farmsteads, and finding that they could fish seasonally
for profit as well as subsistence, or work occasionally at the yards and mills
during boom periods. While yard and mill work gave people experience with
specialist traditions, daily life kept many of them in tune with "the old traditional way of life."[37] While some yard workers continued to specialize in one
skill, others branched out—learning all the jobs in the yard and opening their
own small, complete boat works, or experimenting with an entire range of
waterfront jobs before settling into a speciality—thus keeping a more pastoral
form of occupational behavior alive and part of the waterfront traditions.

Today's commercial fishing has its roots in this more pastoral way of life.
Local fishing has not been supported by moneyed interests, and very few
specialized waterfront shops have ever been able to depend on the fishing
industry alone. Like farming the British uplands, fishing still proves a means of
making a modest living only with very hard work. (Fish processing has had the
backing of big business since World War II, but the plants do not own or
otherwise subsidize fishermen's boats and gear; fishermen own their boats and
equipment, and run their enterprises as small independent businesses.) Without maintaining a strong sense of independence, individualism, and self-
sufficiency, without remaining somewhat diversified in his skills and relying as

much as he can on his own abilities and materials on hand to create and keep up his boat and equipment, the Charleston fisherman could not survive. His adoption of larger boats for ocean fishing has also been necessary for his survival, however. But accordingly, he has had to sacrifice some of his diversification and self-sufficiency, depending more on the specialized waterfront work force and acquiring another set of traditions to heed.

Riding on the prosperity of the wood products industry, most craftsmen adhere to a specialist model, while veterans clearly have diversified during their lives in order to survive. However, to survive as specialists in a somewhat urban, impersonal setting where they do not know most of their customers through family, friends, and long-time residence, craftsmen use impersonal, specified forms of transacting business most of the time. Equally for survival, they extend open, personal business methods to select friends and familiars, recognizing their interdependence.

The state of Charleston's commercial fishboat technology and upkeep indicates that fishermen, craftsmen, and waterfront workers in general subscribe uneasily to urban and rural, specialist and nonspecialist traditions. Between pure specialist and self-sufficient man of many skills lies a spectrum of individuals uniquely combining the two extremes in their own lives and work, achieving neither extreme, vacillating between them, and making life troublesome for each other. The healthy continuance of rural and urban, specialist and nonspecialist traditions ties present-day Coos Bay to its past, attesting to the lasting "effect of first settlement,"[38] and perhaps accounting for the rebounding resourcefulness of Coos Bay waterfront workers, who, often third- and fourth-generation Oregonians, "provide for their own" when the economic boom inevitably lowers.

Conclusion

Fully decked over, containing completely enclosed pilothouses, and built on pre-erected frames, Charleston fishboats are ships in construction, complexity of design, and somewhat in size. Indeed, Charleston fishermen invoke ship traditions by blessing their boats; giving them names, personalities, and life histories; treating them as large, awesome, almost human artifacts; and not trusting themselves alone to maintain and repair them. These fishermen do not use their boats in true shipmaster fashion, however: They operate them alone or with only one or two other men who are often friends or relatives, and they do not relinquish all maintenance and repair chores to specialists. Instead they integrate specialized and nonspecialized fishing traditions. Coming from backgrounds where fishing was one of many occupations (specialized and non-specialized) that a family might pursue during the year, formerly dispersed geographically around the bay and throughout the population, Charleston's fishermen bring individualism and self-sufficiency, thus diversification in skills, to an occupation that has become increasingly specialized (one's sole line of work) as well as geographically and socially concentrated, isolable from most other jobs and settlements in the area.

In order to use the fishing equipment that they do and keep it suitably maintained, Charleston's fishermen depend on shoreside experts: As specialists fishers cooperate with crafters on specific projects, and as nonspecialists they compete with and oppose them by accomplishing certain skilled tasks on their own. With craftsmen, these fishermen create an interdependent maritime occupational community of diversified village specialists brought together by kinds of work and fostered by family connections, ties to Coos Bay's past, and traditional ways of doing business.

This co-existence of diverse traditions is perhaps not so much a unique aspect of Coos Bay and maritime occupational communities as it is both a product of American settlement and a phenomenon of the "industrialized backwoods." Wherever they located, settlers created similar ferments of the rural and urban, preindustrialized and industrialized models they brought with them. With such beginnings, and less isolation due to geography, rural nodes like Coos Bay have remained better integrated in larger communicative webs than in days past when geography more severely circumscribed the transmittal of information and goods. After a fashion, the backwoods keep up with and contribute to mainstream culture and technological developments in distant major industrialized centers. Still constrained by geography as well as by a delicate local economy and ecosystem, self-restrained by choice and hard-earned wariness, modern backwoodsmen do not give up the old for the new, wholesale. Rather, they selectively absorb new information while keeping older, reliable systems intact.[1] Hence, while a few fishermen have had brand new boats built using modern business methods to cover their lack of capital, most Charleston fishermen conservatively retain and often flamboyantly update older, primitive boats (carts vs. wagons), reflecting the economic unpredictability of the local fishing industry, the spareness of the region's fishing grounds, yet a desire to find better solutions to old problems and an accompanying thirst for new ideas.

In this context, where the preservation of existing boats is of vital importance, boat upkeep and modification take on a significance equal to the creation of new boats. In fact, in Coos Bay the regeneration of existing boats for continued use represents a user-based building tradition — with its own customs and aesthetic dimensions — distinct from, yet interdependent with the builder-based, new boatbuilding tradition, and founded on the involvement of the independent, self-sufficient fisherman in the routine maintenance and repair of his boat. According to this tradition, the Charleston fisherman buys an existing boat that he can "get into" — that he can afford — and that is available when he wants to buy one. If he is lucky, his first will be a good boat featuring qualities that he has learned to appreciate through his experiences with boats and exposure to the preferences of peers and elders (both fishermen and boat builders). Usually by his second boat he can obtain a reasonably good boat: one that is sufficiently large and sturdily built for the fishing operations desired and the driving use given, one that feels comfortable, and one that is not too "big a mess," run down and beat up. More specifically, a good Charleston fishboat is about 35 to 50 feet long; fairly deep for a good roll and plenty of hold space; fairly broad for ample room on deck for work and accommodations; heavy, overconstructed, with tall topsides for resistance to the abuses of the environment, work, and enhancements of equipment; and well kept, if not good-looking and well articulated in its structural details.

Rarely does any one boat feature all of the desirable traits, however. Thus, through personal use and attention to trends among peer and elder fishermen and builders, the Charleston fisherman characteristically makes alterations to improve the boat's feel (roll), sturdiness (structural resistance to stresses of the environment, work, and equipment), deflection of water, and the condition, quality, and appearance of all of its parts down to fine detail. Also he often tries to improve boat spaces for on-the-job comfort, and he adds, replaces, or upgrades equipment and work areas for efficiency and fishing success; in this realm he is most likely to try out new ideas. To remedy spatial limitations of an existing hull, the fisherman generally procures another boat, usually second-hand, sometimes new, and typically a bit larger and broader to allow him greater fishing capacity (more fishing gear and more powerful equipment) and extra room for more comfortable accommodations, ampler work space, and a larger hold.

Like the traditional boat builders of Winterton, Trinity Bay, Newfound-land, the Charleston fisherman generally implements change on a subsystem by subsystem basis, altering one while keeping all others stable.[2] Aware of the interrelatedness of the boat's subsystems, however, he often makes changes in one component realizing that specific changes may simultaneously be necessary in one or more of the other subsystems, and that the performance of the entire fishboat may change in certain ways accordingly. As with the traditional barn builders in Otsego County, New York, the majority of changes the fisherman makes are additive and subtractive; basically they do not affect the form of the existing hull base.[3] But the fisherman's changes may indeed alter the composition of members supporting the hull shape, and his experiences with the form may lead him to search for a slightly different shape and construction, that is, a recomposition of the entire base structure. Thus, due to the complex nature of the typical Charleston fishboat and the experienced fisherman's thorough involvement in boat upkeep, some if not all Charleston fishermen appear to comprehend change in the fishing boat in geometric as well as arithmetic ways.

In terms of Glassie's "Individual-Centered Diagram of the Functional Field," maintenance, repair, and alteration not only further the mediating capacity of the boat, but like the boat, they mediate as well.[4] Practices like replacing planks and worn or broken fittings and equipment, and obligatory modifications like bolstering or replacing structures that have proven inade-quate, clearly mediate between the fisherman and nature. More precautionary measures—semi-annual hull check-ups, propellor "blessings," or replacements of gas engines and fittings and reinforcements of boat structures before disaster has struck—look practical and common-sensible on the surface, but border on superstitiousness, and thus mediate between the fisherman and the supernatu-ral. Boat upkeep and modification also offer the fisherman vehicles for self-expression—mediating between the individual and his personality—through which he can demonstrate mastery of skills like carpentry, mechanics, or weld-ing. In modifying interior structures and in juggling equipment, he can also express his concern for the efficiency, comfort, order, and cleanliness of his operation. The fisherman can also use his choice of alterations, his involvement in boat work, and his attentiveness to boat appearance to state his adherence to specific ways of fishing and doing business, acknowledging his affiliations with certain fishermen and craftsmen (in-groups), his differences with others (out-groups), and expressing his individuality among peers. Importantly, the fisherman uses all aspects of boat upkeep and alteration to keep his operation competitive and to guarantee a living from his work—to secure a competitive position with respect to other fishermen in vying for a shared but (self-)limited resource. That is, he uses boat upkeep as mediator between self and nature, and self and the supernatural, to mediate between self and self, and self and others, on the one hand to compete against others, on the other, to cooperate with others in maintaining certain rules of the fishing game or limits to the competition.

Thus an existing fishboat at any given moment is like one recitation of an heroic epic, a tall tale, a joke, or a ballad by a folk performer. Changes due to common maintenance and repair procedures can be seen as differences in word selection or word order from recitation to recitation. Alterations and significant maintenance and repair changes are like personal embellishments and localizations, substitutions and deletions of words, sentences, story segments, or motifs, making the song or tale more relevant to the time and place and more effective from the performer's point of view and in terms of audience response, and representing stages in the performer's development.[5]

Importantly, besides performing basic utilitarian functions, boat alterations, maintenance, and repair serve "expressive and projective" functions in the Coos Bay waterfront occupational community.[6] Boat upkeep is a means of "artistic communication in small groups."[7] By keeping a boat competitive, by keeping it in good working order, and by keeping it looking neat, trim, and well-loved, a fisherman can demonstrate his overall professional ability to other professionals. By simultaneously making a boat more comfortable for personal use, a fisherman can further exhibit his mastery of the fishing business. By showing expertise in the specialized skills of mechanics and boat builders, the fisherman can upstage the specialists and prove himself more than a mere fisherman.

The fisherman does these things as much to impress other fishermen and gain status by artfully executing common practices as to convince himself of his personal control. Like the fisherman's elaborate occupational terminology that details all aspects of his work, equipment, and the environment in which he works, expressions of technological competence give the fisherman the impression that he is in control of the weighty forces that counter him—the fickleness of nature and of the commercial fishing industry, the uncertainty of making a good catch.[8] By carefully following sanctioned guidelines of boat-related behavior, the fisherman hopes he can guarantee his safety and fishing success, and psychologically face an environment that is full of surprises. His failure to follow these practices will be blamed for mishaps at sea: Charleston fishermen fault themselves for unfortunate occurrences like losing fingers to equipment, and they explain disasters like losing boats and lives as the mistakes of the human beings involved and their lack, or the momentary lapsing, of technological control.

Boat upkeep functions not only as an art form through which the individual fisherman can sublimate personal anxieties and fears about his work, but it also operates rather like Malinowski says magic does for the Trobriand Islanders in building their most elaborate, seagoing canoes:

> . . . magic clearly puts order and sequence into the various activities, and . . . it and its associated ceremonial are instrumental in securing the co-operation of the community, and the organisation of communal labour. . . . it inspires the builders with great confidence in the efficiency of their work, a mental state essential in any enterprise of complicated and difficult character. . . .
>
> Magic, far from being a useless appendage, or even a burden on the work, supplies the psychological influence, which keeps people confident about the success of their labour. . . .[9]

By following a "ritual" of boat care prescribed and practiced "religiously" by the great diversity of individuals engaged in maritime occupations and ministered in its most esoteric aspects by highly respected specialists (shaman), the fisherman gains confidence, obtains the approval and help of others, and affirms community and his membership in it. Indeed, while alterations prove divisive as a fisherman uses them to better his odds against others, state his opinions, align himself with some individuals and take a stand against others (specialists in particular), maintenance and repair routines serve to unite in confirming among peers commonly followed procedures and in requiring cooperation across groups as the fisherman defers to shoreside experts, acknowledges his debts to them for the complicated equipment he uses, and thereby gains their continued support in making fishing boats suitable for their many uses.

Basically, boat upkeep offers optimistic, psychologically sound ways through art and magic for the individual to maintain both his mental well-being and his social support system in a very risky activity. Moreover, the collective nature of this cultivation of rational methods for coping with the unknown fosters "attitudes" that are perhaps as essential as they are endemic to maritime groups: a strong community, a willingness to confront the irrational, and a confidence that the unknown can become known. Without these attitudes and a system that supports them, the would-be mariner might never get beyond the shoreline, or stepping beyond it, might not survive psychologically or physically as well as could be.

Not unlike the inextricability of rational and irrational folk medicine, what some would call the secondary and optional functions of boat upkeep, "far from being a useless appendage, or even a burden on the work," ensure that the primary or more utilitarian functions will be met.[10] In this respect, I suggest that the expressive dimensions of what Abrahams calls "material folklore," while operating in a less obvious fashion than the basic utilitarian ones, are no less important or utilitarian themselves in shaping objects.[11] (Indeed, one might argue that American folklorists and cultural geographers, in stressing the role of the overtly utilitarian artifact as a mediator between the individual and nature, have accordingly restricted most explanations of form to that function alone.)

In view of the importance of maintaining one's social support system but also of asserting one's independence from it in order to go to sea, group politics and the persuasive powers of individuals perceived to be successful or otherwise worthy of emulation can promote the acceptance and perpetuation of ideas—in existing as well as new boats—that are not necessarily functional or utilitarian in the usual sense. In maritime communities in particular, these factors may well underlie the retention of much archaic fishing technology as well as the quick acceptance of an idiosyncratic or revolutionary idea.

For example, in Charleston's case, one has to ask why boats built anew locally to be extremely efficient fishing tools well suited to local oceanographic conditions basically did not work. Fred Anderson, for instance, sought to give form to a technologically ideal bottomfishing trawler for the Charleston area, bolstered by his financial success as a fisherman, the spirit of optimism that prevailed in the port during the 1960s and 1970s, and the encouragement of two local shipbuilders who clearly wished to experiment with the latest in steel fishboat design and bring the local fishing fleet "up" to current Seattle standards. Ultimately, however, Anderson's boats, which in their capacities as fishing machines appealed to a lot of local fishermen, proved the unrealistic products of a boom-time mentality—an unusual period where the fisherman could work free of the usual constrictions and actually articulate the dream boat of the moment. Anderson had to take the boats to fish areas where he got many of his ideas in the first place. The local shipyards, which could support only occasional production of such boats in the best of times, collapsed in the worst of times, overextended with too many contracts and not enough financial wizardry. Clearly Anderson's boats did not meet greater economic and ecological requirements. The cost of the new and large-size tool proved prohibitive due to the limitations of local markets and the resource, but as well, not to be overlooked, due to the numbers of people who by long-term commitment and proven ability to earn a living from fishing had an equal right to exploit the resource. Anderson's boats needed a richer resource base, more aggressive marketers, and fewer community-imposed limits, so that their full use would not threaten the abilities of colleagues to make at least modest livings.

Nevertheless, because of Anderson's fishing success, his standing in the fishing community, and the high visibility of having new boats built, his example served to reshape the ideology of probably every fisherman in port, prompting each to reevaluate existing structures, think about their dream machines more optimistically, and ultimately, to reform concepts of what works. Particularly within his own coterie of bottomfishermen, Anderson encouraged the acceptability and adoption of steel boats, larger boats, more and greater fishing equipment (including larger nets of polyester web) demanding ever more complex installations and more powerful horsepowers, and fancier, more commodious accommodations. His experience of having to take his boats elsewhere to fish also had an impact, reconfirming the habits of those who held to other, more conservative strategies with boats and equipment, and compelling some who emulated Anderson's example but sought to remain in Charleston to rework their ideals further and fall back on secondhand or smaller boats with less elaborate outfits.

Further, while Charleston fishermen touted Wilbur Humbert's wooden fishing boats as near to perfect articulations of the ideal local fishboat, very few mainstream fishermen in fact owned one. Rather, part-timers with stabler sources of nonfishing income tended to acquire them, being better able to afford the price of a new boat or of a highly desirable but costly used one. While "perfection" in physical form was available, fishermen opted instead for what may have seemed less ideal working tools that overtly satisfied their pockets but that less obviously substantiated the customs of the local fishing community.

While Humbert was eloquent in the articulation of an ecologically appropriate boat for the local crab-salmon/tuna fisherman — and folklorists would seize him as the perfect example of a folk artisan producing artifacts of best fit to function — the cost of his boats were prohibitive for the kind of fisherman he addressed. In a way, his boats were good resolutions to past, not current, problems. Had he approached the emerging bottomfisher constituencies instead, he may have entertained a more thriving business. But other factors played important parts in the apparent lack of support that fishermen gave the old man for his "new-work." Demoralized about the availability of suitable materials and therefore his ability to build the kind of boat he wished, capricious in the production of boats, Humbert encouraged neither his sons' interests in perpetuating the boatbuilding business nor the potential client's confidence that he could convince the old codger to build a new boat. As an important figure in the maritime occupational community, Humbert used his persuasive powers in a negative way, in fact discouraging the building of new boats well articulated for local circumstances, yet simultaneously, and perhaps unwittingly, encouraging and responding all along to fisher-based boat modification practices. Indeed, fishermen relied strongly upon Mr. Humbert as an instructor and "priest" to educate them about boats and to supervise and approve maintenance, repair, and alterations of boats not of his manufacture. They seemed to find comfort in the availability of his knowledge and the presence of boats which they could use as models towards which to work, against which to compete, or with which to compare their own boat work and the work of others. If they could not own one of Humbert's boats, at least they could internalize the principles that made them such exceptional works of art, and project them as well as they could, but of course idiosyncratically and circumstantially, on to existing and future boats.

The study of artifacts "alive" in context, with the people who use them available for comment and observation, allows us to witness their "design climate" in all its complexity and to seek a full range of explanations for the shapes of things. In particular, this kind of investigation gives us access to the individual, "the unit which through its life establishes society and creates and represents culture."[12] With such recourse, we can see how the individual cultivates certain design features and practices affecting design with respect to friends, colleagues, family members, and other significant individuals. We can observe more clearly how the individual gives visual expression not only to important, self-conscious associations with others, but also to a philosophy of life and work that represents a unique and ongoing interpretation of all the forces in the person's life. We can look at boats in a port or buildings on the land as concrete statements of specific interactions between certain individuals. We can thus group artifacts according to human networks and contemplate a variety of strategies that give rise to variant physical expressions and divergent design directions within the same community. While the individual in association with others allows us to see, within a group, a number of often conflicting orientations to the same artifacts, the individual through word and deed also gives us a glimpse of the dilemmas he finds in his own mind between forms as he would like to see them and forms as they must be given present circumstances—a conversation of ideas to which he gives varied and perhaps conflicting expression throughout his life. Thus, as folklorists, perhaps we can learn to cope with whole "communities" of artifacts that are diverse in forms, similar in functions, experimental one and all whether new or old, and subject to constant reinterpretation.

Background on the Eleven Fishermen

Fred Anderson

Fred Anderson was born May 11, 1927, in Portland, Oregon, to a nonfishing family. He does not remember quite when he and his family moved to Alaska, but when he was about 17 he started fishing off Alaska, first halibut fishing (longlining probably), then purse seining. In 1948 he moved to Eureka, California, and started dragging, and he has been dragging pretty steadily ever since. At first he dragged in the summer and fished crabs the rest of the year. In fact he came to Charleston in 1953 because the crab fishing was a little better there than it was in Eureka. For the first three years in Charleston, however, he fished salmon instead of bottomfish in the summer.

Until the mid-1960s, he either worked on someone else's boat, or he leased one:

> . . . at that time financing on a fishboat was very, very hard . . . . the banks wouldn't loan you any money, or it was just hard to finance a boat, it was hard to save up enough money when you're raising a family. And so it took all that time before I finally got enough money to buy the *Trego*. . . . I could get into it pretty reasonable, and the guy that owned it was a guy I've known for a long time, and he wanted out of the boat, he was tired of fishing or something, a local fellow here . . . and he let me into the boat pretty easy, and I only had ten thousand dollars. He let me have the boat for five thousand dollars down, and I put drag gear on it and went fishing, and he made the payments so that we'd have no problem making it, you know.

Four years later, Anderson began having new boats built for him at Hillstrom's.

Cecil Crockett

Cecil Crockett was born in Salem, Oregon, in 1937, a fifth-generation Oregonian. When he was eight years old he started fishing with his father, who had quit working as a painter in Portland, Oregon, shipyards (1942–45) to follow his uncles (Cecil's great uncles, the Littles) to Charleston to fish. Cecil fished with his father summers, weekends, vacations, and even during school until he was 17. He married when he was 18 and "moved to town" (Coos Bay) for four to five years where he worked at Safeway (a West Coast grocery store chain). Then he returned to commercial fishing. For four years he worked for one of his uncles, fishing salmon, crab, then shrimp. Then he went to work for Oscar Hanson, a veteran fisherman and second-generation Norwegian born in Ballard (Seattle) whose father had fished salmon during summers and made shoes during the winter. For two years Crockett worked on Hanson's 70-foot halibut schooner — which had been converted for dragging — until Hanson took it to Alaska. For another two and a half years, Cecil ran a purse seiner — converted for dragging — for Hanson until the boat sank on the Coos Bay bar in January

1969. And for six more years he worked another halibut schooner—converted for dragging—for Hanson, until he could buy his own boat, the *Lou-R*.

Charlie Ells

Charlie Ells was born June 15, 1909, of Scotch-Irish descent, in Bellingham, Washington. No family members preceded him in the fishing business, but he began fishing in Seattle in 1934–35 during the Depression, when it seemed to him fishing was "all there was to do that made any sense." For the next several years he worked as a puller on several boats out of Seattle and California ports, including sardine boats out of Monterey. In 1939 he bought the *Amak*.

Floyd Green

Floyd Green was born in Portland, Oregon, December 10, 1926. His family moved to Coquille (25 miles inland from Coos Bay on the Coquille River) in 1932, and his father began fishing in 1934. His grandfather, a shipwright in Portland, Oregon, originally from North Carolina, soon joined them and opened a short-lived boatbuilding shop in Charleston. One of Floyd's uncles also fished out of Charleston for many years. As a youngster, Floyd started fishing with his father, baiting boxes for him when he fished crabs, and later trip fishing with him during summers for tuna and salmon, from San Francisco to the Queen Charlotte Islands. When he got out of high school, he went to college for a year, but since he did not know what he wanted to do there, he quit. About then he got married. Feeling like he had to get to work earning a living, he continued fishing with his father during summers and got other kinds of work during off-seasons. In 1951 he finally bought his own boat; but soon he sold it to move to Eugene to work year-round for a firm for which he had been working during off-seasons. He rose in the ranks there, but not finding Eugene to his liking, he transferred to Port Orford. There he bought another boat; then he bought his present boat in 1955, when he could go to year-round, full-time fishing. For a while during the '50s he worked as a crab puller for Arnold Hockema, who found it ironic to have a subordinate whom he felt knew more about fishing than he did!

Leonard Hall

Leonard Hall was born October 6, 1907, to a nonfishing family in Seattle, where he lived in the University District. He did not get involved in fishing while he lived there, but, as he puts it:

> . . . up around Puget Sound, why practically all the halibut fleet's Norwegian. . . . I lived in Seattle long enough to know that Ballard is the capital of Norway. . . . I had a cousin who lived in the Ballard District, so I'd hike over there and visit him. All his neighbors were halibut fishermen.

Hall went through college in Seattle, then got work as a printer and linotype operator, and during the Depression started his own newspaper in Jacksonville, Oregon, moving eventually to Ashland, Oregon. And then:

> Went down to the coast with a friend of mine up at Chetco, and one day sport fishing, first time I'd ever had a sport rod in my hand, I caught a 40-pound chinook. So I started really paying attention then. And I found out that people were making a living on the ocean. I liked the water, so, and someone wanted the newspaper worse than I did.

In 1940 Hall sold his newspaper, moved to Charleston, bought a boat, and started fishing commercially:

> Funny thing was, well, my wife's brother had a salmon and tuna boat before I got into it, and we went up to Astoria one time and went out with him . . . at Newport. I'd been on Puget Sound but I'd never been on the ocean before, and after I got out on the ocean I just had the feeling I'd been there before, first time. So there's a little Norwegian blood back in the family there somewhere. It surfaced then.

Jake Harlan

Jake Harlan was born a third-generation Oregonian near Newport; his grandfather had homesteaded along the Siletz River. While fishing was not "in the family," Harlan began commercial fishing in the early 1950s out of Newport, when he was 17 and still in high school. At first he only worked summers, trolling for other people until he could afford to buy a small troller of his own, first a 26-footer, and later a 32-footer. Since salmon fishing was not doing too well back then, and since he got married and started a family, he quit fishing for 12 years to raise his family. During this period he did some logging and worked at sawmills as a sawyer, mostly in the Coos Bay area. He says he had all kinds of jobs, but he did not like the 40-hour week, and with his temper, he had gotten mad on the job several times and quit. So he returned to fishing in 1963, out of Coos Bay, working for an old-timer, fishing crab and shrimp. Several years later he bought his own boat, a 64-foot wooden dragger. He began bottomfishing with it in 1971 because "there were too many bozos getting into the shrimp business." Then in 1973 he bought the *Puget*.

Carl Harrington

Born June 14, 1937, Carl Harrington grew up in Corvallis, Eugene, and Coos Bay. His father was a logger and moved with his jobs. Carl fished occasionally during summers for relatives when he was still in high school; an uncle and a grandfather were both fishermen, and his grandfather was a Norwegian who had come from the Old Country. After high school, Carl tried logging and millwork, but he did not like either, so he began fishing for his uncle in 1959 out of Coos Bay. He subsequently worked for one of the local old-time fishermen (Virginia Walker's father, Dusty Rhoades), and owned several salmon trollers one after another, including the boat which Cyrus Little, Sr., had built for himself in 1942 and sold in 1948.

Arnold Hockema

Arnold Hockema was born in Myrtle Point, Oregon (35 miles inland from Coos Bay on the Coquille River), November 2, 1919. He was raised on a farm in the area, and then he moved with his family to the Alsea River area (Waldport) to farm. There he logged, before and after World War II, forming a cooperative with his father and brother. When he was still in the service in 1945, he married Doris Walker, Norman Walker's sister. Norman was not yet working full-time for Doris's father, when her brother Frank, then working with her father on the *Rambler* out of Coos Bay, was killed in a car accident. So Arnold started fishing with Doris's father to replace Frank, and in 1947–48, Doris and Arnold moved to Charleston. Arnold worked for Doris's father for three or four years, and then bought his first boat, the salmon troller *Cleora*, in 1953–54. He sold the boat six years later for the *Elaine Dell* because he needed a larger one.

Dick Lilienthal

Dick Lilienthal was born in North Bend, December 10, 1928, and he has lived in the Coos Bay area ever since:

> One of my first cradles was a net boat, too, believe it or not. Mom and Dad used to take me fishing in the gillnetter . . . . That sounds silly, but they did. . . . they ran a big ranch, Dad did, and then they gillnetted when the fish were running. And then the hired man had enough work to do, so they just took me in the boat with them.
>
> The family had a big ranch in Minnesota, and they came here and then they fished in the river for part of their living, logging and fishing both . . . . In fact . . . they built a boat here and took it down to Eureka and Gold Beach, and they panned gold at Gold Beach, and fished down there, crabbed and fished salmon . . . before the First World War.
>
> But in the thirties, Dad would work in the mill, you know, in the winter. And then we'd come down here [Charleston] and rent a cabin . . . and we'd spend the summer down here. Then he'd go back to the mill, move back to our other house in the wintertime again. And then we built right next door here, in '36. We moved down here permanently. . . . He fished salmon and ringed in the bay for crabs, and he had a few crab pots. He was partners with Ed Brown, Gordon Brown's dad. . . .
>
> We had an old converted Coast Guard boat, a life boat, and converted [it] into a troller. And they seined, they had a big beach seine. . . . Gordon and I used to go out with Dad and Ed and learned how to work the gear and get seasick at the same time. . . . I got seasick the first 26 times I went out, took me 'til the 27th time before I finally had it. Believe it or not. . . . Course that old boat was a old two-cylinder gas engine and it was pretty stinking. I could just walk up to it on the dock and get sick, pretty near, just from the smell of it. In fact, Gordon could get sick in the bay on it if we shut the doors.
>
> But then Dad bought Ed out when I was about 10 or 11, and Ed went and worked at the mill 'cause it was steadier, and then I worked with Dad in the summer, starting when I was 11 or 12. In fact, I made a thousand dollars the summer I graduated from grade school, which was a lot of money in those days. . . . We were saving and I put it into the, we were saving to buy a bigger boat, and I bought a 22-foot seine boat and Dad bought the net, and then we went beach-seining and everything. I fished anything I could catch. . . . We could sell anything we caught in the bay. . . . Anything we caught in the bay was legal in those days, and we filleted it, and most of it went to Hawaii. . . .
>
> But then we fished those two boats until I was 18, and then we got the big boat built at Hillstrom's. . . . we sold the troller after we got the big boat going, and my Dad, my brother, and I all worked on the bigger boat, starting in '46. We fished tuna mostly the first year, tuna and crabs. And then we put the drag gear on in '48. Hallmarks wanted to try filleting, so Dad bought a winch and doors and net, we rigged up our drag gear, and we learned how not to do that, we set the net on the rocks first time, tore a great big hole in it. . . . Hallmarks couldn't sell the stuff, so we went back to crabbing and salmon fishing. And then we got a bunch of mink ranchers called us up and wanted fish. . . . we were fishing for six mink ranchers in 1950. . . . and then we filleted what we could ourselves. There was no market for filleted fish here locally. . . . We did that for six years. . . . and then we messed around with shrimp a little bit. . . . for three or four years . . . we were the only boat out there, fishing shrimp. . . . then another boat came up and there was just the two of us, and then a couple more started in it. For a few years it was just four or five, and now there's forty . . . there's lots of people now. I get about so much [shrimp], and then I put on the bottomfishing gear and go off where you get off by yourself, get some peace and quiet for a while. . . .
>
> But over the years we've fished just about every kind of fish in the ocean and the bay and

sold 'em, even bullheads. Seriously, we sold the bullheads out of the seine to a mink ranch. . . . We tried fishing shark a little bit, longlining, gillnetting, beach-seining, we even had set lines in the bay when I was a boy, did real good at it, too. Tried everything.

Cyrus Little, Sr.

Cyrus Little, Sr., was 78 years old when I spoke with him in April 1978. He was born in Salem, Oregon, a third-generation Oregonian, whose family had not been involved in commercial fishing. Cyrus got his first job at the age of eight milking cows at a dairy farm. He quit school when he did not see much point in continuing. Around the beginning of World War I when he was eighteen, he got a job at a sporting goods store in Salem where he was a locksmith who also repaired guns and umbrellas. After three years at the store, he began trucking logs and lumber; he worked the next fifteen years at sawmills. The Depression found him running his own mill, but because of the times, he was forced to close down. He then followed one of his brothers to Waldport on the coast and began fishing in the bay, gillnetting for salmon, ringing for crabs, and selling to a local plant. In November 1941 he followed his elder brother to Charleston and seriously began his commercial fishing career.

Norman Walker

Norman Walker was born in Waldport, Oregon, September 23, 1925. His family had moved from Creswell, Oregon, to Waldport in 1902, where they fished from a small boat in the Alsea Bay in the early days. Norman's father did not start fishing for real, however, until he moved to Charleston in 1940. In 1940, Hallmarks, who had been keeping an eye out for a good fishboat for Norman's father, located what seemed to be a good deal. Walker came down to Charleston to try it out, bought the *Rambler* for $4,000, and took up fishing for crab and salmon, longlining and netting for sharks during the war. Norman began helping his father fish on weekends and during summers while he was still in high school (1941–43) and before he joined the service. Out of the service in 1946, he then began fishing steadily with his father, buying his own boat in 1951. Also in 1946, Norman married Virginia Rhoades, whose father had taken up commercial fishing when the family had moved to Coos Bay in the mid-1930s; Norman helped Virginia's father fish off and on during the 1950s and 1960s.

Descriptive Data on Eleven Fishboats

The following boat descriptions have been compiled from information culled from the U.S. Coast Guard's annual publication of *Merchant Vessels of the United States* (see chap. 3, n. 28); from boat abstracts available to the public at the U.S. Coast Guard Marine Safety Detachment Office in Coos Bay (see Introduction, n. 8); from my photographs (figs. 46, 56–59, 61, 63, 65, 67, 69, 71, 72), boat tours, and observations (see chap. 3, n. 2); and from information supplied by the boat owners.

The *Oregon, Rambler*, and *M. S. Electron* are medium-size, older crabber-trollers built during the 1920s and 1930s. The *Oregon* and *Rambler* were built to be salmon trollers; they are presently used for crabbing and trolling for both salmon and tuna. The *Electron* was not primarily intended for fishing, but she was built along fishboat lines; she was converted first for salmon trolling (1942?) and later for crabbing as well (1946).

The *Oregon* (figs. 64, 65)

Master Carpenter: Matt Tolonen.
Place Built: Columbia River Boat Shop, Astoria, Oregon.
Date Completed: 1926.
Material: Wood—oak frame and white cedar planking.
Shape: Double-ended, Finnish style (see chap. 3).
Plan: Engine sits amidships in its own compartment directly aft of the house. Both quarters and galley are in the fo'c'sle, and passage to them is through the forward part of the house and not the engine compartment.
Measurements: 37 feet, overall length
    33.3 feet, registered length
    9.6 feet, registered breadth
    4.3 feet, registered depth
    8 tons, gross
    6 tons, net
    110 horsepower (diesel)
Color Scheme: All white with black trim and additional turquoise trim on the house.

The *Rambler* (figs. 62, 63)

Master Carpenter: M. E. "Slim" Brown.
Place Built: North Bend, Oregon.
Date Completed: 1938.
Material: Wood—Port Orford cedar ribs and Douglas fir planking and decking.

Shape: Seems to be modeled somewhat after a Finnish double-ender, but the stern is finished off
   with a transom. Square stern; V bottom; bow stem is spooned and especially curved at
   forefoot; sheer is marked and graceful.
Plan: House sits forward of amidships with flying bridge on top. Galley on deck. Engine rests
   beneath galley. Quarters in fo'c'sle may be reached directly from house, not via engine room.
Measurements: 45 feet, overall length
                  39.9 feet, registered length
                  12.9 feet, registered breadth
                  5.9 feet, registered depth
                  21 tons, gross
                  16 tons, net
                  165 horsepower, diesel
Color Scheme: All white with black trim.

The *M. S. Electron* (figs. 60, 61)

Master Carpenter: G. E. Goudie.
Place Built: Seattle, Washington, in a "regular shipyard."
Date Completed: 1935.
Material: Wood—"1 5/8 fir."
Shape: Rounded tugboat stern; round bottom; vertical bow stem that angles slightly outward;
   graceful sheer. She is broad for her length and looks slightly tuggy.
Plan: House extends forward from just aft of amidships and looks large for the hull. Flying bridge
   sits on house top; galley on deck incorporated into house. Engine lies directly beneath galley.
Measurements: 40 feet, overall length
                  35.8 feet, registered length
                  10.7 feet, registered breadth
                  5.6 feet, registered depth
                  19 tons, gross
                  16 tons, net
                  80 horsepower (diesel)
Color Scheme: House and bulwarks, white; house and hull trim, dark red. Says Leonard Hall: ". . .
   the hull was always green, that was a mixed green. I've been using that for probably 12, 15
   years. Three quarts of rustoleum green and one quart of white, all stirred up together . . . the
   boat had a green hull when it was launched, and it's always been green. . . . Just kind of a sea
   foam green on the inside [of the cabin]."

The next three boats are medium- to large-size boats, all built during the 1940s and 1950s. The *Nel
Ron Dic* and *Maria E* were intended as combination boats to fish tuna, salmon, and crab; the *Nel
Ron Dic* has been used additionally to fish for shrimp and bottomfish, and the *Maria E* for shrimp.
The *Elaine Dell* was probably intended as a general purpose boat; she was first used for crab
fishing, and Arnold Hockema used her for shrimp, salmon, and tuna fishing as well.

The *Nel Ron Dic* (fig. 71)

Master Carpenter: J. W. Hillstrom, Sr.
Place Built: Hillstrom Shipbuilding Company, original North Bend, Oregon, location.
Date Completed: 1946.
Material: Wood—Douglas fir.

Shape: Low rounded stern; deep round bottom; high, slightly spooned bow stem; graceful
sheerline. Dick Lilienthal says, "the hull is more like a schooner type. And it's real deep and
narrower than it should be."

Plan: House sits over engine well forward of amidships. Flying bridge is on top of house. Galley
extends aft of house to amidships. Quarters in fo'c'sle are reached through engine room.

Measurements: 56.8 feet, overall length
               51.6 feet, registered length
               14.5 feet, registered breadth
                6.3 feet, registered depth
                 31 tons, gross
                 18 tons, net
                200 horsepower (diesel)

Color Scheme: All white with black and dark blue trim.

The *Maria E* (figs. 58, 59)

Master Carpenter: Richard T. Boyles.
Place Built: Winchester Bay, Oregon.
Date Completed: 1948.
Material: Wood—Douglas fir throughout.
Shape: Square stern, very flat rectangular transom, V bottom.
Plan: House sits forward of amidships with flying bridge on top. Galley is on deck just aft of house.
Engine rests below galley floor. Quarters are in fo'c'sle and are reached through engine room.

Measurements: 50.5 feet, overall length
               45.7 feet, registered length
               14.2 feet, registered breadth
                6.3 feet, registered depth
                 27 tons, gross
                 13 tons, net
                225 horsepower (diesel)

Color Scheme: Hull, dark green with black trim; bulwarks and house, white with green trim.
Author's note: According to Paul Heikkila, August 1, 1985, the *Maria E* sank in 1981 with the loss
of four lives including a Coast Guardsman.

The *Elaine Dell* (figs. 67, 74)

Master Carpenter: Swin Carpenter.
Place Built: Corvallis, Oregon.
Date Completed: 1958.
Material: Wood—red oak frames, Douglas fir planking.
Shape: Rounded stern, round bottom. High bow gives boat distinctive, marked forward curve to
sheer uncharacteristic of West Coast fishboats. Bow stem angles outward; it is tall and straight
except at the waterline where you can see the beginning of the forefoot curve.
Plan: House sits forward of amidships with galley on deck. Engine rests directly beneath galley.
Gear locker in bow is reached through wheelhouse, not engine room.

Measurements: 48 feet, overall length
               40.3 feet, registered length
               13.7 feet, registered breadth
                7.3 feet, registered depth

Figure 74.   Allocation of Space in the *Elaine Dell*.
Drawings by Tom Hockema, Arnold and Doris's eldest fisher-son (not to scale).

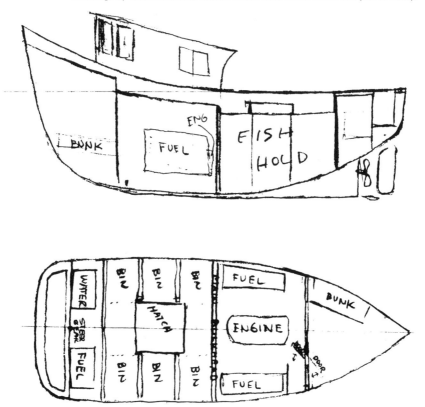

29 tons, gross
19 tons, net
187 horsepower (diesel)
Color Scheme: White with light grey trim, house and hull.

The remaining five boats are large-size boats quite variegated in ages and origins. All were used as draggers in 1977–78. The *Amak*, built as a cannery tender, and the *Kodiak*, built as a purse seiner, were used to fish bottomfish and shrimp. The *Puget*, built as a halibut schooner, and the *Lou-R*, built as a Coast Guard icebreaker, were used to fish only for bottomfish. The *Sleep Robber* was built as a bottomfisher and was used as such.

The *Amak* (fig. 69)

Master Carpenter: E. W. Heath.
Place Built: Seattle, Washington.
Date Completed: 1915.
Material: Wood—Douglas fir throughout.
Shape: Modeled on old-time halibut schooner—rounded fantail tugboat stern, round bottom, slightly spooned bow stem comparatively much taller than the stern, sheer slopes gracefully from stem to stern. Topsides lie closer to water in tender rather than schooner fashion.
Plan: House sits aft over engine on stern. Since 1940s, galley sits on deck just aft of house, and, says Charlie Ells: ". . . on this particular boat there's two holds, there's one aft, and then there's one forward of the house—one aft of the house, one forward of the house—and the engine room is right below the house. Then the fo'c'sle is right in the bow. . . . You have to go across the deck, the forward deck, and then down a hatch."
Measurements: 70 feet, overall length
65.2 feet, registered length
16.0 feet, registered breadth
6.6 feet, registered depth
47 tons, gross
37 tons, net
300 horsepower (diesel)
Color Scheme: Hull, dark grey with black trim; bulwarks and house, white with reddish brown trim; white horizontal stripe painted just above rub rail on each side of hull.

The *Kodiak* (fig. 57)

Master Carpenter: M. A. Petrich, probably a Yugoslavian (Dalmatian).
Place Built: Western Boat Building Company, Tacoma, Washington.
Date Completed: 1926.
Material: Wood—Douglas fir hull, Alaskan cedar house.
Shape: High, rounded stern; round bottom; bow stem tall and vertical; sheer rather flat and not as sweeping as other older boats like the *Oregon* and the *Amak*. Resembles some of older wooden Puget Sound schooner types, but seems bulkier in shape—lines are not as delicate.
Plan: House sits over engine forward of amidships. Flying bridge on top of house. Galley on deck attached to after end of house and extending aft to amidships. Quarters in fo'c'sle reached from engine room. Engine room reached from galley floor above.
Measurements: 70 feet, overall length
62.1 feet, registered length

16.1 feet, registered breadth
7.8 feet, registered depth
49 tons, gross
33 tons, net
275 horsepower (diesel)

Color Scheme: All white with black trim; light blue horizontal stripe on each side of hull above rub rail (cf. *Amak*).

The *Puget* (figs. 55, 56)

Master Carpenter: Edward E. Johnson.
Place Built: Tacoma, Washington.
Date Completed: 1928.
Material: Wood—oak, cedar, and fir.
Shape: Apparently takes after halibut schooner design—high, rounded stern; round bottom; high vertical bow stem; graceful sheer.
Plan: Small house sits just forward of amidships over engine and engine room unlike the *Amak*'s and old-time halibut schooner style. Galley still part of quarters in fo'c'sle, reached through engine room.
Measurements: (cf. *Nel Ron Dic*)
60 feet, overall length (approximate)
51.6 feet, registered length
14.8 feet, registered breadth
7.5 feet, registered depth
39 tons, gross
26 tons, net
300 horsepower (diesel)

Color Scheme: Hull, dark green; bulwarks and house, white; hull and house trim, black; white horizontal stripe above rub rail to each side of hull (cf. *Amak* and *Kodiak*).
Author's note: According to Jake Harlan, May 1, 1985: "In 1982 my vessel the *Puget*, which was under charter, was sunk with no loss of life. All the safety equipment worked like it was supposed to."

The *Lou-R* (figs. 55, 56)

Master Carpenter: Edsel E. Peacock.
Place Built: San Juan Island Shipyard, Friday Harbor, Washington.
Date Completed: 1968.
Material: Steel.
Shape: High rounded stern with stern ramp set into it; short (not deep) hull to run up on ice; probably hard-chine V bottom. Bow profile straight and angles slightly forward; lines angular and sheer flat and slightly sloping.
Plan: House sits well forward of amidships. Galley on deck extending aft of house to amidships.
Measurements: 62 feet, overall length
60.0 feet, registered length
18.9 feet, registered breadth
8.6 feet, registered depth
74 tons, gross

50 tons, net

330 horsepower (twin diesel)

Color Scheme: Hull, black; house, white with black trim.

Author's note: According to Doris Hockema, March 4, 1985, the *Lou-R* sank "a couple or three years ago, up the coast, off Astoria."

The *Sleep Robber* (figs. 46, 73; cf. fig. 72)

Master Carpenter: J. Wm. Hillstrom, Jr.

Place Built: Hillstrom Shipbuilding Company, Coos Bay, Oregon.

Date Completed: 1978.

Material: Steel.

Shape: Medium-height rounded square stern with stern ramp set into it; hard-chine V bottom. Bow profile flares outward some; sheer gentle and graceful.

Plan: House sits well forward of amidships, two stories high above deck. Top story contains wheelhouse, first story commodious living quarters and galley. Engine rests below deck under house in spacious area incorporating what would normally be fo'c'sle space and containing work bench and freezer besides engine components.

Measurements: 77.5 feet, overall length   (cf. *Betty A*)
                68.5 feet, registered length   (66.8)
                22.4 feet, registered breadth   (22.0)
                11.6 feet, registered depth   (10.3)
                144 tons, gross   (99)
                111 tons, net   (70)
                450 horsepower (diesel)   (350)

Color Scheme: Dark blue set off with orange trim, house and hull.

Notes

Introduction

1. Stephen Dow Beckham, *Coos Bay: The Pioneer Period 1851–1890*.

2. Members of the Society for the Survey of North American Culture, personal communication.

3. Jim Wright, Susie Nevill, June Grussendorf, Joan Baker, Kelly Coughlin, Ruth Schellbach, and Robin McManamin made an inspiring lot of observations from their sometimes difficult ventures into the field.

4. Burley Young, a student in the 1974 spring program who subsequently got work on a crab boat and is currently fishing his own boat, pointed out and explained local fishing gear types. Bruce Cunningham, of the 1975 program, observed varied adaptations of a particular Coast Guard life boat hull for commercial fishing. Joe Parker, of the 1976 program, investigated the kinds of materials and related construction techniques used in fishboat building, and discovered a variety of opinions among builders and fishers justifying one material over another.

5. His project, "Every Boatbuilder and Every Fisherman is Biased Toward His Own Material," is available for reference at the Oregon Institute of Marine Biology, filed with the spring 1976 projects.

6. Interview with Paul Heikkila, Coquille, Oregon, September 20, 1976; David S. Liao and Joe B. Stevens, *Oregon's Commercial Fishermen*.

7. Letter from Darrell Demory, Department of Fish and Wildlife biologist, Newport, Oregon, January 13, 1977, in which he enclosed a table listing crab boats that had worked out of Charleston from 1952 through 1972. Mike Hosie, Department of Fish and Wildlife biologist, Charleston, made available lists of "Vessels Landing Groundfish and Shrimp in Oregon by Port by Fishery," printed in the "Otter Trawl Investigative Progress Report," "Trawl Investigation Progress Report," "Otter Trawl Investigations, Annual Report," and "Groundfish and Shrimp Investigations, Annual Report," as it is variously titled, and published "annually" since 1956 by the Oregon Fish Commission Research Division, termed since 1975, The Oregon Department of Fish and Wildlife Marine Region. Gerald Lukas, Department of Fish and Wildlife biologist, Newport, sent me advance lists of the more recent statistics as they were prepared for publication.

8. Current names, addresses, and phone numbers of the owner-operators of most of these boats were available in the Charleston Boat Basin office. Additional information regarding each boat — the master carpenter who built the boat or supervised its construction, the person

who originally requisitioned the construction, the year when and the place where the boat was built, the kind of engine that propels the boat, the hull material, changes in the boat name if any, and changes in ownership and financing through the years—could be had from the "abstract of the bill of sale" filed at the Coos Bay Marine Safety Detachment Office of the U.S. Coast Guard. The office maintains abstracts for all vessels measuring five net tons or more that work between Newport, Oregon, and Eureka, California. Fuller records exist, often including plans drawn to calculate federal measurements, but they are either confidential or inaccessibly located in federal depositories such as the Sand Point facility in Seattle, Washington.

9. Only seven of the fishermen I interviewed were actually fishing the boats with which they were associated on my list. Three had just retired—two had turned their boats over to their sons and continued to help them occasionally; the third had sold his boat, but continued to help his sons who each owned a boat. During the course of my study, the set of brothers sold their boat—one then began working for one of the other fishermen I interviewed; the other allegedly was having a new fiberglass boat built. Another fisherman, who had previously worked the boat these brothers sold, was sitting the year out while he waited for his new steel boat to be built, while a co-owner-operator was fishing his boat in Alaskan waters to help pay off the expenses they were incurring in building the new boat. Meanwhile another one of my informants was trying to sell his steel boat so he could buy an older wooden boat. And in the meantime, one boat on my main list, and another on an auxiliary list, sank. During the time that has transpired since the interviews and the publication of this account, another fisherman has retired, selling his boat to an outport client; two others have procured new second-hand boats, selling their former boats, one to an outport client; another, still based in Coos Bay, now fishes his boat in the Bering Sea for a firm engaging in joint U.S.–foreign fleet fishing; and another has temporarily abandoned fishing for other fisheries-related work in another port. Three of the boats that led me to fishermen have sunk not while under the respective skipper's command; and a related boat has been lost to the bank. Only five of the eleven boats remain in the hands of the same skippers as they did in 1978. This kind of flux is fairly standard in the Coos Bay fishing industry.

10. Many Charleston fishermen rendezvous in eastern Oregon at "Little Charleston," so named because so many people from Charleston converge at the spot to hunt during the season. This "hunting break" habit supports the connection often made between fishing and hunting. See, for example, Raoul Andersen, "Hunt and Deceive," p. 131, n. 13; and Raoul Andersen and Cato Wadel, "Comparative Problems in Fishing Adaptations," pp. 153–54.

11. Richard Wilhelm, trans., *The I Ching or Book of Changes*, pp. 689–90.

12. Boat studies typically start (and end) with boat form(s) as the focus. The boat is generally viewed rather like a racing car, as a very specific form that has evolved to fulfill one very specific task. The methods of constructing the boat and the materials used are of preeminent concern; the builder is of interest mainly insofar as he can demonstrate and explain the technology. The works of Howard I. Chapelle and the revivalist builders who he has so inspired are especially of this nature, for example: his *American Small Sailing Craft*, "Migrations of an American Boat Type," and *Boatbuilding*; The Apprenticeshop, *Norse Boat Building in North America*; and Tom Beard, *The Poulsbo Boat*. Edwin Tappan Adney (the original materials upon which *The Bark Canoes and Skin Boats of North America* is based) and James Hornell (*Water Transport*) went further with their preponderantly historic-geographic work in proposing cultural affinities among widely dispersed groups of people on the basis of shared boat forms and construction techniques. Cultural geographers such as Malcolm Comeaux, John Earnest Damron, and William P. Knipmeyer have greatly

improved upon the specification of the social context of the boat in their studies of boat types within fairly well-defined regions. But still, as in most boat studies, the social context, all of the people involved with the boat, as well as boat form and construction techniques are treated in a highly generalized, "generic" way. Folklorists like C. Richard K. Lunt, David A. Taylor, and Paula Johnson, and maritime archaeologists like Basil Greenhill have concentrated as much on individual builders, idiosyncracies of their creations and technique, and the expressive use of traditional ideas, as on the traditional nature of boat form and construction; they often pay attention to users and client-craftsman relationships again in a rather generic way as they influence the shape a particular builder's boat takes. By starting with water-oriented people as the focus, Raymond Firth (*Malay Fishermen*) and Bronislaw Malinowski (*Argonauts of the Western Pacific*) have produced insightful studies of boats that deal successfully with the human experience of the boat and social relations that revolve around it, in addition to some of the more taxonomic and technical aspects.

13. What Iain A. Crawford says of fishing culture in Scotland in "The Tidal Fishing Pound," p. 111, very likely applies to fishing communities everywhere:

> Fishing has been the basis, clearly, of local economy in much of Scotland from the neolithic period until the present and as man's exploitation of the sea's resources is still virtually at the "hunter-fisher" stage, there is a high degree of conservatism causing the retention of much archaic technology, either still in evidence, or at least surviving in oral tradition.

Ole Crumlin-Pedersen substantiates this idea referring to the antiquity of forms and constructions of boats built, and "terminology connected with the process of building and the individual parts of the boat . . ." used, at some West Norway yards today in "Skin or Wood? A Study of the Origin of the Scandinavian Plank Boat," p. 221. Henry Glassie in his introduction to William P. Knipmeyer's "Folk Boats of Eastern French Louisiana," p. 105, Béla Gunda in his introduction to *The Fishing Culture of the World*, p. 18, and Malcolm Comeaux in "Origin and Evolution of Mississippi River Craft," p. 73, also refer to the conservative retention of cultural elements among fishing peoples.

14. Interview with Richard and Verna Lilienthal, Charleston, September 20, 1977. Andersen, "Hunt and Deceive," and "Those Fisherman Lies"; R. Geoffrey Stiles, "Fishermen, Wives and Radios," pp. 42, 46–51; and Michael K. Orbach, *Hunters, Seamen, and Entrepreneurs*, pp. 104–31.

15. Interview with Charles C. and Jessie Ells, Port Orford, February 6, 1978.

16. Ibid., and interviews in Charleston with Fred Anderson, August 24, 1977; Leonard Hall, July 27, 1977; Jake Harlan, September 1, 1977; Arnold and Doris Hockema, March 7, 1978; and Richard and Verna Lilienthal, September 20, 1977. Visit, accompanying Jens Lund, with one of his stellar Ohio Valley fisher informants, Orval Loven, Grayville, Illinois, October 30, 1977.

17. Béla Gunda, *The Fishing Culture of the World*, pp. 15, 18, for starters.

18. Most anthropological, sociological, psychological, and medical research dwells on fishermen (and seamen in general) in this context. See, for example, Leif C. W. Landberg, comp., *A Bibliography for the Anthropological Study of Fishing Industries and Maritime Communities*, particularly pp. 48–52 and 56–74. More specifically, see Joseba Zulaika, *Terranova*; Bernard H. Russell, "Greek Sponge Boats in Florida"; Jeremy Tunstall, *The Fishermen*; as well as Orbach, *Hunters, Seamen, and Entrepreneurs*, and Stiles, "Fishermen, Wives, and Radios."

19. Cf. David Maurer, "Speech Peculiarities of the North Atlantic Fishermen;" Orbach, *Hunters, Seamen, and Entrepreneurs*, throughout pp. 36–131; Stiles, "Fishermen, Wives, and Radios," p. 54; and Horace Beck, *Folklore and the Sea*, p. 58 ff. On the whole, however, most on-board communication is probably nonverbal; see Orbach, pp. 219–36.

20. See Orbach, *Hunters, Seamen, and Entrepreneurs*, pp. 271–88; Tunstall, *The Fishermen*, pp. 135–75; Zulaika, *Terranova*, pp. 33–64; and Andersen and Wadel, "Comparative Problems in Fishing Adaptations," pp. 144–45.

21. Cf. Stewart F. Sanderson, "The Tweed Salmon Coble," p. 279–80; Basil Greenhill, *The Archaeology of the Boat*, p. 38; and in a general way, Willy Elmer, *The Terminology of Fishing*.

22. Linda Dégh and Andrew Vázsonyi, "The Hypothesis of Multi-Conduit Transmission in Folklore," pp. 211–15.

Chapter 1

1. Interview with Coos County Marine Extension Agent Paul Heikkila, Coquille, Oregon, September 20, 1976.

2. See John J. Poggie, Jr., and Carl Gersuny, *Fishermen of Galilee*, p. 7.

3. James M. Acheson, "Technical Skills and Fishing Success in the Maine Lobster Industry," pp. 111–12, points out that in spite of a growing anthropological literature on North Atlantic and Pacific fishermen and fishing traditions, there is a dearth of scholarly publications regarding the technological expertise of fishermen.

4. For example, see Jens Lund, "Fishing as a Folk Occupation in the Lower Ohio Valley"; the North Carolina skiff builder and the part-time Norwegian farmer and pram builder in Basil Greenhill, *The Archaeology of the Boat*, pp. 34–37, 48–50; Lawrence Sommers, "Commercial Fishing in Norway," p. 237; and Robert H. Squires, "The Fisheries Training Programme of Newfoundland," p. 79.

5. For examples of fishing ships and highly specialized fishermen, see Raoul Andersen, "Hunt and Deceive," p. 132; Virgil J. Norton and Morton M. Miller, *An Economic Study of the Boston Large-Trawler Labor Force*, p. 6; Michael K. Orbach, *Hunters, Seamen, and Entrepreneurs*, pp. 14–21, 27, for starters; Jeremy Tunstall, *The Fishermen*, pp. 45–47, 119–29; William W. Warner, *Distant Water*; and Joseba Zulaika, *Terranova*, pp. 1–32.

6. Cf. James M. Acheson, "Fisheries Management and Social Context," p. 663.

7. John Earnest Damron, "The Emergence of Salmon Trolling on the American Northwest Coast," especially pp. 6–7, 28–33, 122; and personal communication, March 6, 1982: My second cousin, Peter Knutson—a gillnet fisherman based in Seattle who fishes off the southeastern Alaska coast, and a doctoral candidate in the Department of Anthropology at the University of Washington completing a dissertation regarding a mutiny on a Puget Sound purse seiner working Alaskan waters—claims that Norwegian fishermen in the Puget Sound-Alaskan areas are typically known to be fiercely independent, competitive, solitary workers, in contrast to the other predominant ethnic force in the fisheries, Yugoslavs who dominate purse seining operations and work more cooperatively between boats and within fairly large (family) crews. See Wilbur Zelinsky, *The Cultural Geography of the United States*, pp. 13–14, for an explanation of the "Doctrine of First Effective Settlement."

8. Or, in McCarl's terms, he begins to demonstrate the "technique" or "working knowledge" of the "work group." Cf. Robert S. McCarl, "Occupational Folklife," pp. 5–7. Also with respect

to McCarl (p. 6, his quote of Carl B. Kaufmann), I use the term "technical skills" in a narrow sense, ". . . to signify . . . the things that a man can do with his hands . . ."

9. Cf. David A. Taylor's application of Christopher Alexander's subsystem concept to traditional boatbuilding and the evolution of boat form in *Boat Building in Winterton, Trinity Bay, Newfoundland*, pp. 120, 126 especially.

10. Cf. Ibid., especially "Performance Correlatives," pp. 114–19, and "Timber Placement and Other Measurement Formulas," pp. 106–14.

11. See Ibid., p. 106 and "Work Technique," pp. 169–74.

12. George Sturt, *The Wheelwright's Shop*, p. 176.

13. Ibid.

14. R. Geoffrey Stiles's notion of a "crowd network" applies fairly well in this case. See his "Fishermen, Wives, and Radios," p. 45.

15. This concept is an expanded version of Poggie and Gersuny's appraisal of "the fishing population of Galilee as an occupational culture distinct from the shoreside world of work in which it is located" (*Fishermen of Galilee*, p. 78). Cf. Archie Green's mention of "occupation functioning to form an enclave" and of William Pilcher's "notion that occupation defines a community as much as does territory" in "Industrial Lore: A Bibliographic-Semantic Query," p. 76 and p. 93 respectively.

Chapter 2

1. Paul Heikkila, marine extension agent for the southern Oregon coast, defines the marine region from Eureka, California, to Grays Harbor, Washington, with Coos Bay at its center (interview, Coquille, Oregon, September 20, 1976). A Coos Bay insurance company insured one local crab, salmon, and shrimp fisherman from Cape Mendocino, California, to Cape Flattery, Washington (tape-recorded interview with Arnold and Doris Hockema, Charleston, March 7, 1978). The range of salmon trollermen sometimes exceeds this limit, extending from Monterey and San Francisco to Neah Bay, Washington, or farther yet, to the Queen Charlotte Islands off British Columbia or even to Middleton Island in the Gulf of Alaska:

   The California troll fleet fishes mainly off its own coast, but a few boats have fished as far north as the southern coast of Washington.

   Although the Oregon salmon troll fleet fishes primarily off the coast of Oregon, some vessels, particularly larger ones, follow the salmon runs from northern California to northern Washington.

   The Washington troll fleet fishes waters from northern California to southeastern Alaska. (Pacific Fishery Management Council, *Draft Fishery Management Plan*, p. 26.)

   Below Santa Barbara and Point Concepcion, California, salmon is seldom fished (Coos Bay *World*, March 16, 1978, p. 19). For ranges of trollermen, see also, John Earnest Damron, "The Emergence of Salmon Trolling on the American Northwest Coast," pp. 141–45; Robert J. Browning, *Fisheries of the North Pacific*, p. 201; and interview of Richard J. Anderson by Lloyd Lyman, Southwestern Oregon Community College Living History Series cassette, no. 435 (Coos Bay, May 20, 1975).

2. From statistics culled from the National Marine Fisheries Service's *Fishery Statistics of the United States 1977* [hereafter, N.M.F.S.], I infer that the coastal stretch has the distinction of being the poorest of United States Pacific Coast fishing regions. Concurrently, according

to Browning, *Fisheries of the North Pacific*, pp. 7–58, and 93–98, it also appears to lack both the variety of species available to southern California fishermen as well as the sheer quantities of the more limited number of species available in Alaskan waters. While the Pacific Coast overall was the most productive commercial fishing region in the United States in 1977 in total poundage and ex vessel value of fish landed, the coastal districts of Oregon, Washington, and northern California together accounted for only 11 percent of the volume (203,812,700 pounds), 13 percent of the value ($86,692,830), yet approximately one-fourth of all Pacific Coast fishermen (ca. 8,000) and one-third of the fishboats (ca. 14,000).

3. Oregon Coastal Conservation and Development Commission [hereafter, O.C.C.D.C.], *Economic Survey and Analysis of the Oregon Coastal Zone*, p. D-15, although for 1973 the ranking was salmon, tuna, shrimp, bottomfish, and crab (p. D-29). Comparatively, in Oregon perhaps until the late 1970s, more pounds of shrimp were landed than any other fish, followed in decreasing total poundage by tuna, bottomfish, salmon, and Dungeness crab (p. D-29); according to N.M.F.S. statistics, the order was shrimp, bottomfish, crab, salmon, and tuna, for the entire state, and shrimp, crab, bottomfish, salmon, and tuna for the coastal district alone in 1977. According to Paul Heikkila (personal communication of August 1, 1985), bottomfish are now probably first in quantity and value and crab is stable (perhaps second in quantity and value?). Due to weather, economic conditions, and fishery cycles, shrimp, salmon, and tuna landings have taken severe nose dives and crab is at a low ebb also. There has been some local success harvesting scallops with dredges; taking black cod with otter trawls, longlines, and pots; capturing Pacific whiting with otter and some mid-water trawls; and gathering squid with otter trawls.

4. Alaska and Puget Sound account for the remaining four-fifths of the salmon catch. Between 1961 and 1970, Oregon albacore tuna averaged 38 percent of the entire Pacific Coast catch, including British Columbia catches, Dungeness crab around 25 percent, bottomfish around 17 percent, shrimp 16 percent, and salmon between 11 and 24 percent (calculated from a chart "Annual Catch Statistics for Some Oregon and Pacific Coast and Marine Fisheries in Pounds Round," prepared by the Fish Commission of Oregon Research Division, October 29, 1971, a copy of which appears in Bruce H. McLain, "Commercial Fishing and Its Related Industries"). These statistics may still hold to some extent, but they must be taken with a grain of salt. The 1970s represented a boom period for most of the fisheries, while the 1980s have thus far proven a bust for all but the crab and bottomfish enterprises (personal communication with Paul Heikkila, August 1, 1985).

5. For the older statistics on all ports: interview with Paul Heikkila, September 20, 1976; O.C.C.D.C., pp. D-30, D-34, D-38; and using N.M.F.S., *Fishery Statistics of the United States 1974*. For the updates: personal communication with Paul Heikkila, August 1, 1985.

6. F. C. Cleaver, ed., *Fishery Statistics of Oregon*, p. 71; cf. William G. Loy, *Atlas of Oregon*, p. 62.

7. On bottomfish, Cleaver, *Fishery Statistics of Oregon*, p. 10, and Browning, *Fisheries of the North Pacific*, pp. 95–98: Cleaver says between 5 and 90 fathoms, Browning between 5 and 250 fathoms. On shrimp: Browning, p. 53. Cf. Loy, *Atlas of Oregon*, p. 62, for chart and different figures yet.

8. Browning, *Fisheries of the North Pacific*, p. 202 on salmon, p. 11 on albacore. According to Loy, *Atlas of Oregon*, p. 62, most of the salmon catch comes from between 5 and 30 kilometers out (3 to 20 miles); most of the tuna is taken within 320 kilometers (200 miles) of the coast, but some boats operate up to 1600 kilometers (1000 miles) out.

9. Browning, *Fisheries of the North Pacific*, pp. 11–12.

10. Ibid., pp. 37–39, 40.

11. O.C.C.D.C., p. G-4, map G-1, and chap. G, "Ports and Other Economic Support Systems;" also Wilsey and Ham, Inc., *Estuarine Resources of the Oregon Coast*, p. 3.

12. These two fishing ports are additionally unique to the region. Cape Kiwanda near Pacific City protects an exclusive dory fishery where dories are launched and landed directly through the surf. As such, no moorage facilities exist in the water for the local dories or transient commercial boats. Fish produced from this fishery are transported overland to nearby Kiwanda and Pacific City for processing. At Port Orford, however, moorage facilities do exist, but during the winter they are exclusively dry dock. All boats contributing to the winter fisheries there—mostly crab—must be small and light enough to be hoisted into the water to start a day of fishing and hoisted out on to a boat trailer to be parked at the facility at the end of the fishing day. Boats can measure no longer than 37 feet and weigh no more than 7 tons, I believe.

13. The condition of the bar figures in many fishermen's reasonings for fishing out of one port or another. Coos Bay's bar has a reputation for being good, and many fishermen have thus switched to Coos Bay from other ports in recent years. Design and amount of upkeep, in addition to the geographical nature of the estuary and predominant weather conditions of the area, seem to be important in producing a good bar. But tide changes also influence passability such that though Eureka's bar is not as well maintained as Coos Bay's, it is easier to cross because the amount of tide change is less. Hypothetically, if the Eureka bar were in better condition, it would be a better, easier bar all around to cross than the Coos Bay bar. Each bar along the coast has idiosyncracies and each fisherman seems to be knowledgeable of them and the best ways in which to cross a particular bar—or he knows how to find out its quirks through observation and shop talk.

14. See, for instance, the description of Bishop Wells's trip to southern Oregon in Erik Bromberg, "Frontier Humor," pp. 316–17; E. R. Jackman, ed., "After the Covered Wagons: Recollections of Russel C. and Ellis S. Dement"; and Stephen Dow Beckham, *Coos Bay: The Pioneer Period 1851–1890*.

15. Tape-recorded interview with Ruth Hallmark Day, fish plant manager, Charleston, July 28, 1977.

16. Interview with Jake Harlan, fisherman, Charleston, September 1, 1977; panel discussion at a "Workshop on Commercial Fisheries," held at the Oregon Institute of Marine Biology, Charleston, April 28, 1977.

17. Browning, *Fisheries of the North Pacific*, p. 111; interview with Paul Heikkila, September 20, 1976; N.M.F.S., *Fishery Statistics 1974*.

18. Tape-recorded interview with Jack Wilskey, marine architect and engineer, Nelson Log Bronc/Mid-Coast Marine, Eastside, Oregon, September 13, 1977.

19. Tape-recorded interview with Fred Anderson, fisherman, Charleston, August 24, 1977.

20. Ibid.; personal correspondence with Betty Anderson, April 1985; and personal communication with Paul Heikkila, August 1, 1985.

21. Interview of September 20, 1976, and personal communication of August 1, 1985, with Paul Heikkila.

22. Cf. O.C.C.D.C., p. D-20 (Coos County ranked second, Lincoln County [Newport] third, in 1973); Ken Roberts, *Diversity—Characteristic of Oregon's Year 'Round Fishery*, p. 2 (Coos Bay ranked third, Newport second in 1970). According to Mike Hosie, Coos Bay ranked first

in 1977, with 25 percent of the total Oregon catch, and 20 to 30 percent each of the salmon, crab, bottomfish, and shrimp catches (discussion, Charleston, January 30, 1978). Updated information: personal communication with Paul Heikkila, August 1, 1985.

23. O.C.C.D.C., p. D-38: Lincoln County (Newport) comparatively claimed 20 percent of the landings and 23 percent of the value in 1973.

24. Ibid., p. D-20. In 1973, Coos County contributed the major proportion of the Oregon salmon catch (35 percent), yet in terms of the entire Coos County catch for that year, salmon represented only 18.4 percent, and shrimp and bottomfish combined, 68.5 percent (Ibid., p. D-38).

25. Ibid., p. D-30.

26. Ibid., p. D-13, map p. D-11 puts Coos County's 1973 employment at 405. According to McLain, Paul Heikkila reported 360 employees for the seven Coos County plants in 1969.

27. Tape-recorded interview with Leonard Hall, fisherman, Charleston, July 27, 1977. Also 75 boats served Hallmark's in 1942, according to William T. McLean, ed., *An Historical Sketch of Coos County — Its Cities and Industries*, p. 171.

28. Marc Firestone, "An Examination of the Coastal Changes of Charleston, Oregon," pp. 8, 9–10.

29. According to my inventories, January 17, 23, 24, and 26, 1978; February 22, 1978; and March 9, 1978; and in comparison with Helen Cardwell's estimates of boat basin numbers (discussion, Charleston, November 8, 1976).

30. Ibid.

31. Personal communication with Paul Heikkila, August 1, 1985.

32. For 1945 and 1960–64 figures, Firestone, "An Examination of the Coastal Changes," pp. 8, 9–10. Figures for 1977–78 are inferentially drawn from statistics presented in Frederick J. Smith, *Some Characteristics of Oregon Fishermen*, pp. 1–4; Oregon State University Cooperative Extension Service, Sea Grant Advisory Program, *Fisheries-Related Marine Career Training Needs on the Oregon Coast, 1971–1975*, pp. 8–11; O.C.C.D.C., pp. D-2–D-3; and personal correspondence with Elmer C. Case, Oregon Department of Fish and Wildlife, Portland, Oregon, October 1, 1979, which included information regarding numbers of Oregon commercial fisheries licenses, 1971–79.

33. Ibid., excluding Firestone.

34. Interview with Ruth Hallmark Day, July 28, 1977; and interview with Leonard Hall, July 27, 1977.

35. Comparing statistics with Firestone, "An Examination of the Coastal Changes," pp. 9–10, and O.C.C.D.C., pp. D-3–D-4.

36. O.C.C.D.C., p. D-50, and personal communication with Paul Heikkila, August 1, 1985.

37. David S. Liao and Joe B. Stevens, *Oregon's Commercial Fishermen*, pp. 6–8, 13–16.

38. Ibid.; also testimony of Jake Harlan, interview, September 1, 1977.

39. Arthur L. Throckmorton, *Oregon Argonauts*, pp. 39, 222.

40. Cleaver, p. 33.

41. Emil R. Peterson and Alfred Powers, *A Century of Coos and Curry*, p. 439.

42. U.S. Works Progress Administration [hereafter, W.P.A.], *Inventory of the County Archives of Oregon; No. 6, Coos County*, p. A-61—they quote John N. Cobb's *Pacific Salmon Fisheries*, p. 436, and A. G. Walling, comp., *History of Southern Oregon*, p. 489. Census figures: U.S. Census Office, *Census Reports: Twelfth Census of the United States*, vol. 1, pp. 36, 324–325.

43. W.P.A., p. A-61.

44. Throckmorton, *Oregon Argonauts*, p. 310; Damron, "The Emergence of Salmon Trolling," p. 19; Courtland L. Smith, *Fish or Cut Bait*, p. 5.

45. Damron, "The Emergence of Salmon Trolling," pp. 19–20; Peterson and Powers, *A Century of Coos and Curry*, p. 439.

46. Peterson and Powers, *A Century of Coos and Curry*, p. 439; W.P.A., p. A-61; Walling, *History of Southern Oregon*, pp. 488–89; Orvil Dodge, *Pioneer History of Coos and Curry Counties, Oregon*, p. 252; and Cobb, *Pacific Salmon Fisheries*, p. 435. See n. 42, above, for census sources.

47. See n. 42, above, for census sources.

48. W.P.A., p. A-61; McLean, pp. 170–71.

49. Just to mention a very few sources: Elizabeth Coover and Ellen Garner, *Life and Legend in the Coos Bay Area*, p. 102, 111–12; interview of Martin Steckel by Angie Word and Sheila Cassidy, Living History Series cassette, no. 306 (Coos Bay, 1972).

50. Interview of John L. Koontz by Jeff Galbraith, Living History Series cassette, no. 321 (November 1972).

51. Shad: Cleaver, *Fisheries Statistics of Oregon*, p. 53. Bass: McLean, *An Historical Sketch of Coos County*, pp. 236–43, and interview with Lorance Eickworth, Coos Bay, August 29, 1977. Varieties of fish sought: undated pamphlet put out jointly by Charles Feller, Inc., Salmon Packers and Shippers, and the Marshfield Chamber of Commerce, Marshfield [Coos Bay], Oregon (I put the date roughly at 1925) and located in the Charles Feller Papers, Oregon Collection, University of Oregon, Eugene.

52. Tape-recorded interview with Richard and Verna Lilienthal, Charleston, September 20, 1977.

53. Interview of Carl Sandstrom by Lloyd Lyman, Living History Series cassette, no. 458 (May 24, 1975), side one.

54. Interview with Lorance Eickworth, August 29, 1977.

55. Charles Feller Papers, ledger 1916–17.

56. Interview of Carl Sandstrom, Living History Series cassette, no. 458; interview of Joseph P. DeCosta by Lloyd Lyman, Living History Series cassette, no. 411 (March 28, 1975); author's interview of Lorance Eickworth, August 29, 1977; interview of Harold Ott by Bessie Gavick, Living History Series cassette, no. 328 (May 1974); interview of Arthur Pederson by Lloyd Lyman, Living History Series cassette, no. 403 (April 4, 1975); interview of Orville C. Barrows and Ruth Barrows Lennon by Lloyd Lyman, Living History Series cassette, no. 417 (April 19, 1975); and author's interview of Cyrus, Sr., and Violet Little, Charleston, April 17, 1978.

57. Ibid.

58. Closure of Coos Bay: Cleaver, *Fisheries Statistics of Oregon*, p. 42. Closure of the Coquille: interview of Carl Sandstrom, Living History Series cassette, no. 458. These boats were one-

to two-man dayboats with gas or diesel engines, no mechanized gear, no depth finder, no Loran, only a compass and a small radio, according to Ruth Hallmark Day (author's interview, July 28, 1977), Richard J. Anderson (Living History Series cassette, no. 435), and Alice Hallmark and Ruth Hallmark Day (interview by Lloyd Lyman, Living History Series cassette, no. 409 [March 19, 1975]).

59. Damron, "The Emergence of Salmon Trolling," pp. 9–11, 43–45.

60. Ibid., pp. 46–48; and interview of John Koontz, Living History Series cassette, no. 321.

61. Damron, "The Emergence of Salmon Trolling," pp. 50–53.

62. Cleaver, *Fisheries Statistics of Oregon*, p. 47.

63. The Feller pamphlet (see n. 51, above) propounded the virtues of salmon caught inside as opposed to that caught outside. This propaganda suggests the processor's resistance to change rather than the fishermen's, however, for by the 1930s some local fishing families had begun to summer near the mouth of the estuary where they had readier access to fishing in the open ocean (interview with Richard and Verna Lilienthal, September 20, 1977).

64. Interview with Fred Humbert, boat builder, Haynes Inlet, March 16, 1978.

65. Cleaver, *Fisheries Statistics of Oregon*, p. 73; Courtland L. Smith, *Fish or Cut Bait*, p. 20; and Kenneth D. Waldron, *The Fishery and Biology of the Dungeness Crab (Cancer Magister Dana) in Oregon Waters*, p. 9.

66. Cleaver, *Fisheries Statistics of Oregon*, p. 31; author's interview with Lorance Eickworth, August 29, 1977; and interview of Lorance Eickworth by Lloyd Lyman, Living History Series cassette, no. 420 (April 25, 1975).

67. Courtland L. Smith, *Fish or Cut Bait*, p. 23.

68. Cleaver, *Fisheries Statistics of Oregon*, pp. 9 and 26; see George Y. Harry, Jr., and Alfred R. Morgan, "History of the Oregon Trawl Fishery, 1884–1961," pp. 5–9.

69. Interview with Ruth Hallmark Day, July 28, 1977; interview of Alice Hallmark and Ruth Hallmark Day, Living History Series cassette, no. 409.

70. Interview with Ruth Hallmark Day, July 28, 1977.

71. Ibid.

72. Firestone, "An Examination of the Coastal Changes," pp. 7–9.

73. Interview with Richard and Verna Lilienthal, September 20, 1977; interview with Ruth Hallmark Day, July 28, 1977; interview with Fred Anderson, August 24, 1977; interview with Leonard Hall, July 27, 1977; and interview with Norm Anderson, manager, Oregon-Pacific Company, North Bend, March 28, 1978.

74. Charles Feller Papers.

75. Firestone, "An Examination of the Coastal Changes," p. 8.

76. Ibid., p. 9.

77. McLain, *An Historical Sketch of Coos County*, p. 26.

78. Ibid., p. 25; interview with Leonard Hall, July 27, 1977.

79. McLain, *An Historical Sketch of Coos County*, pp. 24, 26; Harry and Morgan, "History of the Oregon Trawl Fishery," p. 24.

80. Harry and Morgan, "History of the Oregon Trawl Fishery," p. 24, say 1957; Courtland L. Smith, *Fish or Cut Bait*, p. 23, says 1955–56.

81. McLain, *An Historical Sketch of Coos County*, p. 25; interview with Fred Anderson, August 24, 1977; and personal communication with Paul Heikkila, August 1, 1985.

82. McLain, *An Historical Sketch of Coos County*, pp. 26–27; personal communication with Paul Heikkila, August 1, 1985.

83. Personal communication with Paul Heikkila, August 1, 1985.

84. McLain, *An Historical Sketch of Coos County*, p. 26.

85. Personal communication with Paul Heikkila, August 1, 1985.

86. From my own calculations based on inventories and observations.

87. Interview with Floyd Green, fisherman, Charleston, February 23, 1978; and interview with Lorance Eickworth, August 29, 1977.

88. Interview with Jack Kelley, Charleston, March 11, 1978; and interview with Louise and David Hanson, Charleston, April 4, 1978.

89. Firestone, "An Examination of the Coastal Changes," pp. 9–10; O.C.C.D.C., pp. D-26–D-27; Harry and Morgan, "History of the Oregon Trawl Fishery," pp. 23–24.

90. Beckham, *Coos Bay: The Pioneer Period*, pp. 31–44.

91. Dodge, *Pioneer History of Coos and Curry*, pp. 147–68, 205; Peterson and Powers, *A Century of Coos and Curry*, pp. 405–24, 428, 429; W.P.A., pp. A-59–A-60; interview of Mary Banks Granger by Lloyd Lyman, Living History Series cassette, no. 431 (May 6, 1975); interview with Fred Humbert, March 16, 1978; interview of William A. and Ena McKeown Josephson by Lloyd Lyman, Living History Series cassette, no. 446 (May 22, 1975); interview of John Arthur Mattson by Lloyd Lyman, Living History Series cassette, no. 453 (May 24, 1975); and interview of Arthur Pederson, Living History Series cassette, no. 403.

92. Interview of Harold Ott, Living History Series cassette, no. 328; and interview of Richard J. Anderson, Living History Series cassette, no. 435.

93. Interview with Fred Humbert, March 16, 1978.

Chapter 3

1. Here is the breakdown of boats at various Coos Bay area docks:

Location	Conventional Fishboats	Comm. Rigged Pleasure Boats	Pleasure & Miscellaneous	Approximate No. of Spaces
Boat Basin	(305)	(54)	(83)	(520)
Inner Basin	85	50	70	296
Outer Basin	120	4	13	224 +
Barbey Fisheries	7	2	—	15
Hallmark Fisheries	4	—	—	4
Peterson Seafood	21	7	2	33
Hanson's Landing	14	7	6	40 +
Joe Ney Slough	10	4	6	24
Coos Bay City Dock	9	2	2	16
Hillstrom Shipbldg.	11	—	2	14

Table (cont.)

Location	Conventional Fishboats	Comm. Rigged Pleasure Boats	Pleasure & Miscellaneous	Approximate No. of Spaces
Koontz Machine Shop	4	—	2	6
Eureka Fisheries*	1	**	**	8*
Mid-Coast Marine	**	**	**	4*
Humbert's, et al.	**	**	**	10*
Totals	286	76	103	694 +

*means estimated, an actual inventory of the boats docked at these locations was not carried out.

2. Inventories taken January 17, 1978 (Inner Basin), January 23, 1978 (Outer Basin), January 24, 1978 (Barbey's, Hallmark's, Peterson's, Hanson's, Joe Ney Slough), and January 26, 1978 (Coos Bay City Dock, Koontz's, Hillstrom's); rechecked February 22, 1978, and March 9, 1978.

3. According to my estimates, comparing figures with Helen Cardwell's estimates, the boat basin had a maximum of 580 berths in January 1978, all of which are used during the summer months, but 60 of which are not available for winter use. Sixty-five to 70 percent of the boats are commercial fishboats, 30 to 35 percent are sports fishing or other types of boats.

4. Tape-recorded interview with Leonard Hall, fisherman, Charleston, July 27, 1977.

5. Actually, two boats carried only crab gear. I put one of them in the salmon/crab group, the other in the drag/crab group. One other boat carried tuna trolling, crab, and shrimp trawling gear—I put this boat in the drag/crab group.

6. Robert J. Browning, *Fisheries of the North Pacific*, p. 205.

7. Ibid., pp. 219–22.

8. Ibid., p. 211.

9. For full discussion and illustrations of salmon trolling components, rigging, and operation of gear, see Ibid., pp. 201–17, especially pp. 205–6, 210, 211–14; see also, Harold R. Ingebrigtsen, *Roaming with Reta*, pp. 11–17, 54–57, 97–102, 115–16.

10. For full discussion and illustrations of albacore trolling, see Browning, *Fisheries of the North Pacific*, pp. 217–24, especially pp. 219–22, 223; also see Ingebrigtsen, *Roaming with Reta*, p. 96.

11. I have thus inferred information from a copy made of a list of boats that landed tuna in Charleston the summer of 1976, which was compiled by Larry Goodman, then employed by the Charleston branch of the Oregon Department of Fish and Wildlife.

12. See Browning, *Fisheries of the North Pacific*, p. 243. He quotes a crab pot description of Robert M. Meyer's from "The Dungeness Crab Fishery Around Kodiak," *Commercial Fisheries Review* (September 1968). A closer description of Coos Bay type pots may be found in Kenneth D. Waldron, *The Fishery and Biology of the Dungeness Crab (Cancer Magister Dana) in Oregon Waters*, pp. 14, 15 (illustration).

13. See Browning, *Fisheries of the North Pacific*, pp. 121–22, 239–40, 243–44, for discussion of Dungeness crab fishing gear and its operation; also, Waldron, *The Fishery and Biology*, pp. 13–16.

14. Much of this description has been culled from Browning, *Fisheries of the North Pacific*, pp. 143–44. For full description and illustration of trawling gear and its operation, see Browning, pp. 123–44, especially pp. 125–26, 128 (description of the otter trawl and its operation from Fish and Wildlife Circular 109 [1961] of the Bureau of Commercial Fisheries, and from W. L. Scofield, "Trawl Gear in California," California Department of Fish and Game [1947]), and pp. 140–43. Also see George Y. Harry, Jr., and Alfred R. Morgan, "History of the Oregon Trawl Fishery, 1884–1961," pp. 10–12, 16–18. For a vivid comparative sketch of trawling, see Jeremy Tunstall, *The Fishermen*, pp. 64–65.

15. Tape-recorded interview with Fred Anderson, Charleston, August 24, 1977. For these and following horsepower figures, I averaged the horsepowers of a selection of Charleston boats as given in U.S. Department of Transportation, U.S. Coast Guard, *Merchant Vessels of the United States 1970 (Including Yachts)*. I also referred to horsepower figures given in R. Barry Fisher, *An Effective Combination Trawl for West Coast Draggers*.

16. According to Browning, *Fisheries of the North Pacific*, pp. 217, 219; also according to fisherman Neil Gilbertson as reported in Joe Parker, "Every Boatbuilder and Every Fisherman is Biased Towards His Own Material," p. 83.

17. Interview with Leonard Hall, July 27, 1977.

18. Tape-recorded interview with Richard and Verna Lilienthal, fishercouple, Charleston, September 20, 1977.

19. John Earnest Damron, "The Emergence of Salmon Trolling on the American Northwest Coast," pp. 85, 87, 91, 118, 159.

20. C. Richard K. Lunt, "Lobsterboat Building on the Eastern Coast of Maine," pp. 42–46, especially figs. 3–8.

21. Ibid., figs. 18–27 (pp. 127, 129, 131, 133, 135, 136), figs. 70, 71 (p. 200); also cf. the "S-shape stern post" mentioned by Kari Helmer-Hansen, "Growth of a Fishing Village," pp. 203–4.

22. Damron, "The Emergence of Salmon Trolling," p. 53, quotes O. Smith on Monterey clipper antecedents; pp. 59–68, discusses the Columbia River gillnet boat and its development into a motorized boat.

23. Ibid., pp. 120, 159.

24. Ibid., pp. 85–91, 95–97.

25. Ibid., p. 87.

26. Ibid., pp. 80–84.

27. Ibid., p. 81.

28. Other Charleston boats of this type are *Nickey, Sandy, Ila-B*, and fiberglass take-offs, *Little Star, Karla*, and *Wherever*. The information in this section comes from Damron, "The Emergence of Salmon Trolling," pp. 53–59. The clipper dimensions he gives (29-foot length, 9-foot beam, 3-foot draft) may not be the boat's registered measurements. I have used registered measurements in some descriptions in this chapter, usually in captions to photographs. Generally when I refer to boat lengths, however, I use their overall lengths, which fishermen quote, rather than their registered lengths. Registered length measures from the top of the "deck from the fore part of the outer planking or plating at the bow to the after part of . . . the rudder post," and thus usually falls short of the overall length of the boat by several feet. One fisherman said it basically measures the length of the keel. Registered breadth measures the widest part of the boat from the outside of the planking or plating on one side to the corresponding point on the opposite side; it may be identical to

a boat's beam. Registered depth, however, is measured "from the underside of the tonnage deck, amidships, to the bottom of the hold," and thus differs greatly from draft, which is measured from the waterline to the bottom of the keel at its deepest point. Registered measurements and their definitions appear in the annual publication of the U.S. Department of Transportation, U.S. Coast Guard, *Merchant Vessels of the United States.* The measurements are used to determine the net tonnage of a vessel to see whether it is large enough (five net tons) to be federally documented; otherwise the boat must be registered with the state. Under federal documentation, a boat is considered a merchant vessel of the United States and therefore federal property during wartime; but otherwise the fisherman is entitled to certain benefits such as excellent medical insurance.

29. Damron, "The Emergence of Salmon Trolling," p. 159.

30. Lunt, "Lobsterboat Building," fig. 67 (p. 195), fig. 72 (p. 210), fig. 31 (p. 142).

31. Inventory of bow profiles and stern shapes of the 48 fishing boats that were resting out of water at Port Orford, Oregon, February 6, 1978.

32. Cf. Lunt, "Lobsterboat Building," pp. 52–56.

33. Cf. Damron, "The Emergence of Salmon Trolling," p. 159; see also nn. 56, 90, 91 of chap. 2, above.

34. Cf. Lunt, "Lobsterboat Building," pp. 51–52.

35. Damron, "The Emergence of Salmon Trolling," p. 159.

36. Lunt, "Lobsterboat Building," pp. 52–54; Damron, "The Emergence of Salmon Trolling," p. 91; Parker, "Every Boatbuilder," p. 68 (testimony of fisherman Gary Wassom).

37. Lunt, "Lobsterboat Building," figs. 4, 5 (pp. 42, 43); Howard I. Chapelle, *The National Watercraft Collection*, p. 153 (description and illustration of model of *Thomas E. Moran*), p. 119 (standard American harbor tug), pp. 149–54 (selected boats, especially the *Rattler* and *Conestoga*), p. 259 (*Aqua Pura*, a Gloucester water boat), p. 357 (*The Spray*), and p. 358 (*The Brooklyn*).

38. Cf. Browning, *Fisheries of the North Pacific*, p. 103, for descriptions of halibut schooners. A. K. Larssen and Sig Jaeger in *The ABC's of Fo'c'sle Living*, p. 91, say that the Pacific halibut schooner is "a crossbreed, of sorts, between a Gloucester schooner and a Norwegian *kutter*." Fisherman Charlie Ells says that cannery tenders like the *Amak* were schooners, more or less," but they were "lower to the water . . . the stern is much higher in the halibut boat. But they had them low so that they could be a tender to the smaller gillnet boats, they could come alongside . . ." (tape-recorded interview, Port Orford, February 6, 1978).

39. Damron, "The Emergence of Salmon Trolling," p. 99.

40. Interview with Lorance Eickworth, Coos Bay, August 29, 1977; interview of Lorance Eickworth by Lloyd Lyman, Southwestern Oregon Community College Living History Series cassette, no. 420 (Coos Bay, August 25, 1975); interview with Charlie and Jessie Ells, February 6, 1978.

41. Cf. what Browning, *Fisheries of the North Pacific*, has to say about the "Western Combination," pp. 103–4, and see photograph p. 115. Regarding ethnic groups, see Damron, "The Emergence of Salmon Trolling," pp. 11–16, 20–25, 120–22; Browning, p. 4; and Larssen and Jaeger, *The ABC's*, pp. 94–95.

42. Damron, "The Emergence of Salmon Trolling," p. 118; Lunt, "Lobsterboat Building," pp. 41–46, 51–52.

43. Joe Parker, "Every Boatbuilder," pp. viii, 38–39, relates the following:

> A fisherman who owns a wood boat was telling me how several years ago there was a wooden boat caught in the breaking surf near the north jetty. A fiberglass boat saw the trouble and called the Coast Guard. The owner of the fiberglass boat then went to offer assistance. Within seconds the fiberglass boat was being thrown into the rocks. Both boats were destructed [*sic*] and nine people died. There was nothing left of the fiberglass boat. The wood boat was broken up, yet there were still large pieces to cling on to, if they only could have been found. The person who was telling me the story, praised wood because it was a material that floated, not only when it was together, but when it was torn apart.
>
> Two days later an owner of a fiberglass boat was telling me how two boats were crossing the bar this winter under rough conditions. One boat was wood and the other was fiberglass. One set of waves had no backsides to them, and when the two boats reached the peak of the wave, they dropped down 20′ and both boats cracked open their hulls. The wood boat sank immediately, yet with a good pumping system the fiberglass boat got back to the dock in time to put a temporary patch on the hull. The person who told me this story no doubt believed in fiberglass all the way.

44. Interview with Fred Anderson, August 24, 1977.

45. Ibid.

46. As told to Joe Parker, "Every Boatbuilder," by many fishermen and locals, p. 23 (Fred and Wilbur Humbert), p. 32 (Blair Samuelson), p. 55 (Bob Bernhart), p. 76 (Gary Wassom), p. 84 (Neil Gilbertson), and p. 108 (Orion Wells, who refuted the noisy coldness of iron boats). Also, interview with Cecil Crockett, fisherman, Charleston, January 18, 1978; and tape-recorded interview with Arnold and Doris Hockema, fishercouple, Charleston, March 7, 1978, who reported that wood was softer, quieter, friendlier, and easier to stand on all day.

47. Parker, "Every Boatbuilder," p. 38 (Jim Peterson), p. 46 (Ron Allison), p. 76 (Gary Wassom), and p. 83 (Neil Gilbertson).

48. Basil Greenhill, *Archaeology of the Boat*, p. 287; also see his chaps. 3 and 19.

49. Ibid. Also see Olof Hasslöf, "Main Principles in the Technology of Ship-Building," pp. 27–72.

50. Greenhill, *Archaeology*, p. 292, 298; Hasslöf, "Main Principles," pp. 27–72.

51. Greenhill, *Archaeology*, p. 268.

52. Parker, "Every Boatbuilder," p. 96.

53. Parker, "Every Boatbuilder," pp. 62–67; cf. Lunt, "Lobsterboat Building," pp. 225–26.

54. Damron, "The Emergence of Salmon Trolling," pp. 85, 100.

55. Parker, "Every Boatbuilder," pp. 105–9 (Orion Wells), pp. 112–13 (Bob Jackson), pp. 114–17 (Ron Warren).

56. Henry Glassie, "The Variations of Concepts within Tradition," p. 178.

57. Interview with Paul Heikkila, marine extension agent for the southern Oregon coast, Coquille, Oregon, September 20, 1976.

58. Interview with Charlie and Jessie Ells, February 6, 1978; interview with Cyrus, Sr., and Violet Little, fishercouple, Charleston, April 17, 1978.

59. Parker, "Every Boatbuilder," pp. 43–45; Don Holm, "The Dory Story in Oregon."

60. Parker, "Every Boatbuilder," p. 30 (Blair Samuelson).

61. Ibid., pp. 17–18; also, interview with Norman and Virginia Walker, fishercouple, Charleston, April 11, 1978.

62. Parker, "Every Boatbuilder," pp. 20–21.

63. Cf. Browning, *Fisheries of the North Pacific*, p. 103, regarding sturdy halibut schooner construction; tour of the *Husky*, Charleston Boat Basin, May 12, 1975; discussion of the *Zebra*, Charleston, February 5, 1978.

64. Interview with Fred Humbert, Haynes Inlet, March 16, 1978.

65. Interview, July 27, 1977.

66. Interview, August 24, 1977.

67. Interview, February 6, 1978.

68. Interview with Fred Humbert, March 16, 1978; interview with Fred Anderson, August 24, 1977.

69. Tape-recorded interview, Charleston, July 28, 1977.

70. Damron, "The Emergence of Salmon Trolling," p. 108. Peter Anson, *Fisher Folk-Lore*, p. 98, observed:

    > Just as fishermen in most parts of Europe were very particular about the fashion, cut and colour of their clothes until modern times, so were they even as conservative in the colours used on their vessels, which were painted according to traditions handed down from one generation to another. The selection of colours varied, so it was easy to tell at a glance the district to which a vessel belonged, even if her lines were no different to those of other boats in a harbour.

    Also cf. Horace Beck, *Folklore and the Sea*, pp. 16–17, who draws color distinctions mainly on the basis of broad geographical/climatic regions and the nature of paints.

71. Howard I. Chapelle, *The American Fishing Schooners, 1825–1935*, pp. 559–60.

72. Interview with Ruth Hallmark Day, July 28, 1977.

73. Horace Beck, *The Folklore of Maine*, p. 56.

74. Interview with Richard and Verna Lilienthal, September 20, 1977; interview with Charlie and Jessie Ells, February 6, 1978; also see Ingebrigtsen, *Roaming with Reta*, p. 18.

75. Beck, *Folklore of Maine*, pp. 57–58; Beck, *Folklore and the Sea*, pp. 5–6, 12, and throughout chap. 1. Also see Patrick B. Mullen, *I Heard the Old Fishermen Say*, pp. 156–60, Beliefs nos. 102, 103, 104, also 62, 31, 43.

76. The launching was also reported in Coos Bay's *World*, May 6, 1978, p. 5.

77. Most Charleston fishboats are large enough to be registered with the federal government as merchant vessels (see n. 28), and thus are officially required to bear names, in addition to federal registration numbers. In contrast, commercial boats that do not measure up to the requisite minimum of five net tons and can only be registered with the state of Oregon, frequently go unnamed, like most of the world's small boats, marked on the bow only with state registration numbers. Many small, state-registered commercial fishboats, however, have been named in the tradition of the federally documented vessels. Greenhill, *Archaeology*, p. 44, also mentions that big ships must have a name "under the successive Merchant Shipping Acts since 1786."

78. I compared: 1) the names of all of the Charleston fishboats appearing in my 1977–78 inventories (see n. 2); 2) the names of all Oregon trawlers appearing in the Oregon Department of Fish and Wildlife annual reports from 1955 to the present (cf. introduction, n. 7); and 3) the names of all large wooden vessels that were built in Coos County shipyards from the 1850s through the 1940s according to Victor West's list printed in Emil R. Peterson and Alfred Powers, *A Century of Coos and Curry*, pp. 405–24.

79. Interview with Ruth Hallmark Day, July 28, 1977.

80. Ibid.

81. Interview with Richard and Verna Lilienthal, September 20, 1977.

82. Interview with Ruth Hallmark Day, July 28, 1977; interview with Leonard Hall, July 27, 1977.

83. Damron, "The Emergence of Salmon Trolling," p. 99: "Knowledge of how each individual boat performed was common around fishing ports, hence the fishermen/designers gleaned knowledge from the boats they knew, both those professionally designed and those which were envisioned in backyard workshops." Ingebrigtsen, *Roaming with Reta*, p. 31, substantiates this behavior:

    Another storm and the boys, blowed in again, drift into the Inshore Bar, most of them all set to catch their load of fish all over again. In between fish and drinks they take a hand at finding flaws in other boats and picking them to pieces. If their words could become factual instead of figurative, there would be a hell of a looking fleet of boats in the cove.

84. Talk with Kurt Swanson, draughtsman, Nelson Log Bronc/Mid-Coast Marine, Eastside, September 7, 1977.

85. Interview with Cyrus, Sr., and Violet Little, April 17, 1978.

86. Interview with Fred Anderson, August 24, 1977.

87. Interview with Fred Humbert, March 16, 1978.

88. Lunt, "Lobsterboat Building," p. 329, defines a half-model thus: "The wooden model carved by a traditional builder as he fashions the designed hull shape. Measurements are taken from this model which are expanded geometrically to full-size hull dimensions." For an elaborate discussion of half-models, their construction, and their use in boatbuilding, see Chapelle, *The National Watercraft Collection*, pp. 2–12.

89. Talk with Kurt Swanson, Eastside, September 7, 1977.

90. Interview with Cecil Crockett, January 18, 1978.

91. Interview with Fred Anderson, August 24, 1977.

92. Ibid.

93. Tape-recorded interview with Jack Wilskey, marine architect and engineer, manager, Nelson Log Bronc/Mid-Coast Marine, Eastside, September 13, 1977.

94. Interview with Richard and Verna Lilienthal, September 20, 1977.

95. Interview with Ruth Hallmark Day, July 28, 1977.

96. Interview with Art Horton, propellor repairman, Koontz Machine Shop, Coos Bay, April 6 and 7, 1978.

97. Interview with Arnold and Doris Hockema, March 7, 1978.

98. Ibid.

99. Interview with Richard and Verna Lilienthal, September 20, 1977; Interview with Floyd Green, fisherman, Charleston, February 23, 1978.

100. Interview with Cecil Crockett, January 18, 1978; and interview with Carl and Lynne Harrington, fishercouple, Charleston, February 9, 1978.

Chapter 4

1. David S. Liao and Joe B. Stevens, *Oregon's Commercial Fishermen*, p. 10, t. 5.

2. Tape-recorded interview with Leonard Hall, Charleston, July 27, 1977.

3. Tape-recorded interview with Arnold and Doris Hockema, Charleston, March 7, 1978.

4. Tape-recorded interview with Jack Wilskey, marine architect and engineer, Nelson Log Bronc/Mid-Coast Marine, Eastside, September 7, 1977.

5. Interview with Leonard Hall, July 27, 1977.

6. Interview with Jake Harlan, Charleston, March 29, 1978.

7. Interview with Carl and Lynne Harrington, Charleston, February 9, 1978.

8. Interview with Leonard Hall, July 27, 1977.

9. Tape-recorded interview with Richard and Verna Lilienthal, Charleston, September 20, 1977.

10. Ibid.

11. Interview with Art Horton, propellor repairman, Koontz Machine Shop, Coos Bay, April 6 and 7, 1978.

12. Interview with Richard and Verna Lilienthal, September 20, 1977.

13. Ibid.

14. Interview with Arnold and Doris Hockema, March 7, 1978.

15. Interview with Cecil Crockett, Charleston, January 18, 1978; actually, my notes say he got nine days out of three *months* at the yard when he could paint and sandblast the boat.

16. Interview with Leonard Hall, July 27, 1977.

17. Interview with Richard and Verna Lilienthal, September 20, 1977.

18. Tape-recorded interview with Fred Anderson, Charleston, August 24, 1977.

19. Interview, July 27, 1977.

20. Interview with Floyd Green, Charleston, February 23, 1978.

21. Interview with Art Horton, April 6 and 7, 1978.

22. Interview with Floyd Green, February 23, 1978. Also see John Earnest Damron, "The Emergence of Salmon Trolling on the American Northwest Coast," pp. 70–71, 109–13, 123; and Harold R. Ingebrigtsen, *Roaming with Reta*, pp. 115–16.

23. Interview with Jake Harlan, March 29, 1978; and interview with Bill Hillstrom, Jr., manager and draughtsman, Hillstrom Shipbuilding Company, Coos Bay, September 28, 1977.

24. Cf. Leonard Hall's comment, n. 19; also see Damron, "The Emergence of Salmon Trolling," p. 112.

25. Interview with Leonard Hall, July 27, 1977.

26. Interview with Norman and Virginia Walker, Charleston, April 11, 1978.

27. Interview with Leonard Hall, July 27, 1977.

28. Interview with Arnold and Doris Hockema, March 7, 1978.

29. Interview with Leonard Hall, July 27, 1977. Floyd Green (interview, February 23, 1978) said he loses about 50 of 165 pots per year. Arnold Hockema (interview, March 7, 1978) lost never less than 40 to 50 pots when he fished 300 of them.

30. Interview with Arnold and Doris Hockema, March 7, 1978; interview with Cyrus, Sr., and Violet Little, April 17, 1978; interview with Leonard Hall, July 27, 1977; interview with Floyd Green, February 23, 1978; and interview with Norman and Virginia Walker, April 11, 1978.

31. Interview with Floyd Green, February 23, 1978.

32. Ibid.; interview with Arnold and Doris Hockema, March 7, 1978; interview with Leonard Hall, July 27, 1977; and cf. Horace Beck, *The Folklore of Maine*, p. 127.

33. Interview with Richard and Verna Lilienthal, September 20, 1977.

34. Tape-recorded interview with Charles C. and Jessie Ells, Port Orford, February 6, 1978; interview with Cecil Crockett, January 18, 1978; interview with Jake Harlan, March 29, 1978; and interview with Carl and Lynne Harrington, February 9, 1978.

35. Interview with Richard and Verna Lilienthal, September 20, 1977.

36. Interview with Fred Anderson, August 24, 1977.

37. Interview with Carl and Lynne Harrington, February 9, 1978; interview with Norman and Virginia Walker, April 11, 1978; interview with Charles C. and Jessie Ells, February 6, 1978; and interview with Floyd Green, February 23, 1978.

38. Interview with Arnold and Doris Hockema, March 7, 1978.

39. Interview with Richard and Verna Lilienthal, September 20, 1977.

40. Interview with Keith Ott, machinist, mechanic, welder, and hydraulics expert, Charleston, March 13, 1978.

41. Interview with John Knutson, manager, Knutson Diesel and Machine, Coos Bay, September 7, 1977.

42. Interview with Cyrus, Sr., and Violet Little, April 17, 1978.

43. Interview with Keith Ott, March 13, 1978.

44. Interview with Arnold and Doris Hockema, March 7, 1978.

45. Interview with Fred Anderson, August 24, 1977.

46. Interview with Cecil Crockett, January 18, 1978.

47. Interview with "Bud" Hartley, manager, George's Marine Electronics, Charleston, March 15, 1978.

48. Interview with Arnold and Doris Hockema, March 7, 1978.

49. Ibid.

50. Interview with Richard and Verna Lilienthal, September 20, 1977; cf. Raoul Andersen, "Those Fisherman Lies," and "Hunt and Deceive"; also see Ingebrigtsen, *Roaming with Reta*, p. 51.

51. Interview with Arnold and Doris Hockema, March 7, 1978.

52. Interview with Fred Anderson, August 24, 1977; and interview with Carl and Lynne Harrington, February 9, 1978.

53. Interview with "Bud" Hartley, March 15, 1978.

54. Interview with Leonard Hall, July 27, 1977.

55. Interview with Bill Hillstrom, Jr., September 28, 1977.

Chapter 5

1. Information in this section comes from an interview with Cecil Crockett in his home, with his wife listening in from the kitchen, Charleston, January 18, 1978. See app. A for additional background on Crockett.

2. See A. K. Larssen and Sig Jaeger, *The ABC's of Fo'c'sle Living*, p. 91.

3. Information in this section comes from an interview with Carl and Lynne Harrington on the *Kodiak*, Charleston, February 9, 1978. See app. A for additional background on Carl.

4. Information in this section comes from an interview with Cyrus, Sr., and Violet Little in their home, Charleston, April 17, 1978. See app. A for additional background on Cyrus.

5. Information in this section comes from a tape-recorded interview with Leonard Hall in his home, with his wife present, Charleston, July 27, 1977. See app. A for additional background on Hall.

6. Information in this section comes from an interview with Norman and Virginia Walker in their home, Charleston, April 11, 1978. See app. A for further background on Norman and some on Virginia.

7. Information in this section comes from an interview with Jake Harlan on his boat, Charleston, September 1, 1977, and a long talk with him on the docks, Charleston, March 29, 1978. See app. A for more background on Harlan.

8. Information in this section comes from an interview with Floyd Green in his home, his wife within earshot, Charleston, February 23, 1978. For additional background on Floyd, see app. A.

9. Information in this section comes from a tape-recorded interview with Arnold and Doris Hockema in their home, Charleston, March 7, 1978. For further background on Arnold and some on Doris, see app. A.

10. Information in this section comes from a tape-recorded interview with Charles C. and Jessie Ells in their home, Port Orford, February 6, 1978. See app. A for more background on Charlie.

11. Information in this section comes from a tape-recorded interview with Richard and Verna Lilienthal in their home, Charleston, September 20, 1977. For additional background on Dick, see app. A.

12. Information in this section comes from a tape-recorded interview with Fred Anderson in a dockside cafe, Charleston, August 24, 1977. For more background on Anderson, see app. A.

13. Interview with Charlie and Jessie Ells, February 6, 1978.

14. H. C. Hanson, *Combination Fishing Vessel of the Pacific*, p. 1: "The stern sheer must be adjusted to the service intended since the boat deck has to be low for such fishing as trolling, dragging and longlining. It has to be high to support the heavy nets for seining." Also, p. 3, "The steel bulwarks are installed when dragging as indicated."

15. Ibid., p. 1: "The sheer is a matter of individual choice; my own is to give a good sheer forward for a dry boat; see fig. 1 — Outboard Profile and particularly the high chock rail for house protection. . . . The bow has a fair flair for keeping a dry boat."

16. R. B. Wood-Jones, *Traditional Domestic Architecture in the Banbury Region*, chap. 10, "The Process of Improvement, 1600–1800."

17. Robert J. Browning, *Fisheries of the North Pacific*, pp. 146–48, regarding Mario Puretic and his famous invention; and Damron, "The Emergence of Salmon Trolling," p. 108, for discussion of Wood Freeman's invention of the iron mike in the 1930s.

18. Browning, *Fisheries of the North Pacific*, p. 125.

19. Ibid., p. 104; and H. C. Hanson, *Combination Fishing Vessel of the Pacific*.

20. Interview with Richard and Verna Lilienthal, September 20, 1977.

21. Ibid.

22. Interview with Fred Anderson, August 24, 1977.

23. Verna Lilienthal used this phrase: "It's all a game. It still is. They compete with different nets out there yet, you know, *They all have to have a new wrinkle* [author's italics]." Interview with Richard and Verna Lilienthal, September 20, 1977. Fisherman Harold Inge-brigtsen also uses the phrase repeatedly in *Roaming with Reta*.

24. Elizabeth Mosby Adler, "Little Houses Made of Ticky-Tacky"; Petr Bogatyrev, *The Functions of Folk Costume in Moravian-Slovakia*, especially pp. 85, 93; Anne Louise Gjesdal Christensen, "Dwelling as Communication," and Gösta Arvaston's "Commentary"; Priscilla Denby, "The Automobile"; Susan Tosaw Marks, "Low Riding"; and Michael Ann Williams, " 'Old Home Place,' " and "Rethinking the House."

Chapter 6

1. Information on Hillstrom Shipbuilding mainly comes from an interview with Bill Hillstrom, Jr., draughtsman and manager, Coos Bay, September 28, 1977.

2. Information on Nelson Log Bronc mainly comes from a tape-recorded interview with Jack Wilskey, marine architect and engineer, manager, Eastside, September 13, 1977.

3. Information on Kelley Boat Works mainly comes from an interview with Jack Kelley, boatwright and manager, Charleston, March 11, 1978.

4. Information on Humbert's boat shop mainly comes from interviews with Fred Humbert, Haynes Inlet, March 11 and 16, 1978.

5. Information on Koontz Machine Shop mainly comes from interviews with Mr. Smith, co-manager, Coos Bay, March 28, 1978, and Art Horton and Elmer Jorgensen, propellor repairman and blacksmith, respectively, Coos Bay, April 6 and 7, 1978.

6. Information on Knutson Diesel and Machine comes from talks with John Knutson, manager, Harold Knutson, manager of Knutson Towboat, and Virginia Maine, accountant, Coos Bay, September 7, 1977.

7. Information on Ott's business comes from an interview with Keith Ott, Charleston, March 13, 1978.

8. Information on Bill's Machine and Welding comes from an interview with Bill Chard, Charleston, March 15, 1978.

9. Information on George's Marine Electronics comes from an interview with George Hartley's son "Bud," manager, Charleston, March 15, 1978.

10. Information on Oregon-Pacific Company comes from interviews with Norm Anderson, manager, North Bend, March 28 and 30, 1978; information on Hanson's Landing comes from an interview with Louise and David Hanson, Charleston, April 4, 1978.

11. Warren E. Roberts, "Folk Crafts," pp. 233–52; see also Carl Bridenbaugh, *The Colonial Craftsman*, pp. 126–30.

12. Interview with Lorance Eickworth, Coos Bay, August 29, 1977.

13. Jim Bottom, "Fred Nelson—Inventor of the 'Bronc,'" and Anonymous, "Hanson Serves Both Sports and Commercial Fishermen."

14. Tape-recorded interview of John L. Koontz by Jeff Galbraith, Coos Bay, Southwestern Oregon Community College Living History Series cassette, no. 321 (November 1972).

15. Interview with Jack Wilskey, September 13, 1977.

16. Ibid.

17. George Sturt, *The Wheelwright's Shop*, p. 69, also pp. 3–4.

18. C. Richard K. Lunt, "Lobsterboat Building on the Eastern Coast of Maine," pp. 102, 113–17.

19. Cf. Roger D. Abrahams, "Personal Power and Social Restraint in the Definition of Folklore," p. 28:

    If folklore is the embodiment of the wisdom of the group and, therefore, the key to its value system, self-conceptions, and anxieties, then the ones who know and perform items of traditional expression have the group's most powerful weapons at their disposal. The fact that the performer knows the lore, can perform it effectively, and is permitted to perform it gives him a status and a power role in the community that would be unavailable to him through any other channel.

20. Interview with Jack Wilskey, September 13, 1977.

21. Interview with Floyd Green, Fisherman, Charleston, February 23, 1978.

22. Tape-recorded interview with Richard and Verna Lilienthal, Charleston, September 20, 1977.

23. Tape-recorded interview with Leonard Hall, Charleston, July 27, 1977.

24. Interview with Jack Wilskey, September 13, 1977.

25. Louis J. Chiaramonte, *Craftsman-Client Contracts*.

26. See chap. 2, nn. 51–54, 56, above; Wolfgang Rudolph, *Inshore Fishing Craft on the Southern Baltic from Holstein to Curonia*, p. 3; and I. M. Killip, "Crofting in the Isle of Man," pp. 68–69.

27. See Jeremy Tunstall, *The Fishermen*; Michael K. Orbach, *Hunters, Seamen, and Entrepreneurs*; and cf. Joseba Zulaika, *Terranova*.

28. Cf. Bridenbaugh, *The Colonial Craftsman*, pp. 153-54; Roberts, "Folk Crafts," p. 236; and Sturt, *The Wheelwright's Shop*, pp. 197-98.

29. See Chiaramonte, *Craftsman-Client Contracts*, pp. 51-62, for definition and discussion of open and specified contracts.

30. Ibid.

31. See Rudolph, *Inshore Fishing Craft*, p. 3; Bridenbaugh, *The Colonial Craftsman*, pp. 65-66; and Roberts, "Folk Crafts," pp. 234-36, 240.

32. For example, J. Geraint Jenkins, *The English Farm Wagon* and *Traditional Country Craftsmen*; Roberts, "Folk Crafts," p. 240; and Sturt, *The Wheelwright's Shop*, in general.

33. Jenkins, *English Farm Wagon*, p. 74.

34. Ibid., pp. 53-54; also throughout his book Bridenbaugh, *The Colonial Craftsman*, makes a similar distinction in contrasting crafts of the southern United States with village crafts of the northern United States, and northern village crafts with northern urban crafts.

35. Chiaramonte, *Craftsman-Client Contracts*, p. 58.

36. Cf. Bridenbaugh, *The Colonial Craftsman*, pp. 92-95.

37. Warren E. Roberts develops this concept in his "Indiana Folklore" course at Indiana University. See Roberts, "Folk Crafts," pp. 246-50, for a rough idea of what he means.

38. Wilbur Zelinsky, *The Cultural Geography of the United States*, pp. 13-14, explains the "Doctrine of First Effective Settlement." Fred B. Kniffen's earlier statement and application of the same concept, which he terms "initial occupance" in "Folk Housing: Key to Diffusion," is particularly applicable.

Chapter 7

1. Cf. Ronald H. Buchanan, "Tradition and Change in Rural Ulster;" Gwyn E. Jones, "The Nature and Consequence of Technical Change in Farming;" and G. B. Thompson, "Rural Industry in Modern Ulster Society."

2. David A. Taylor, *Boat Building in Winterton, Trinity Bay, Newfoundland*, p. 120.

3. Henry Glassie, "The Variation of Concepts within Tradition," pp. 184, 231.

4. Henry Glassie, "Structure and Function, Folklore and the Artifact," pp. 335-38.

5. Cf. Glassie, "The Variation of Concepts within Tradition," p. 231.

6. Roger D. Abrahams, "Personal Power and Social Restraint in the Definition of Folklore," p. 17.

7. Dan Ben-Amos, "Toward a Definition of Folklore in Context," p. 13.

8. For example, see Willy Elmer, *The Terminology of Fishing*; Jerry Eunson, "The Fair-Isle Fishing Marks;" James C. Faris, *Cat Harbour*, pp. 23-28; Horace Beck, *Folklore and the Sea*, p. 58; David W. Maurer, "Speech Peculiarities of the North Atlantic Fishermen;" and R. Geoffrey Stiles, "Fishermen, Wives and Radios," p. 46. For a contrary opinion clearly not grounded in fieldwork and the fisherman's experience, see Eugene B. Vest, "Names on the Ocean Bottom, or Some Observations on the Invisible Landscape."

9. Bronislaw Malinowski, *Argonauts of the Western Pacific*, p. 116.

10. Respective to the order of the references, Don Yoder, "Folk Medicine," p. 199; Malinowski, *Argonauts*, p. 116; and Abrahams, "Personal Power," pp. 18-19.

11.   Abrahams, "Personal Power," pp. 17–18.

12.   Sigurd Erixon, "An Introduction to Folklife Research or Nordic Ethnology," *Folk-Liv* 14 (1950) p. 15.

Bibliography

Abrahams, Roger D. "Introductory Remarks to a Rhetorical Theory of Folklore." *Journal of American Folklore* 81(1968):143–58.

_____. "Personal Power and Social Restraint in the Definition of Folklore." In *Toward New Perspectives in Folklore*, edited by Américo Paredes and Richard Bauman, pp. 16–30. Austin: University of Texas Press, 1972.

Acheson, James M. "Fisheries Management and Social Context: The Case of the Maine Lobster Fishery." *Transactions of the American Fisheries Society* 104:4(1975):653–68.

_____. "The Lobster Fiefs: Economic and Ecological Effects of Territoriality in the Maine Lobster Industry." *Human Ecology* 3:3(1975):183–207.

_____. "Technical Skills and Fishing Success in the Maine Lobster Industry." In *Material Culture: Styles, Organizations, and Dynamics of Technology*, edited by Heather Lechtman and Robert Merrill, pp. 111–38. St. Paul, MN: West Publishing Co., 1977.

_____. "Territories of the Lobstermen." *Natural History Magazine* 81:4(1972):60–69.

Adler, Elizabeth Mosby. "Little Houses Made of Ticky-Tacky: Personalization and Conformity in Expansion Architecture." Paper presented at the annual meeting of the American Folklore Society, Pittsburgh, PA, October 1980.

_____. " 'My Mother Had One of Those': The Experience of the Pie Safe." In *American Material Culture and Folklife: A Prologue and Dialogue*, edited by Simon J. Bronner, pp. 119–28. Ann Arbor, MI: UMI Research Press, 1985.

Adler, Elizabeth Mosby, and Adler, Thomas A. "Folk Architectural Teratology: Problems in the Study of an Indiana Farm." *Folklore Forum* 12:2/3(1979):199–221.

Adler, Thomas A. "Musical Instruments, Tools, and the Experience of Control." In *American Material Culture and Folklife: A Prologue and Dialogue*, edited by Simon J. Bronner, pp. 103–11. Ann Arbor, MI: UMI Research Press, 1985.

Adney, Edwin Tappan, and Chapelle, Howard I. *The Bark Canoes and Skin Boats of North America*. U.S. National Museum Bulletin, no. 230. Washington, DC: Smithsonian Institution, 1964.

Andersen, Raoul. "Hunt and Deceive: Information Management in Deep-Sea Trawler Fishing." In *North Atlantic Fishermen: Anthropological Essays on Modern Fishing*, edited by Raoul Andersen and Cato Wadel, pp. 120–40. Newfoundland Social and Economic Papers, no. 5. St. John's: Memorial University of Newfoundland Institute of Social and Economic Research, 1972.

_____. "Those Fisherman Lies: Custom and Competition in North Atlantic Fisherman Communication." *Ethnos* 38(1973):153–64.

Andersen, Raoul, and Wadel, Cato. "Comparative Problems in Fishing Adaptations." In *North Atlantic Fishermen: Anthropological Essays on Modern Fishing*, edited by Raoul Andersen and Cato Wadel, pp. 141–65. Newfoundland Social and Economic Papers, no. 5. St. John's: Memorial University of Newfoundland Institute of Social and Economic Research, 1972.

_____, eds. *North Atlantic Fishermen: Anthropological Essays on Modern Fishing*. Newfoundland Social and Economic Papers, no. 5. St. John's: Memorial University of Newfoundland Institute of Social and Economic Research, 1972.

Andrews, R. W., and Larssen, A. K. *Fish and Ships*. Seattle, WA: Superior Publishing Co., 1955.

Anonymous. "Hanson Serves Both Sports and Commercial Fishermen." In *The World*. Coos Bay, OR, September 27, 1975.

Anson, Peter F. *Fisher Folk-Lore: Old Customs, Taboos, and Superstitions among Fisher Folk, Especially in Brittany and Normandy, and on the East Coast of Scotland*. London: Faith Press, 1965.

_____. *Fishermen and Fishing Ways*. London: George G. Harrap, 1932.

_____. *Scots Fisherfolk*. Banff: Banffshire Journal for the Saltire Society, 1950.

The Apprenticeshop. *Norse Boat Building in North America*. Bath, ME: Maine Maritime Museum, 1981.

Arvaston, Gösta. "Commentary." *Ethnologia Scandinavica* 8(1979):88–91.

Baldwin, Leland D. *The Keelboat Age on Western Waters*. Pittsburgh, PA: Pittsburgh University Press, 1941.

Bamford, Edwin F. *Social Aspects of the Fishing Industry at Los Angeles Harbor*. Sociological Monograph, no. 18. *Studies in Sociology* 5:2(1921).

Bárdarson, Hjalmar R. "Icelandic Fishing Vessels." *Iceland Review* 2:4(1969):29–36; 3:1(1965):19–24.

Barnett, H. G. "Culture Element Distributions: VII, Oregon Coast." *Anthropological Records* 1:3(1937):155–203.

_____. *Innovation: The Basis of Cultural Change*. New York: McGraw-Hill Book Co., 1953.

Beard, Tom. *The Paulsbo Boat*. Traditional Small Craft of the Northwest, vol. 1. Seattle, WA: The Center for Wooden Boats, 1981.

Beattie, John. *Understanding an African Kingdom: Bunyoro*. New York: Holt, Rinehart, and Winston, 1965.

Beck, Horace P. *Folklore and the Sea*. Mystic Seaport Marine Historical Association American Maritime Library, vol. 6. Middletown, CT: Wesleyan University Press, 1973.

_____. *The Folklore of Maine*. Philadelphia: J. B. Lippincott, 1957.

_____. "Sea Lore." *Northwest Folklore* 2:2(1967):1–13.

Beckham, Stephen Dow. *Coos Bay: The Pioneer Period 1851–1890*. Coos Bay: Arago Books, 1973.

_____. "Oregon's South Coast: A Selected Bibliography." Spring 1975. Dittoed.

_____, ed. *Tall Tales from Rogue River: The Yarns of Hathaway Jones*. Bloomington: Indiana University Press, 1974.

Ben-Amos, Dan. "Analytical Categories and Ethnic Genres." *Genre* 2:3(1969):275–301. Also in *Folklore Genres*, edited by Dan Ben-Amos, pp. 215–42. Austin: University of Texas Press, 1976.

_____. "Toward a Definition of Folklore in Context." In *Towards New Perspectives in Folklore*, edited by Américo Paredes and Richard Bauman, pp. 3–15. Austin: University of Texas Press, 1972.

Bogatyrev, Petr. *The Function of Folk Costume in Moravian Slovakia*. Translated by Richard G. Crum. Approaches to Semiotics, no. 5. The Hague: Mouton and Co., 1971.

Bottom, Jim. "Fred Nelson—Inventor of the 'Bronc.'" In *Horizon '79*, pp. 92–93. Coos Bay: Southwestern Oregon Publishing Co., May 1979.

Brewington, Marion V. *Chesapeake Bay Log Canoes and Bugeyes*. Cambridge, MD: Cornell Maritime Press, Inc., 1963.

Bridenbaugh, Carl. *The Colonial Craftsman*. 1950. Paperback ed. Chicago: University of Chicago Press, Phoenix Books, 1961.

Bromberg, Erik. "Frontier Humor: Plain and Fancy." *Oregon Historical Quarterly* 61(1960):261–342.

Bronner, Simon J. " 'Visible Proofs': Material Culture Study in American Folkloristics." *American Quarterly* 35:3(1983):316–38.

Bronner, Simon J., and Poyser, Stephen J., eds. *Approaches to the Study of Material Aspects of American Folk Culture. Folklore Forum* 12:2/3(1979).

Brooks, Alfred A. "The Boats of Ash Point, Maine." *American Neptune* 2(1942):307–23.

Browning, Robert J. *Fisheries of the North Pacific: History, Species, Gear and Processes.* Anchorage: Alaska Northwest Publishing Co., 1974.

Brunvand, Jan Harold. "Sailors' and Cowboys' Folklore in Two Popular Classics." *Southern Folklore Quarterly* 29:4(December 1965):266–83.

Buchanan, Ronald H. "Tradition and Change in Rural Ulster." *Folk-Life* 3(1965):39–45.

Burgess, John. *Fishing Boats and Equipment.* London: Fishing News, 1966.

Butler, Victor. *The Little Nord Easter: Reminiscences of a Placentia Bayman.* Edited by Wilfred W. Wareham. Community Studies, no. 1. St. John's: Memorial University of Newfoundland Folklore and Language Archive, 1975.

Byington, Robert H., ed. *Working Americans: Contemporary Approaches to Occupational Folklife.* Smithsonian Folklife Studies, no. 3. Los Angeles: California Folklore Society, 1978.

Carey, George. *A Faraway Time and Place: Lore of the Eastern Shore.* Washington, DC: Robert B. Luce, 1971.

Carranco, Lynwood. "A Miscellany of Folk Beliefs from the Redwood Country." *Western Folklore* 26:3(1967):169–76.

Chapelle, Howard I. *The American Fishing Schooners 1825–1935.* New York: W. W. Norton and Co., 1973.

———. *American Small Sailing Craft: Their Design, Development, and Construction.* New York: W. W. Norton and Co., 1951.

———. *Boatbuilding: A Complete Handbook of Wooden Boat Construction.* New York: W. W. Norton and Co., 1941.

———. "Migrations of an American Boat Type." Contributions from the Museum of History and Technology, U.S. National Museum Bulletin, no. 228, Paper 25, pp. 133–54. Washington, DC: Smithsonian Institution, 1961.

———. *The National Watercraft Collection.* U.S. National Bulletin, no. 219. Washington, DC: Smithsonian Institution, 1960.

Chiaramonte, Louis J. *Craftsman-Client Contracts: Interpersonal Relationships in a Newfoundland Fishing Community.* Newfoundland Social and Economic Studies, no. 10. St. John's: Memorial University of Newfoundland Institute of Social and Economic Research, 1970.

Christensen, Anne Louise Gjesdal. "Dwelling as Communication." *Ethnologia Scandinavica* 8(1979):68–88.

Cleaver, F. C., ed. *Fisheries Statistics of Oregon.* Oregon Fish Commission Contribution, no. 16. Portland, OR, September 1955.

Cluff, Dohn A. "Lobster Fishing on the Maine Coast: Past and Present." *American Neptune* 14(1954):203–8.

Cobb, John N. *Pacific Salmon Fisheries.* Washington, DC, 1930.

Comeaux, Malcolm. "Origin and Evolution of Mississippi River Fishing Craft." *Pioneer America* 10:1(June 1978):73–97.

Commercial Fishermen's Wives Association of the Port of Coos Bay, *Cook Book Presented by the Fishwives of Charleston, Oregon.* North Bend, OR: Wegford Publications, 1972.

Coover, Elizabeth, and Garner, Ellen. *Life and Legend in the Coos Bay Area: A Story of the Indians and Pioneers Who First Settled on Coos Bay.* Coos Bay: School District 9, 1961.

Coppedge, Robert O., and Smith, Frederick J. *Background on Oregon's Marine Industry.* Oregon State University Cooperative Extension Service Circular, no. 750. Corvallis, OR, August 1970.

Coull, James R. *Crofter-Fishermen in Norway and Scotland.* Aberdeen: Department of Geography, University of Aberdeen, 1971.

———. "Fisheries in the North East of Scotland before 1800." *Scottish Studies* 13(1969):17–32.

———. "Melness, a Crofting Community on the North Coast of Scotland." *Scottish Studies* 7(1963):180–98.

Cove, John James. "A Comparative Approach to Decision-Making: Risk-Taking by Fish Boat Captains in Two Canadian Fleets." Ph.D. diss., University of British Columbia, 1971.

Crawford, Iain A. "The Tidal Fishing Pound." *Scottish Studies* 5(1961):110–11.

Crumlin-Pederson, Ole. "Skin or Wood? A Study of the Origin of the Scandinavian Plank Boat." In *Ships and Shipyards, Sailors and Fishermen: Introduction to Maritime Ethnology,* edited by Olof Hasslöf, Henning Henningsen, and Arne Emil Christiansen, Jr., pp. 208–34. Copenhagen: Rosenkilde and Bagger, 1972.

Damron, John Earnest. "The Emergence of Salmon Trolling on the American Northwest Coast: A Maritime Historical Geography." Ph.D. diss., University of Oregon, 1971.

Deetz, James. *Invitation to Archaeology.* New York: The Natural History Press, 1967.

Dégh, Linda, and Vázsonyi, Andrew. "The Hypothesis of Multi-Conduit Transmission in Folklore." In *Folklore: Performance and Communication,* edited by Dan Ben-Amos and Kenneth S. Goldstein, pp. 207–52. The Hague: Mouton, 1975.

Denby, Priscilla. "The Automobile: Folklore and Connotative Experience." Paper presented at the annual meeting of the American Folklore Society, Detroit, MI, November 1977.

Dodge, Orvil. *Pioneer History of Coos and Curry Counties, Oregon: Heroic Deeds and Thrilling Adventures of the Early Settlers.* Salem, OR: Capital Printing Co., 1898.

Douthit, Nathan. "Local History of Southwestern Oregon" and "Additions to Local History of Oregon." Southwestern Oregon Community College Learning Resource Center. Coos Bay, Spring 1974. Mimeographed bibliography, 31 pp.

Eberhart, Beth. *A Crew of Two.* New York: Doubleday, 1961.

Elísson, Már. "The Fishing Fleet and Its Equipment." *Iceland Review* 2:3(1964):36–39.

Elmer, Willy. *The Terminology of Fishing: A Survey of English and Welsh Inshore Fishing Things and Words.* Cooper Monographs, English Dialect Series, no. 19 (Basel, Switzerland). Bern: Francke Verlag, 1973.

Erixon, Sigurd. "An Introduction to Folklife Research or Nordic Ethnology." *Folk-Liv* 14(1950):5–15.

Eunson, Jerry. "The Fair-Isle Fishing-Marks." *Scottish Studes* 5(1961):181–98.

Evans, George Ewart. *Tools of Their Trade: An Oral History of Men at Work c. 1900.* New York: Taplinger Publishing Co., 1970.

Eydal, A. "Fisheries." *Proceedings of the Association of American Geographers* 2(1970):56–58.

Faris, James C. *Cat Harbour: A Newfoundland Fishing Settlement.* Newfoundland Social and Economic Studies, no. 3. St. John's: Memorial University of Newfoundland Institute of Social and Economic Research, 1972.

Firestone, Marc. "An Examination of the Coastal Changes of Charleston, Oregon." Oregon Institute of Marine Biology. Charleston, OR, Spring 1973.

Firth, Raymond. *Malay Fishermen: Their Peasant Economy.* London: Kegan Paul, Trench, Trubner and Co., 1946.

Fisher, R. Barry. *An Effective Combination Trawl for West Coast Draggers: Atlantic-Western Trawls.* Oregon State University Sea Grant College Program Publication, no. ORESU-T1-74-001. Agricultural Experiment Station Bulletin, no. 615. Corvallis, OR, July 1974.

Fricke, Peter, ed. *Seafarer and Community.* British Sociological Association Proceedings. London: Croom Helm, 1973.

Gersuny, Carl, and Poggie, John J., Jr. "Danger and Fishermen's Taboos." *Maritimes* 16:1(1972):3–4.

_____. "Harbor Improvements and Fishing at Point Judith." *Rhode Island History* 32:1(1973):22–32.

Glassie, Henry. "The Double-Crib Barn in South Central Pennsylvania." Part one, *Pioneer America* 1:1(1969):9–16; part two, *Pioneer America* 1:2(1969):40–45; part three, *Pioneer America* 2:1(1970):47–52; and part four, *Pioneer America* 2:2(1970):23–34.

_____. "Folk Art." In *Folklore and Folklife: An Introduction*, edited by Richard M. Dorson, pp. 253–80. Chicago: University of Chicago Press, 1972. Also in *Material Culture Studies in America*, edited by Thomas J. Schlereth, pp. 124–40. Nashville, TN: The American Association for State and Local History, 1982.

_____. *Folk Housing in Middle Virginia: A Structural Analysis of Historic Artifacts*. Knoxville: University of Tennessee Press, 1975.

_____. "The Nature of the New World Artifact: The Instance of the Dugout Canoe." In *Festschrift für Robert Wildhaber*, edited by Walter Escher, Theo Gantner, and Hans Trümpy, pp. 153–70. Basel: G. Krebs, 1973.

_____. *Pattern in the Material Folk Culture of the Eastern United States*. Philadelphia: University of Pennsylvania Press, 1968.

_____. "The Pennsylvania Barn in the South." *Pennsylvania Folklife* 15:2(Winter 1965–66):8–19; and 15:4(Summer 1966):12–25.

_____. "Structure and Function, Folklore and the Artifact." *Semiotica* 7:4(1973):313–51.

_____. "The Variation of Concepts within Tradition: Barn Building in Otsego County, New York." In *Man and Cultural Heritage: Papers in Honor of Fred B. Kniffen*, edited by H. J. Walker and W. G. Haag, pp. 177–235. Geoscience and Man, vol. 5. Baton Rouge: Louisiana State University, 1974.

_____. "The Wedderspoon Farm." *New York Folklore Quarterly* 22:3(1966):165–87.

Golde, Peggy, ed. *Women in the Field: Anthropological Experiences*. Chicago: Aldine Publishing Co., 1970.

Goldstein, Kenneth S. *A Guide for Field Workers in Folklore*. Hatboro, PA: Folklore Associates, 1964.

Goode, William J., and Hatt, Paul K. *Methods in Social Research*. New York: McGraw-Hill, 1952.

Green, Archie. "Industrial Lore: A Bibliographic-Semantic Inquiry." In *Working Americans: Contemporary Approaches to Occupational Folklife*, edited by Robert H. Byington, pp. 71–102. Smithsonian Folklife Studies, no. 3. Los Angeles: California Folklore Society, 1978.

Greenhill, Basil. *The Archaeology of the Boat*. Middletown, CT: Wesleyan University Press, 1976.

Gunda, Béla, ed. *The Fishing Culture of the World: Studies in Ethnology, Cultural Ecology and Folklore*. 2 vols. Budapest: Akadémiai Kiadó, 1984.

Guthorn, Peter J. *The Sea Bright Skiff and Other Jersey Shore Boats*. New Brunswick, NJ: Rutgers University Press, 1971.

Guthrie, Besse L. "Index to Living History Series." Southwestern Oregon Community College Learning Resource Center. Coos Bay, 1976.

Hage, Karl Per. "On Some Formal and Substantive Properties of a Maritime Communication System." Ph.D. diss., University of Washington, 1971.

Hanson, H. C. *Combination Fishing Vessel of the Pacific*. Seattle, WA, 1953. Private publication.

_____. *The Gillnet Boat and Its Operations in the Pacific Coast*. Seattle, WA, 1954. Private publication.

_____. *The Tuna Clipper of the Pacific*. Seattle, WA, 1953. Private publication.

Harry, George Y., Jr., and Morgan, Alfred R. "History of the Oregon Trawl Fishery, 1884–1961." Oregon Fish Commission Research Brief, no. 9:1(Portland, OR, 1963):5–26.

Hasslöf, Olof. "Main Principles in the Technology of Ship-Building." In *Ships and Shipyards, Sailors and Fishermen: Introduction to Maritime Ethnology*, edited by Olof Hasslöf, Henning

Henningsen, and Arne Emil Christiansen, Jr., pp. 27–72. Copenhagen: Rosenkilde and Bagger, 1972.

Hasslöf, Olof; Henningsen, Henning; and Christiansen, Arne Emil, Jr., eds. *Ships and Shipyards, Sailors and Fishermen: Introduction to Maritime Ethnology*. Copenhagen: Rosenkilde and Bagger, 1972.

Helmer-Hansen, Kari. "Growth of a Fishing Village. The Economy of the Community in Utgårdskilen on Hvaler 1900–1965." In *Ships and Shipyards, Sailors and Fishermen: Introduction to Maritime Ethnology*, edited by Olof Hasslöf, Henning Henningsen, and Arne Emil Christiansen, Jr., pp. 189–207. Copenhagen: Rosenkilde and Bagger, 1972.

Holm, Don. "The Dory Story in Oregon." *The Oregonian* (Portland, OR), May 2, 1976.

Hornell, James. *Fishing in Many Waters*. Cambridge: The University Press, 1950.

———. *Water Transport, Origins, and Early Evolution*. Cambridge: Cambridge University Press, 1946. Reprint. Newton Abbot: David and Charles, 1970.

Hunt, Charles B. *Natural Regions of the United States and Canada*. San Francisco: W. H. Freeman and Co., 1974.

Ingebrigtsen, Harold R. *Roaming with Reta; Trolling for Salmon and Keeping Up with Affairs on Shore with Commercial Fishermen Working the Northwest Waters*. New York: William-Frederick Press, 1954.

Ives, Edward D. *Joe Scott: The Woodsman Songmaker*. Urbana: University of Illinois Press, 1978.

———. "A Manual for Field Workers." *Northeast Folklore* 15 (1974).

Jackman, E. R., ed., "After the Covered Wagons: Recollections of Russel C. and Ellis S. Dement." *Oregon Historical Quarterly* 63 (1962):5–40.

Jaresh, Elissa. "Fish Sniffers." *Western Folklore* 26:3(1967):188.

Jenkins, J. Geraint. *The English Farm Wagon*. Lingfield, Surrey: The Oakwood Press, 1961.

———. *Traditional Country Craftsmen*. London: Routledge and Kegan Paul, 1965.

Jensen, William S. *The Salmon Processing Industry, Part One: The Institutional Framework and Its Evolution*. Oregon State University Sea Grant Publication, no. ORESU-T-76-003. Agricultural Experiment Station Circular, no. 654. Corvallis, OR, May 1976.

Johnson, Paula. " 'This is the way they like 'em around here': Workboat Building in Southern Maryland." Paper presented at the annual meeting of the American Folklore Society, Nashville, TN, October 1983.

Jones, Gwyn E. "The Nature and Consequences of Technical Change in Farming." *Folk-Life* 3(1965):79–87.

Jones, Michael Owen. "Chairmaking in Appalachia: A Study in Style and Creative Imagination in American Folk Art." Ph.D. diss., Indiana University, 1970.

———. *The Handmade Object and Its Maker*. Berkeley: University of California Press, 1975.

———. "L. A. Add-Ons and Re-Dos: Renovation in Folk Art and Architectural Design." In *Perspectives on American Folk Art*, edited by Ian M. G. Quimby and Scott T. Swank, pp. 325–63. New York: W. W. Norton and Co., 1980.

Jones, Suzi. *Oregon Folklore*. Eugene: University of Oregon Press and the Oregon Arts Commission, 1977.

———. "Regionalization: A Rhetorical Strategy." *Journal of the Folklore Institute* 13(1976):105–20.

Jones, Walter G., and Harry, George Y., Jr. "The Oregon Trawl Fishery for Mink Food—1948–1957." Oregon Fish Commission Research Brief, no. 8:1 (Portland, OR, 1961):14–30.

Jordan, Terry G. *Texas Log Buildings: A Folk Architecture*. Austin: University of Texas Press, 1978.

Junek, Oscar Waldemar. *Isolated Communities: A Study of a Labrador Fishing Village*. New York: American Book Co., 1937.

Killip, I. M. "Crofting on the Isle of Man." *Folk-Life* 9(1971):61–78.

Kniffen, Fred B. "American Cultural Geography and Folklife." In *American Folklife*, edited by Don Yoder, pp. 51–70. Austin: University of Texas Press, 1976.

———. "Folk Housing: Key to Diffusion." *Annals of the Association of American Geographers* 55(1965):549–77.

Kniffen, Fred B., and Glassie, Henry. "Building in Wood in the Eastern United States: A Time-Place Perspective." *The Geographical Review* 56(1966):40–66. Also in *Material Culture Studies in America*, edited by Thomas J. Schlereth, pp. 237–250. Nashville, TN: The American Association for State and Local History, 1982.

Knipmeyer, William P. "Folk Boats of Eastern French Louisiana." Edited by Henry Glassie. In *American Folklife*, edited by Don Yoder, pp. 105–49. Austin: University of Texas Press, 1976.

Landberg, Leif, comp. *A Bibliography for the Anthropological Study of Fishing Industries and Maritime Communities* and *Supplement, 1973–1977*. Kingston: University of Rhode Island, International Center for Marine Resources Development, 1973 and 1979, respectively.

Larssen, A. K., and Jaeger, Sig. *The ABC's of Fo'c'sle Living*. Seattle, WA: Madrona Publishers, 1976.

Lewis, Pierce. "Learning from Looking: Geographic and Other Writing about the American Cultural Landscape." *American Quarterly* 35:3(1983):242–61.

Liao, David S., and Stevens, Joe B. *Oregon's Commercial Fishermen: Characteristics, Profits, and Incomes in 1972*. Oregon State University Sea Grant Publication, no. ORESU-T1-75-001. Corvallis, OR, July 1975.

Loy, William G. *Atlas of Oregon*. Eugene: University of Oregon Press, 1976.

Lund, Jens. "Fishing as a Folk Occupation in the Lower Ohio Valley." Ph.D. diss., Indiana University, 1983.

Lunt, C. Richard K. "Lobsterboat Building on the Eastern Coast of Maine: A Comparative Study." Ph.D. diss., Indiana University, 1975.

———. "The St. Lawrence River Skiff and the Folklore of Boats." *New York Folklore Quarterly* 29(1973):254–68.

———. "They Still Tailor Maine Lobster Boats." *Festival of American Folklife* (1970), pp. 40–42. Washington, DC: Smithsonian Institution, 1970.

Maccoby, E. E., and Maccoby, Nathan. "The Interview: A Tool of Social Science." In *Handbook of Social Psychology*, vol. 1, edited by Gardner Lindzey, pp. 449–87. Reading, MA: Addison-Wesley, 1954.

MacLeish, William H. "New England Fishermen Battle the Winter Ocean on Georges Bank." *Smithsonian* 16:2 (May 1985): 105–17.

Malinowski, Bronislaw. *Argonauts of the Western Pacific*. 1922. Reprint. New York: E. P. Dutton and Co., Dutton Paperback, 1961.

Marks, Susan Tosaw. "Low Riding." Paper presented at the annual meeting of the American Folklore Society, Pittsburgh, PA, October 1980.

Marshall, Howard Wight. "The 'Thousand Acres' Log House, Monroe County, Indiana." *Pioneer America* 3:1(1971):48–56.

Mather, J. Y. "Boats and Boatmen of Orkney and Shetland." *Scottish Studies* 8(1965):19–32.

Maurer, David W. "Speech Peculiarities of the North Atlantic Fishermen." In *Language of the Underworld*, collected and edited by Allan W. Futrell and Charles B. Wordell, pp. 13–14. Lexington, KY: The University Press of Kentucky, 1981.

McCarl, Robert S., Jr. "Occupational Folklife: A Theoretical Hypothesis." In *Working Americans: Contemporary Approaches to Occupational Folklore*, edited by Robert H. Byington, pp. 3–18. Smithsonian Folklife Studies, no. 3. Los Angeles: California Folklore Society, 1978.

———. "The Production Welder: Product, Process and the Industrial Craftsman." *New York Folklore Quarterly* 30:4(December 1974):243–53.

McKee, Eric. "Traditional British Boatbuilding Methods." *Mariner's Mirror* 62(1976):3–14.

McLain, Bruce H. "Commercial Fishing and Its Related Industries." Oregon Institute of Marine Biology. Charleston, OR, Spring 1973.

McLean, William T., ed. *An Historical Sketch of Coos County—Its Cities and Industries.* Marshfield (Coos Bay): Marshfield High School, 1949.

Moe, John F. "Concepts of Shelter: The Folk Poetics of Space, Change and Continuity." *Journal of Popular Culture* 11:1(1977):219/82–253/115.

_____. "The Relation of Personal Narrative and Folk Art and Architecture." Paper presented at the annual meeting of the American Folklore Society, Detroit, MI, November 1977.

Mullen, Patrick Borden. *I Heard the Old Fishermen Say: Folklore of the Texas Gulf.* Austin: University of Texas Press, 1978.

National Marine Fisheries Service. *Fishery Statistics of the United States 1974.* U.S. Department of Commerce, National Oceanic and Atmospheric Administration Statistical Digest, no. 68. Washington, DC, 1976.

_____. *Fishery Statistics of the United States 1977.* U.S. Department of Commerce, National Oceanic and Atmospheric Administration Statistical Digest, no. 71. Washington, DC, February 1984.

Needham, Walter, and Mussey, Barrows. *A Book of Country Things.* Brattleboro, VT: The Stephen Green Press, 1965.

Norton, Virgil J., and Miller, Morton M. *An Economic Study of the Boston Large-Trawler Labor Force.* Bureau of Commercial Fisheries Circular, no. 248. Washington, DC: U.S. Department of the Interior Fish and Wildlife Service, 1966.

Orbach, Michael K. *Hunters, Seamen, and Entrepreneurs: The Tuna Fishermen of San Diego.* Berkeley: University of California Press, 1977.

Oregon Coastal Conservation and Development Commission. *Economic Survey and Analysis of the Oregon Coastal Zone.* Florence, OR, November 1974.

_____. *Summary, Final Report.* Florence, OR, 1975.

Oregon Department of Fish and Wildlife. "Groundfish and Shrimp Investigations, Annual Report." Newport, OR, 1956— .

Oregon State Marine Board. *Boating in Coastal Waters.* Rev. ed. Salem and Corvallis: Oregon State Extension Service and Sea Grant Marine Advisory Program, 1976.

Oregon State University Cooperative Extension Service, Sea Grant Advisory Program, *Fisheries-Related Marine Career Training Needs on the Oregon Coast, 1971–1975.* Corvallis, OR, June 1971.

Oregon State University Department of Agricultural and Resource Economics, *Socio-Economics of the Idaho, Washington, Oregon, and California Coho and Chinook Salmon Industry.* Final Report to the Pacific Fishery Management Council. 2 vols. Corvallis, OR, September 1978.

Pacific Fishery Management Council. *Draft Fishery Management Plan and Environmental Impact Statement for Commercial and Recreational Salmon Fisheries off the Coasts of Washington, Oregon, and California, Commencing in 1978.* Portland, OR, October 19, 1977.

Pacific Sea Grant Advisory Program. *Directory of Services for Mariners: North Pacific Coast.* Seattle: University of Washington Division of Marine Resources, March 1973.

Parker, Joe. "Every Boatbuilder and Every Fisherman is Biased toward His Own Material." Oregon Institute of Marine Biology. Charleston, OR, Spring 1976.

Paul, Benjamin D. "Interview Techniques and Field Relationships." In *Anthropology Today,* edited by A. L. Kroeber, pp. 430–51. Chicago: University of Chicago Press, 1953.

Pederson, Elsa. *Fisherman's Choice.* New York: Atheneum, 1964.

_____. *Petticoat Fisherman.* New York: Atheneum, 1969.

Peterson, Emil R., and Powers, Alfred. *A Century of Coos and Curry: History of Southwest Oregon.* Portland: Binfords and Mort; Coquille: Coos-Curry Pioneer Historical Association, 1952.

Pilcher, William. *The Portland Longshoremen: A Dispersed Urban Community*. New York: Holt, Rinehart, and Winston, 1972.

Poggie, John J., Jr., and Gersuny, Carl. *Fishermen of Galilee: The Human Ecology of a New England Coastal Community*. University of Rhode Island Marine Bulletin Series, no. 17. Kingston, RI, 1974.

_____. "Risk and Ritual: An Interpretation of Fishermen's Folklore in a New England Community." *Journal of American Folklore* 85(1972):66–72.

Rettig, R. Bruce, and Roberts, Kenneth J. *Commercial Seafood Industry of Oregon: A Comparison with Other Regions of the United States*. Oregon State University Sea Grant Special Report, no. 331. Corvallis, OR, July 1971.

Roberts, Kenneth J. *Diversity—Characteristic of Oregon's Year 'Round Fishery*. Oregon State University Sea Grant, Extension Marine Advisory Program, Man and His Ocean Publication, S. G. no. 15. Corvallis, OR, November 1972.

Roberts, Warren E. "Folk Crafts." In *Folklore and Folklife: An Introduction*, edited by Richard M. Dorson, pp. 233–52. Chicago: University of Chicago Press, 1972.

_____. "The Whitaker-Waggoner Log House from Morgan County, Indiana." In *American Folklife*, edited by Don Yoder, pp. 185–207. Austin: University of Texas Press, 1976.

Rudolph, Wolfgang. *Handbuch der volkstümlichen Boote im östlichen Niederdeutschland*. Berlin: Akademie-Verlag, 1966.

_____. *Inshore Fishing Craft on the Southern Baltic from Holstein to Curonia*, translated by T. Max Feininger and edited by Sean McGrail. National Maritime Museum Monographs and Reports, no. 14. Greenwich, England, 1974.

_____. *Segelboote der deutschen Ostseekuste*. Berlin: Akademie-Verlag, 1969.

Russell, Bernard H. "Greek Sponge Boats in Florida." *Anthropological Quarterly* 38(1965):41–54.

Salaman, R. A. "Tools of the Shipwright, 1650–1925." *Folk-Life* 5(1967):19–51.

Sanderson, Stewart F. "The Tweed Salmon Coble." In *Studies in Folklife: Essays in Honor of Iowerth C. Peate*, edited by J. Geraint Jenkins, pp. 274–80. New York: Barnes and Noble, 1969.

Sauer, Carl O. "Seashore—Primitive Home of Man?" In *Land and Life: A Selection from the Writings of Carl Ortwig Sauer*, edited by John Leighly, pp. 300–312. Berkeley: University of California Press, 1962.

Schlereth, Thomas J. "American Studies and Students of American Things." *American Quarterly* 35:3(1983):236–41.

Smith, Courtland L. *Fish or Cut Bait*. Oregon State University Sea Grant College Program Publication, no. ORESU-T1-77-006. Corvallis, OR, 1977.

_____. "Intracultural Variation: Decline and Diversity in North Pacific Fisheries." *Human Organization* 35:1(1976):55–64.

_____. *Oregon Fish Fights*. Oregon State University Sea Grant Publication, no. ORESU-T-74-004. Corvallis, OR, 1974.

Smith, Frederick J. *Some Characteristics of Oregon Fishermen*. Oregon State University Sea Grant, Extension Marine Advisory Program, Commercial Fishing Publication, no. 12. Corvallis, OR, 1970.

Smith, M. Estellie, ed. *Those Who Live from the Sea: A Study in Maritime Anthropology*. St. Paul, MN: West Publishing Co., 1977.

Sommers, Lawrence. "Commercial Fishing in Norway: Aspects of the Changing Geography of a Traditional Industry." *Tijdschrift voor economische en sociale geografie* 53:11(1962):237–42.

Speroni, Charles. "California Fishermen's Festivals." *Western Folklore* 14(1955):77–91.

Squires, Robert H. "The Fisheries Training Programme of Newfoundland." *Canadian Geographical Journal* 56:2(1958):78–82.

Stiles, R. Geoffrey. "Fishermen, Wives and Radios: Aspects of Communication in a Newfoundland Fishing Community." In *North Atlantic Fishermen: Anthropological Essays on Modern Fishing*, edited by Raoul Andersen and Cato Wadel, pp. 35–60. Newfoundland Social and Economic Papers, no. 5. St. John's: Memorial University of Newfoundland Institute of Social and Economic Research, 1972.

Sturt, George. *The Wheelwright's Shop.* 1923. Reprinted paperback ed. London: Cambridge University Press, 1974.

Taylor, David A. *Boat Building in Winterton, Trinity Bay, Newfoundland.* Canadian Centre for Folk Culture Studies Paper, no. 41. Ottawa: National Museum of Man, 1982.

Thompson, G. B. "Rural Industry in Modern Ulster Society." *Gwerin* 2:2(1958):78–84.

Throckmorton, Arthur L. *Oregon Argonauts: Merchant Adventures on the Western Frontier.* Portland: Oregon Historical Society, 1961.

Tunstall, Jeremy. *The Fishermen.* London: MacGibbon and Kee, 1969.

U.S. Census Office. *Census Reports: Twelfth Census of the United States, Taken in the Year 1900.* 3rd ed. Washington, DC, 1906.

U.S. Department of Transportation, U.S. Coast Guard. *Merchant Vessels of the United States 1977 (Including Yachts).* Washington, DC: Government Printing Office, 1978.

———. *Merchant Vessels of the United States 1981 (Including Yachts).* Washington, DC: Government Printing Office, 1981.

U.S. Works Progress Administration. *Inventory of the County Archives of Oregon: No. 6, Coos County.* Portland: Oregon Historical Society, May 1942.

University of Lund Folklivsarkivet. *Ethnologia Scandinavica: A Journal for Nordic Ethnology.* Vol. 1–. Lund, Sweden, 1972–.

Upton, Dell. "The Power of Things: Recent Studies in American Vernacular Architecture." *American Quarterly* 35:3(1983):262–79.

Vest, Eugene B. "Names on the Ocean Bottom, or Some Observations on the Invisible Landscape." *Names* 16:2(1968):79–88.

Vlach, John Michael. "The 'Canada Homestead': A Saddlebag Log House in Monroe County, Indiana." *Pioneer America* 4:2(1972):8–17.

———. "The Shotgun House: An African Architectural Legacy." *Pioneer America* 8(1976):47–70.

Waldron, Kenneth D. *The Fishery and Biology of the Dungeness Crab (Cancer Magister Dana) in Oregon Waters.* Oregon Fish Commission Contribution, no. 24. Portland, OR, May 1958.

Walling, A. G., comp. *History of Southern Oregon.* Portland, OR, 1884.

Warner, William W. *Beautiful Swimmers: Watermen, Crabs and the Chesapeake Bay.* Boston: Little, Brown and Co., 1976. New York: Penguin Books, 1977.

———. *Distant Water: The Fate of the North Atlantic Fisherman.* Boston: Little, Brown and Co., 1983. New York: Penguin Books, 1984.

Whyte, William F. "Observational Field-work Methods." In *Research Methods in Social Relations,* edited by Marie Jahoda, Morton Deutsch, and Stuart W. Cook, vol. 2, pp. 493–513. New York: Dryden Press, 1951.

Wiedeman, Kent Mans. "Commercial Fishing in Oregon: Limits to Growth." Master's thesis, University of Oregon, 1973.

Wilhelm, Gene. "Pioneer Boats and Transportation on the Upper James River." *Pioneer America* 3(1971):39–47.

Wilhelm, Richard, trans. *The I Ching or Book of Changes.* Translated by Cary F. Baynes. 3rd ed. Princeton, NJ: Princeton University Press, 1967.

Williams, Michael Ann. " 'Old Homeplace': Abandonment, Alteration, and the Multiple Purposes of the Dwelling." Paper presented at the annual meeting of the American Folklore Society, Minneapolis, MN, October 1982.

———. "Rethinking the House: Interior Space and Social Change." Paper presented at the annual meeting of the American Folklore Society, Nashville, TN, 1983.

Wilsey and Ham, Inc. *Estuarine Resources of the Oregon Coast. A Natural Resource Inventory*

Report to the Oregon Coastal Conservation and Development Commission. Portland, OR, September 1975.

Wood-Jones, R. B. *Traditional Domestic Architecture in the Banbury Region*. Manchester: University Press, 1963.

Yoder, Don, ed. *American Folklife*. Austin: University of Texas Press, 1976.

_____. "Folk Medicine." In *Folklore and Folklife: An Introduction*, edited by Richard M. Dorson, pp. 191–215. Chicago: University of Chicago Press, 1972.

Zelinsky, Wilbur. *The Cultural Geography of the United States*. Englewood Cliffs, NJ: Prentice-Hall, Inc., 1973.

Zulaika, Joseba. *Terranova: The Ethos and Luck of Deep-Sea Fishermen*. Philadelphia: Institute for the Study of Human Issues, 1981.

Special Collections

Coos Bay, Oregon. Southwestern Oregon Community College Learning Resource Center. Living History Series:

Anderson, Richard J. Interviewed by Lloyd Lyman, May 20, 1975 (no. 435).

Barber, Olive. Interviewed by Abdul Aldus, 1972 (no. 326, side 2).

Barrows, Orville C., and Lennon, Ruth Barrows. Interviewed by Lloyd Lyman, April 19, 1975 (no. 417).

Boyd, Marguerite Therrien. Interviewed by Lloyd Lyman, April 23, 1975 (no. 418).

Byler, Horace. Interviewed by Lloyd Lyman, May 20, 1975 (no. 438).

DeCosta, Joseph P. Interviewed by Lloyd Lyman, March 28, 1975 (no. 411).

Eickworth, Lorance. Interviewed by Lloyd Lyman, April 25, 1975 (no. 420).

Engblom, Sarah. Interviewed by Bernell Meacham, July 1973 (no. 319, side 2).

Granger, Mary Banks. Interviewed by Lloyd Lyman, May 6, 1975 (no. 431).

Hallmark, Alice, and Day, Ruth Hallmark. Interviewed by Lloyd Lyman, March 19, 1975 (no. 409).

Josephson, William A., and Josephson, Ena McKeown. Interviewed by Lloyd Lyman, May 22, 1975 (no. 446).

Koontz, John L. Interviewed by Jeff Galbraith, November 1972 (no. 321).

Mattson, John Arthur. Interviewed by Lloyd Lyman, May 24, 1975 (no. 453).

McGeorge, Charles. Interviewed by Jack Wilson, November 1972 (no. 320, side 1).

Metcalf, Marie. Interviewed by Jack Wilson, October 1972 (no. 319, side 1).

Ott, Harold. Interviewed by Bessie Gavick, May 1974 (no. 328).

Pederson, Arthur. Interviewed by Lloyd Lyman, April 4, 1975 (no. 403).

Sandstrom, Carl. Interviewed by Lloyd Lyman, May 24, 1975 (no. 458).

Scott, Mark. Interviewed by George D. Chick, March 1, 1972 (no. 309).

Smith, Mrs. Henry. Interviewed by Angie Word, 1972 (no. 299).

Spoerle, Stephen J. Interviewed by Lloyd Lyman, June 4, 1975 (no. 459).

Steckel, Martin. Interviewed by Angie Word and Sheila Cassidy, 1972 (no. 306).

Stephenson, Carl, and Melchers, Mrs. Helen Stephenson. Interviewed by Lloyd Lyman, March 28, 1975 (no. 401).

Eugene. University of Oregon. Oregon Collection. Charles Feller Papers.

_____. Photograph: "Pilchard fishing fleet in Coos Bay harbor."

Field Notes and Recordings: Interviews, Discussions, Informants

Fishermen and Associates:

Anderson, Fred. Charleston, August 24, 1977 (3 pp. notes; 95 mins. tape, 35 pp. selectively transcribed).

Boyington, Roger. Charleston, May 5, 1977 (2 pp. notes).

Crockett, Cecil. Charleston, January 18, 1978 (9 pp. notes).

Ells, Charles C. and Jessie. Port Orford, February 6, 1978 (12 pp. notes; 59 mins. tape, 4 pp. transcribed for use in text).

Green, Floyd. Charleston, February 23, 1978 (12 pp. notes).

Hall, Leonard. Charleston, July 27, 1977 (3 pp. notes; 73 mins. tape, 32 pp. transcribed).

Harlan, Jake. Charleston, September 1, 1977, and March 29, 1978 (24 pp. notes).

Harrington, Carl and Lynne. Charleston, February 9, 1978 (10 pp. notes).

Hockema, Arnold and Doris. Charleston, March 7, 1978 (19 pp. notes; 97 mins. tape, 5 pp. transcribed for use in text).

Irick, Terry. Charleston, February 18, 1977 (4 pp. notes).

Lane, Mike. Charleston, January 13, 1978 (3 pp. notes).

Lilienthal, Richard and Verna. Charleston, September 20, 1977 (6 pp. notes; 96 mins. tape, 30 pp. selectively transcribed).

Little, Cyrus, Sr., and Violet. Charleston, April 17, 1978 (12 pp. notes).

Walker, Norman and Virginia. Charleston, April 11, 1978 (18 pp. notes).

Young, Burley. Charleston, May 9, 1975 (4 pp. notes).

Others. Charleston, 1977–1978 (9 pp. notes).

Marine Support Personnel:

Bill's Machine and Welding: Chard, Bill. Charleston, March 15, 1978 (10 pp. notes).

George's Marine Electronics: "Bud" Hartley. Charleston, March 15, 1978 (3 pp. notes).

Hallmark Fisheries: Day, Ruth Hallmark. Charleston, July 28, 1977 (3 pp. notes; 84 mins. tape, 28 pp. transcribed).

Hanson's Landing: Hanson, Lucille and David. Charleston, April 4, 1978 (5 pp. notes).

Hillstrom Shipbuilding: Hillstrom, Bill, Jr. Coos Bay, September 28, 1977 (9 pp. notes). Schroeder, William "Butch." North Bend, April 6, 1978 (5 pp. notes).

Humbert's Boat Shop: Humbert, Fred. Haynes Inlet. March 11 and 16, 1978 (12 pp. notes).

Kelley Boat Works: Kelley, Jack. Charleston, March 11, 1978 (3 pp. notes).

Knutson Diesel and Machine: Knutson, Harold; Knutson, John; and Maine, Virginia. Coos Bay, September 7, 1977 (7 pp. notes).

Koontz Machine Shop: Horton, Art (and Jorgensen, Elmer). Coos Bay, April 6 and 7, 1978 (26 pp. notes). Smith, Mr. Coos Bay, March 28, 1978 (5 pp. notes).

Nelson Log Bronc/Mid-Coast Marine: Swanson, Kurt. Eastside, September 7, 1977 (5 pp. notes). Wilskey, Jack. Eastside, September 7 and 13, 1977 (4 pp. notes; 78 mins. tape, 19 pp. selectively transcribed).

Oregon-Pacific Company: Anderson, Norm. North Bend, March 28 and 30, 1978 (8 pp. notes). Eickworth, Lorance. Coos Bay, August 29, 1977 (7 pp. notes).

Ott's Machine and Diesel: Ott, Keith. Charleston, March 13, 1978 (9 pp. notes).

Officials:

Begeman, Mr. U.S. Coast Guard Marine Safety Detachment Office, Coos Bay, October 4, 1976, and January 26, 1977 (3 pp. notes).

Cardwell, Helen. Charleston Boat Basin Office, November 8, 1976, and January 27, 1977 (5 pp. notes).

Heikkila, Paul. Marine Extension Agent, Coquille, OR, September 20, 1976 (4 pp. notes).

Hosie, Mike. Oregon Department of Fish and Wildlife, Charleston, November 10, 1976, and January 30, 1978 (6 pp. notes).

Index